FAIRNESS AND FUTURITY

FAIRNESS
AND FUTURITY

Essays on Environmental Sustainability
and Social Justice

Edited by
ANDREW DOBSON

OXFORD
UNIVERSITY PRESS

OXFORD

UNIVERSITY PRESS

Great Clarendon Street, Oxford OX2 6DP

Oxford New York

Athens Auckland Bangkok Bogotá Buenos Aires Calcutta
Cape Town Chennai Dar es Salaam Delhi Florence Hong Kong Istanbul
Karachi Kuala Lumpur Madrid Melbourne Mexico City Mumbai
Nairobi Paris São Paulo Singapore Taipei Tokyo Toronto Warsaw
and associated companies in Berlin Ibadan

Oxford is a registered trade mark of Oxford University Press

Published in the United States
by Oxford University Press Inc., New York

British Library Cataloguing in Publication Data

Data available

Library of Congress Cataloging in Publication Data
Fairness and futurity: essays on environmental sustainability and
social justice/edited by Andrew Dobson.
Includes bibliographical references and index.
1. Sustainable development. 2. Social justice.
3. Intergenerational relations. I. Dobson, Andrew.
HC79.E5F25 1999 363.7–dc21 98-49344

ISBN 0–19–829488–3
ISBN 0–19–829489–1 (Pbk.)

1 3 5 7 9 10 8 6 4 2

Typeset in Dante
by J&L Composition Ltd, Filey, North Yorkshire

Printed in Great Britain on acid-free paper by
Bookcraft Ltd, Midsomer Norton, Somerset

ACKNOWLEDGEMENTS

I would like to thank the Economic and Social Research Council (ESRC) for a grant under its Research Seminar competition which made it possible to bring a number of nationally and internationally renowned scholars and activists together at Keele University, UK, on three occasions in 1996. Each of the chapters here was written specially for these seminars and subsequently revised in the light of discussions that took place during—and between—them. A number of people other than those who appear here attended the Keele seminars, either as core or occasional members of the group. I would like to thank, in particular, John Barry, Paula Casal, Avner de-Shalit, Tim Hayward, John Horton, Jonathon Porritt, John Proops, Michael Redclift and Hilary Wainwright for their invaluable contributions to the debates we had.

Editing this book has been a pleasurable it lengthy task. It would have taken even longer had it not been for the tenacity and editorial skills displayed by one of my doctoral students, Tim Arnold, who shouldered the hefty burden of turning ten rather disparately produced contributions into a single text. I am deeply indebted to Tim for his wonderful work. It is appropriate here, also, to thank Dominic Byatt at Oxford University Press, for his faith in this undertaking, and for his assistance in helping to bring it to fruition.

I would like to thank each of the contributors to this book for taking part in the project. The terms of reference for seminar attendance (everyone to attend all three of them) obliged colleagues to set aside scarce time in busy schedules over a relatively short space of time, and they have been patient in waiting to see the fruits of their labours published. I hope and trust that the result is worthy both of their efforts and the reader's attention. All proceeds from the sale of this book will be shared equally between Oxfam and the environmental charity, Forum for the Future.

Finally, permission from Random House and from Peters, Fraser, & Dunlop to quote from Martin Amis's *London Fields* is gratefully acknowledged.

Andrew Dobson
Keele University
May 1998

CONTENTS

PART III

NOTES ON CONTRIBUTORS

BRIAN BARRY is Arnold A. Saltzman Professor in the Departments of Political Science and Philosophy at Columbia University, New York, having previously been Professor of Political Science at the London School of Economics. Among his books are *Theories of Justice* (1989), *Justice as Impartiality* (1995), and *Culture and Equality* (2000).

WILFRED BECKERMAN is an Emeritus Professor of Balliol College, Oxford, where he had taught economics since 1975, having previously been Professor of Political Economy at University College London. He has published on a wide range of economics topics in numerous books and articles in academic journals. He is currently authoring, with Joanna Pasek, a book on our obligations to future generations and their implications for environmental policy.

TED BENTON teaches in the Sociology Department at the University of Essex, UK. He is a member of the Red-Green Study Group, an affiliate of the Green Left. He is author of numerous books and articles, including *Natural Relations* (Verso, 1993), and *The Rise and Fall of Structural Marxism* (Macmillan, 1984). He edited *The Greening of Marxism* (Guilford, 1996), and co-edited (with Michael Redclift) *Social Theory and the Global Environment* (Routledge, 1994).

ANDREW DOBSON teaches in the Politics Department at Keele University, UK. His recent publications include *Green Political Thought* (2nd edn.) (Routledge, 1995), and *Justice and the Environment: Conceptions of Environmental Sustainability and Dimensions of Social Justice* (Oxford University Press, 1998). He is currently working on the idea of environmental citizenship.

CHRIS HEWETT is a Research Fellow at the Institute for Public Policy Research (IPPR). He has been working on environmental taxation for two years and is currently undertaking research into the implications of an energy tax on industry. Joint editor of

Energy'98: Competing for Power and contributor to *Britain in Europe: Initiatives for the 1998 Presidency.*

ALAN HOLLAND is Senior Lecturer in Philosophy at Lancaster University, UK. He edits the journal *Environmental Values* and has recently co-edited an anthology on *Animal Biotechnology and Ethics.*

MICHAEL JACOBS is General Secretary of the Fabian Society. Previously an ESRC Research Fellow in the Centre for the Study of Environmental Change, Lancaster University, and in the Geography Department of the London School of Economics, he is author of *The Green Economy* (Pluto Press, 1989) and *The Politics of the Real World* (Earthscan, 1996), and editor of *Greening the Millenium? The New Problems of the Environment* (Blackwell, 1997).

DAVID MILLER is Official Fellow in Social and Political Theory at Nuffield College, Oxford. His most recent books are *On Nationality* (Clarendon Press, 1995) and (with Michael Walzer) *Pluralism, Justice, and Equality* (Oxford University Press, 1995). He is currently completing a new book entitled *Principles of Social Justice.*

KOOS NEEFJES is Oxfam (GB)'s Policy Adviser on environmental matters, and his main activities include project appraisal and review, training on participatory methodologies and advising Oxfam on food security matters, with a particular focus on the relationship between environmental sustainability and poverty alleviation.

BRYAN G. NORTON is a Professor in the School of Public Policy, Georgia Institute of Technology, USA, and Coordinator of the Philosophy, Science and Technology Program there. His publications include *Ethics on the Ark* (co-editor) (Smithsonian Institution Press, 1995); *Why Preserve Natural Variety?* (Princeton University Press, 1987); and *Toward Unity Among Environmentalists* (Oxford University Press, 1991). He has served on numerous panels, including the Ecosystem Valuation Forum, and the Risk Assessment Forum (US EPA). He was a charter member of the Environmental Economics Advisory Committee of the EPA Science Advisory Board. His current research includes work on intergenerational impacts of policy choices and on community involvement in eco-system management processes.

STEPHEN TINDALE was Director of the Green Alliance and pre-viously a Senior Research Fellow at the Institute for Public Policy Research (IPPR). He has written extensively on environmental issues, in particular on green taxation. He is co-author of *Green Tax Reform* and joint editor of *Energy'98: Competing for Power*, both published by the IPPR. He has recently been seconded to work for the Sustainable Development Unit in the Department of Environment, Transport and the Regions.

MARCEL WISSENBURG is a research fellow and lecturer in political theory at the University of Nijmegen, the Netherlands. His recent publications include *Green Liberalism: The Free and the Green Society* (UCL Press, 1998) and *Imperfection and Impartiality: A Liberal Theory of Social Justice* (UCL Press, 1999).

'It's the confinement. Children like to whirl around. How about forty-five minutes? He needs some fresh air'.

'We all do. But there isn't any.'

There wasn't any. And hard to explain that one away, hard to justify it—to the young (Guy meant), to those who would come after. How would you begin? Well, we suspected that some sacrifices might have to be made, later, for all the wonderful times we had with our spray cans and junk-food packaging. We knew there'd be a price. Admittedly, to you, the destruction of the ozone layer looks a bit steep. But don't forget how good it was for us: our tangy armpits, our piping hamburgers. Though maybe we *could* have got by with just roll-ons and styrofoam . . .

Martin Amis, London Fields

Introduction

ANDREW DOBSON

This book has its origins in a series of three seminars, funded by the Economic and Social Research Council (ESRC), and held at Keele University during 1996. The seminars were organized in the belief that too little attention has been paid to the relationship between the objective of environmental sustainability and other political objectives such as deepening democracy and securing social justice. We should not, I believe, take it for granted that these latter objectives sit in a relationship of seamless harmony with the achieving of environmental sustainability, such that more justice and greater democracy will necessarily lead to greater environmental sustainability, and that all policies for sustainability will enhance justice and democracy. This present set of essays focuses in particular on the relationship between sustainability and justice, and especially—although not exclusively—on the implications for justice of including future generations in the community of justice.

A further intention was to bring together three groups of people associated with the themes of environmental sustainability and social justice who too often seem to be operating on parallel rather than converging tracks. The first two groups are those academics working on sustainability and justice respectively. Despite the interesting connections between these two issues, 'mainstream' justice theorists have long seemed intent on regarding sustainability (or, more generally, 'environmental') questions

The opinions expressed in this Introduction are mine alone and should not be assumed to be shared by any of the other contributors to this volume.

as an optional extra, to be dealt with only when, and if, all the really important work has been done. Likewise, environmental theorists behave as though they can safely ignore 2,000 years of political theory because it cannot possibly have anything useful to say on such a novel and contemporary issue as global environmental degradation. I think that both of these views are wrong, and it was certainly a treat to see sustainability and justice theorists grappling with each other's languages and conceptions as the seminars progressed. (Indeed the distinction between 'sustainability' and 'justice' theorists already sounds forced).

The third group comprises people working in the policy community. It is important for there to be dialogue between the academy and the wider world, and most academics working in this field would probably like to think that their reflections can, or will, make some 'real world' difference. The integration of this group with the other two (or should that be the other way round?) was much harder to achieve, and the success of the enterprise was certainly equivocal: the two essays in the third and last part of this book are therefore exceptional in both senses of the word. I shall have more to say on this towards the end of this Introduction.

As far as the principal themes under discussion here are concerned, there are those who suggest that the languages of justice and sustainability are too divergent to be brought into effective contact; that is, that justice is about distributing benefits and burdens, while sustainability is about maintaining life-support systems (or whatever it is that we are enjoined by any given theory of sustainability to sustain). There is some truth in this claim, I believe. The environmental movement's various and sometimes ill-defined political and social objectives cannot all be captured under the sign of 'social justice', just as those working for social justice will sometimes be frustrated at environmentalists' apparent willingness to put environmental preservation before the creation of jobs (for example).

There are, though, at least three contexts in which the themes of justice and sustainability speak to each other rather than past each other. The first is in terms of the functional relationship between them. There is no doubt that policies for sustainability have distributive implications, and a *locus classicus* of this kind of relationship is that of environmental taxation, some of whose themes are explored here by Chris Hewett and Stephen Tindale in Chapter 9. It is unlikely that any governmental policy (fiscal or otherwise) could be sold simply on the basis of its contribution to sustainability, since such policies will, and should, be examined for their distributive consequences. Likewise, certain regimes and relationships of distribution may well be functional for sustainability, in that they encourage sustainable behaviour. It is, indeed, something of an article of faith in the sustainable development movement that a precondition for global sustainability is a global redistribution of wealth, given the weight of evidence suggesting that poor people are forced into degrading their environment by eking out a living on marginal lands. If this is true—and it almost certainly sometimes, even if not always, is—then part of the answer to unsustainability will lie in policies for social justice.

The second principal context in which justice and environment debates are connected is that of the 'environmental justice' movement in the United States of America. This movement shares the sustainable development belief that 'poor people live in poor environments' and a large body of empirical evidence has been built up to show as much. With some exceptions, though, supporters of the US environmental justice movement do not tend to suggest that greater social justice would result in more environmental sustainability: the focus is rather on the unjust ways in which the environmental 'bads' in society are unfairly shared out across society. Of course, if such 'bads' *were* more fairly shared out, with the consequence that the wielders of power and influence were exposed to environmental degradation rather then shielded from it because of their greater purchasing power, a broader movement to avoid environmental degradation rather than spread it around more fairly might develop. It is also true that some individuals in the environmental justice movement have come to embrace broader sustainability issues through their justice activism, so it would be a mistake to say that environmental justice can never be a 'route' to sustainability. Still, I think it is generally true to suggest the prime focus of the movement is on social justice rather than environmental sustainability.

What the environmental justice movement does make most vivid, though (and this is the third context in which the themes of justice and sustainability come into contact), is that the 'natural' environment can be construed in many different ways, and one of these is in terms of 'something to be distributed'. Once we see this, both the distance between, and the proximity of, the languages and intentions of the justice and the environment movements become clear. They are distant because environmentalists will balk at regarding the environment as simply 'something to be distributed', and they are proximate because the whole of the sustainability debate can be read, precisely, in terms of 'distributing something' across generations, or, in other words, in terms of intergenerational distributive justice.

More precisely, the ideas of social justice and environmental sustainability can be regarded as answers to particular sets of questions—questions that define the subject matter of justice and sustainability, respectively.[1] Not all of the questions to which theories of justice and sustainability must have an answer are directly comparable. For example, one type of sustainability theorist may want to know how much substitutability between human-made and natural capital is possible, so as to be able to determine how much conservation of natural capital is required for long-term sustainability. This is a question which has no real analogue in justice theory (although substitutability does have a bearing on the issue of compensatory justice as Ted Benton points out in his contribution here).[2] Likewise, justice theorists ask whether theories of justice should be procedural or consequentialist (or some combination of the two), and this is a question that has no obvious counterpart in sustainability theory (although if, as I suggested above, it can be argued that different regimes of justice have different implications for environmental sustainability, then whether such regimes are procedural or consequentialist may turn out to be an important question).[3]

There are questions, though, to which sustainability and justice theories have answers which, if not exactly shared, certainly make tandem examination of the two a fruitful exercise. The most important question in sustainability theory is 'what is to be sustained?'. This may seem blindingly obvious, but what is less obvious is that there is no determinate answer to this question. Sustainability theorists argue interminably over this 'what?' (or 'X' as Brian Barry refers to it here in Chapter 4), and conceptions of sustainability can be analytically organized around the different answers that have been given to the question.[4] Justice theorists, on the other hand, are often preoccupied by the issue of what is to be distributed, and a number of different answers to this question have been canvassed over the centuries.[5] What we have then, are two fields of enquiry (environmental sustainability and social justice), both of which are concerned with an 'X', but which ask slightly different questions about it: for sustainability the question is, 'what X is to be *sustained*', while for justice the question is, 'what X is to be *distributed?*'

The point at which these questions come together is the point at which what is to be sustained is also that which is to be distributed—the point, in other words, at which considerations of intergenerational justice begin. Put differently, sustainability obliges us to think about sustaining something into the future, and justice makes us think about distributing something across present and future. These considerations connect the languages and objectives of justice and sustainability, and it is this connection that the present collection of essays seeks principally, although not exclusively, to explore.

The book is divided into three parts, corresponding roughly to the three sets of seminars from which the papers here emerged. The first part deals with the broad themes of sustainability and sustainable development and thus sets the scene for subsequent contributions. The treatment of sustainability here is not entirely divorced from the question of justice, but distributive questions ghost the texts rather than appear centrally in them. The relationship between justice and sustainability is treated more explicitly in Part II, and Part III is devoted to aspects of justice and sustainability policy in widely differing circumstances.

Opening Part I, then, Michael Jacobs notes that sustainable development has come to mean all things to all people and that some critics have concluded from this that it has lost any theoretical or policy-related purchase it might have once had. Jacobs resists this conclusion and argues that the practical consequences of the widespread adoption of sustainable development as a policy goal have been considerable and largely beneficial. He points out that governments often feel obliged to do something rather than nothing, that non-governmental organizations now have a rhetorically accepted measure against which to check and expose governments' actions, and that through a process of institutional learning even deeper greens implicitly endorse sustainable development as an idea when they suggest that 'not enough' is being done. This theme of guarded optimism regarding the idea of sustainable development is picked up again by Ted Benton in Chapter 8.

Jacobs rightly argues that sustainable development is better viewed as a 'contested' rather than as an empty concept, the meaning of which is up for grabs. There are, he says, four identifiable 'faultlines' in competing conceptions of sustainable development, and he suggests that two distinct conceptions can be derived from different positions on these faultlines. Opponents within the sustainable development movement argue about the degree of appropriate environmental protection, about the role of equity, about the degree of political participation required by and for sustainable development, and about the scope of the subject area itself.

Proponents of what Jacobs calls the 'radical' conception of sustainable development will argue for strong environmental protection because of the existence of environmental limits. This contrasts with the 'conservative' conception which accepts that conservation is necessary and that protection might be desirable, but which does not endorse the view that the economy must be constrained within predetermined environmental limits. Along the second faultline, radicals will argue that equity is central to sustainable development, while conservatives will downplay its importance. This distinction maps quite neatly, says Jacobs, onto a North–South reading of sustainable development, which is to say that for those concerned with sustainable development in the South, equity is central to sustainability—for the reasons I referred to in the earlier paragraphs of this introduction. 'Northern' interpretations, on the other hand, will stress environmental protection ahead of social equity.

Third, radicals will argue that political participation is both conducive to greater environmental sustainability and a good-in-itself, while conservatives will conceive sustainable development as a more expert-driven project in which objectives are both determined and met by governments and their agencies. Finally, radicals criticize the conservative view that the objective of sustainable development is primarily environmental protection, and they stress sustainable development's potential for harnessing progressive energies across a range of social, economic, and political issues.

Jacobs' chapter has the great merit of stressing the multiple forms and features of sustainable development, and his original analysis comprises an excellent introduction to the themes of the rest of the book. Not all of its normative conclusions, though, will be enthusiastically endorsed. In particular, his assessment of the 'environmental protection' strand of the final faultline as 'conservative' may generate opposition among those who think that the sustainable development agenda has given too much ground to environmental despoilers, and that environmental protection is the radical line to take. Indeed, Alan Holland devotes the second chapter here to asking whether 'sustainability' will deliver the protection of nature. For most of his essay, Holland assumes that sustainability is about maintaining some conception and level of human welfare into the future, and his view is that, seen in these terms, 'the pursuit of sustainability by no means entails the protection of natural capital'. In some cases this is due to the indeterminacy of the notion of 'human welfare', in others it is due to the fact that the standard invocation of the maintenance of *critical* natural capital does nothing for nature that is not critical, and in still others it is because of the difficulties associated with measuring the level of natural capital.

Towards the end of his chapter Holland picks up this last point and suggests a different object of measurement, that is 'the natural items themselves' rather than any economic value that they may contain or represent. He claims that this has methodological advantages over economic forms of measurement, and while beyond any rough approximations this might be disputed, he is surely right to say that his 'physical stock' approach amounts to a

terms of what we would want for other (future) people, and if we say something general like 'opportunities', we seem to be unable to avoid wondering what the preconditions for these opportunities might be. Barry writes suggestively that, 'Perhaps people in the future might learn to find satisfaction in totally artificial land-scapes, walking on the astroturf amid the plastic trees while the electronic birds sing overhead. But we cannot but believe that something horrible would have happened to human beings if they did not miss real grass, trees and birds.' Does a preference for real trees rather than plastic ones amount to a vision of the good life, or a part of such a vision at least? Less dramatically, choosing between 'critical natural capital' and Alan Holland's 'physical stock' conceptions of sustainability might be regarded as a 'good life' kind of decision, and if it is, then liberalism's neutrality may be in tension with the demands implicit in sustainability decisions.

The 'X' theme is picked up in Bryan Norton's contribution in Chapter 5. He says that he assumes that 'some obligations to future generations exist, and the task accepted is to clarify and explain these obligations.' In his view there are two broad approaches to the 'what should we save for future generations' question: utility comparison (UC) and 'listing stuff' (LS). This latter approach—which Norton favours, and which he believes may entail rethinking 'the role of economic analysis in the search for environmental sustainability'—bears comparison with Holland's 'physical stock' notion in that it seems to entail bequeathing actual and determinate 'things' to future generations. Norton points out that an LS approach suffers from a lack of a unifying theory of value (Barry's 'irreducibly normative' aspect of sustainability) and that therefore any specification of the features to be bequeathed to future generations will embody 'powerful and controversial assumptions'. Norton cuts the Gordian knot by suggesting that protection should be 'of features and sources of value in each particular place': that is, that sustainability rules should be deter-mined in given localities.

A key idea in Norton's chapter is that if these features and sources of value are lost, then this loss must be regarded as *non-compensable* as far as future generations are concerned. This amounts to drawing a line in the sand as far as the perennial issue of substitutability is concerned: non-compensability is to justice as non-substitutability is to sustainability. It also puts some flesh on the bones of the question of what the provision of opportunities for future generations might consist in. In Norton's view 'opportunities' derive from 'keystone natural resources' which 'form the basis for an enduring and place-based cultural identity'. These resources are not, says Norton, 'interchangeable with other forms of capital', and so intergenerational justice from this point of view would seem to entail the mandatory protection, as far as possible, of the physical features of a given locality that are regarded as valuable in and by that locality. Just what these features might be is, of course, a moot point, and Norton himself might be regarded as anticipating a jump too far when he writes that: 'If I cut down a mature tree and plant a seedling of the same species, it seems unlikely that I have significantly harmed people of the future.' In some places and instances it might be that the mature tree contains the sort of socially recognized value to which Norton himself refers, so its loss would indeed amount to harm to future generations.

The next two chapters, by David Miller and Marcel Wissenburg respectively, both grapple with the sustainability question in the context of specifically liberal theories of distributive justice. Miller's view is that environmental goods should not fall 'outside the scope of our theories of justice. We should regard them as potential benefits (often accompanied by restrictions) that need to go into the distributive calculus alongside other goods like opportunity, income and wealth.' He examines the work of John Rawls and Ronald Dworkin for evidence that environmental goods can be accommodated within liberal theories of justice, and concludes that while there is certainly room for accommodation, no systematic attempt has been made to do so. Miller gestures at the boundaries by confirming that no mandatory measures for the protection of wildlife (for example) can be derived from Rawls's theory, and that Dworkin's 'avowed neutralism' 'prohibits him from saying that there is anything of special value about a life lived in harmony with nature'.

However, Miller points out, first, that some sorts of environmental goods can be comfortably incorporated into Rawls's notion of primary goods and, second, that we may be able to generate enough general agreement about the value of some other environmental goods for their preservation/conservation not to present problems of justice. There will, though, be some environmental goods whose value is disputed and whose value will come into conflict with other, non-environmental, values. How are courses of action to be decided upon in such cases of conflict? Miller answers with a defence of a version of cost-benefit analysis (CBA)—a version in which the different valuations that people might put on environmental goods as private persons and as citizens is catered for. Criticisms of CBA come from two sides. From one side, environmentalists worry that people's private preferences are likely merely to reflect the status quo and that CBA is therefore a procedure for reinforcing present environmental practices rather than changing them, and from the other, pragmatists express the concern that preferences expressed from a citizen's point of view will tend towards protection whatever the cost, and therefore paralyse the decision-making process.

Miller makes a virtue of both these positions by incorporating them in a two-stage process whereby private preferences are expressed first, and then, second, these preferences are regarded as information that is taken forward to a second stage of public deliberation. This democratizes the process of decision-making and allows for the transformation of preferences, while allowing that people will value environmental goods differently. Finally, Miller suggests that the state has a significant role to play in the provision and protection of non-disputed (what we might call 'preconditional') environmental goods, but that it should play a more cautious hand in respect of goods of his third, disputed, type.

So Miller concludes that environmental goods can be incorporated into the Rawlsian project: the sorts of goods, moreover, that sustainability theorists might refer to as 'critical natural capital'. Rawls, of course, is also one of the few major theorists of justice who has paid systematic attention to the issue of intergenerational justice itself. This attention has gone through at least two phases, corresponding to his *A Theory of Justice*[6] and, latterly, *Political Liberalism*.[7] In Chapter 7, Marcel Wissenburg argues that Rawls's most recent version of his 'savings principle' is more convincing than his better-known, earlier, version. Rawls's new savings principle does not rely on any of the bloodline altruism that made his first version seem like something of an afterthought: self-interest and mutual disinterest are the motivating factors in the new version, and so the savings principle now has a more secure and consistent (Rawlsian) basis. 'It is simply rational for goal-maximizing individuals to seek the mutual benefit of a savings principle,' writes Wissenburg.

Wissenburg also believes that Rawls can be shown to have done more than he probably intended. In the first place, he argues, not only can Rawls's principle be said to be a satisfactory basis for any liberal theory of justice, even non-contractarian ones, but he can also be used to show that a savings principle is 'a necessary condition of a just society'. This, says Wissenburg, is because 'a savings principle for justice between generations is a necessary condition for the survival of liberal democracy.' If Wissenburg is right about this, then liberalism and sustainability look more compatible than is often claimed, and it is indeed part of Wissenburg's intention to show that this is so. From a sustainability point of view, of course, much depends on what the savings principle demands of the current generation, and Wissenburg develops what he calls a 'restraint principle' which reads as follows in its general form: 'no goods shall be destroyed unless unavoidable and unless they are replaced by perfectly identical goods; if that is physically impossible, they should be replaced by equivalent goods resembling the original as closely as possible; and if that is also impossible, a proper compensation should be provided'. Clearly, much turns on what 'unless avoidable' means, and interpretations of this key phrase will be (as we observed above) as much a normative as a scientific, or descriptive, matter.

In the final chapter of Part II, Ted Benton shifts the focus of attention from liberalism to socialism. Benton gives a guarded welcome to the normative dimensions of the (still-developing) notion of sustainable development, arguing that the 1992 'Rio Summit' commitments to meeting the basic needs of the poor as well as passing on the conditions for needs-meeting to the future, extending grassroots participation, and preserving indigenous ways of life are all worth building on. Like Jacobs in Chapter 1, Benton believes that these commitments can be used as 'regulative ideals' by NGOs and by Green and Left social movements as these progressive forces seek to call governments and commercial interests to environmental and social account. So far, so good, but Benton proceeds to 'expose the deep tensions between these normative aspirations, on the one hand, and key features and tendencies in the global political economy, on the other'. He deploys a number of examples designed to illustrate this fatal contradiction, and at a fundamental theoretical level he takes neoclassical economists to task for their failure to see that capitalism's problematic relationship with environmental protection will not be resolved by 'internalizing the externalities', by organizing surrogate markets in environmental goods, or by commodifying nature. In Benton's view there is a 'dynamic tendency' in market systems for over-exploitation, and 'this is not a consequence of market 'failure', but of the very forms of calculation . . . which constitute markets'.

The problems lie with an economistic ideology and with the global capitalist institutions that produce and reproduce it, argues Benton. So the way forward, he suggests, is to 'adhere to and strengthen the normative aspirations at the core of the Brundtland approach, while using these as a platform from which to argue the case for radical changes in economic organization and ideology'. At least part of this task, he says, will involve reconceptualizing the idea of 'need', to take it away from its connection with basic physical sustenance towards a more inclusive sense of 'human individual and social flourishing'. According to Benton, this would have the merit of taking Brundtland's social needs-based understanding of sustainability further towards accommodation with demands made on behalf of non-human nature, on the grounds that a suitably broadened conception of need would acknowledge 'spiritual', 'ethical', and 'aesthetic' needs, and the role that non-human nature might conceivably play in meeting them. At the same time, and crucially, any social forces that resist 'capitalist globalization' need to be defended and extended.

Benton has been powerfully instrumental for some time in bringing environmental and Leftist concerns into constructive alignment, and his chapter is a typically careful yet vigorous contribution to this project. His is the big picture, and the scale of his far-reaching proposals for changes in the global capitalist economy contrast with the first contribution to Part III, in which Stephen Tindale and Chris Hewett deal with one of the most-discussed policy tools available to politicians for moving towards sustainability in so-called advanced industrial countries: environmental taxation. Such taxation is popularly regarded as regressive and therefore socially unjust, and this is one of the reasons why sustainability and justice are often seen as pulling in different directions. In their chapter, Tindale and Hewett respond to such charges by pointing out, first, that the fiscal consequences of environmental taxes depend on 'the nature of the problem and the nature of the tax', and, second, that *any* taxation can be regressive, but that environmental taxation can be made progressive if designed to be so. Tindale and Hewett point out, for example, that domestic energy taxes are usually regressive, and as the British Conservative Government found out when it raised the Value Added Tax (VAT) on domestic fuel, this is regarded as unacceptable by the justice lobby. But Tindale and Hewett argue that a progressive *package* could be put together by, for example, linking tax on domestic fuel with 'ecobonuses', by allocating tax-free fuel allowances whose regressive effects could be mitigated through the benefits system, and/or by insulating the homes of the poor.

They also examine transport taxes, and argue that increasing motoring costs will be largely progressive because poor people do not own cars. Of course there will be exceptions, but once again any regressive effects of an environmentally oriented transport tax on, for example, the disabled, could be mitigated through special allowances. Finally, Tindale and Hewett point out that 'the greatest cause of poverty in Britain today is unemployment', and that green taxes have a role to play in stimulating environmental industries and therefore reducing unemployment. Overall, they argue for a 'package of reforms which leave both the poor and the environment better off', and it is worth remembering that these are ideas that come from the British Labour Party's most influential 'think-tank'. Many environmentalists, though, have been disappointed at the Labour government's environmental record during its first year in office, and it seems clear that reformers both inside and outside the party have some way to go before packages like those suggested by Tindale and Hewett are integral to Labour government policy.

The final chapter of the collection, by Koos Neefjes of Oxfam (GB), stands in stark and salutary contrast to the other contributions in its insistence on taking turmoil and instability as its starting point. How will the carefully crafted sustainability and justice principles of other contributors fare in zones of conflict? How will some of the measurements for sustainability (Alan Holland's 'physical stock', or Bryan Norton's 'keystone natural resources', for example) be made on the required regular basis under conditions of civil war, or even of genocide? The implied answer is that they won't, and Neefjes' principal focus is on an analysis of the causes of conflict and the role that environmental factors might play in them. In Neefjes' view, what are called 'complex emergencies' are fuelled by a number of factors and it would be a mistake to think that environmental ones are primordial—or even that they are ever-present. The causes of social breakdown are 'multiple and interlinked', and so responses to them must be multiple and interlinked too: bare 'relief' is insufficient, and institutional development, for example, should form part of responses to crisis situations.

Neefjes argues that growth and technology will, and should, have a role to play in poverty relief, and that it is a mistake for environmentalists not to acknowledge this. He backs up these insights with case-study evidence from Rwanda, Sierra Leone, Sudan, Kivu, and Kagera, and suggests that, on balance, 'Environmental degradation and resource distribution play an increasingly important role' in conflicts, and that, 'supporting the (local) management of access and control over natural resources and providing the wider conditions for their sustainable use in a changing world is paramount.'

No book on the vast issues of environmental sustainability and social justice could ever claim to be comprehensive, and there are some very obvious gaps in the treatment offered here: there is no gender analysis, for example, and there is no voice from the developing world, nor from the 'environmental justice' movement in the USA. Some of these gaps are due to the vagaries of individual lives and the consequent unavailability of invitees to attend the seminars that formed the backdrop to this book. It seemed inappropriate to fill these gaps with commissioned papers, since the idea was to publish a collection of papers whose authors had all had the opportunity to read, hear, and discuss each of the contributions. There is, however, a considerable range of opinions and dimensions on show. We have moved from sustaining 'physical stock' to bequeathing 'human institutions', from liberal justice to socialist justice and back again, from justice in the present to justice in the future (and between present and future), from global capitalism to national environmental taxation, and from the hypothetical original position of John Rawls to the killing fields of Rwanda.

In the end, nothing will come of any these reflections unless theory can be translated into practice, and one of the most fascinating aspects of the series of seminars which produced this book was the encounter between academics (mostly political theorists in the broadest sense) and members of the policy community. As far as the chapters in this book are concerned, the ghost at the feast is Jonathon Porritt. Porritt is the best-known figure in the environmental movement in Britain, and he has cut an increasingly large figure on the international stage. He attended all three of the Keele seminars, and by the last encounter he was in considerable despair at the inability or unwillingness of the professional academics to make a useful and usable contribution to the policy debate. Brian Barry makes sympathetic reference to this in his chapter here, and defends the approach of the academy to these questions in perfectly reasonable terms—but ones which might be read as maintaining the division between the academy and the wider world. The challenge would be to bring them together: to ask progressive members of the policy community what they want, and to enjoin academics to deliver it—not slavishly, of course, but merely relevantly and comprehensibly. This, though, is the task for another series of seminars. What we have here is a series of contributions to the task of clarifying the relationship between social justice and environmental sustainability by some of the outstanding figures in each field—and in some cases in both of them. This, in itself, is a commitment to fairness and futurity.

PART I

1

Sustainable Development as a Contested Concept

MICHAEL JACOBS

Introduction

Over the last ten years, the terms 'sustainable development' and 'sustainability'[1] have come to dominate the field of environmental policy and politics. Although they had appeared in environmentalist literature before,[2] these terms first gained political authority and widespread recognition from the so-called 'Brundtland Report' (the report of the United Nations Commission on Environment and Development), published in 1987.[3] In examining the major environmental problems facing the world and appropriate responses to them, the Brundtland Report established the concept of sustainable development as the framework under which the twin requirements of environmental protection and economic development could be integrated. Sustainable development rapidly became the key principle underpinning official environmental policy at both national and international levels. The 1992 'Earth Summit' in Rio de Janeiro (the UN Conference on Environment and Development) generated not only formal endorsement for the concept from over 150 national governments, but a wide range of general and particular policy initiatives under the sustainable development heading. At the same time the huge sales of the Brundtland Report, coupled with the support of non-governmental environment organizations, launched the concepts of sustainable development and sustainability into the wider public domain.

These concepts are now the common currency of almost all players in the environmental arena. Not long ago, environmental policy and politics was a battlefield not just for sharply conflicting interests and world-views—from radical greens through techno-centric environmentalists to capitalists defending economic growth—but correspondingly for competing vocabularies.[4] Yet today nearly all of these groups are using the same language and endorsing the same nominal objective, that of sustainable development.

This state of affairs has not met universal approbation, however. Amongst those participating in environmental debates three forms of resistance are discernible. The first is frustration or irritation, usually expressed from a policy-technocratic standpoint. Sustainable development is never properly *defined,* it is protested; everybody seems to think it means something different. How can the term be adopted as a policy objective unless its meaning is clarified and agreed upon?[5]

The second form of resistance is outright rejection. Not all environmentalists have endorsed the concept of sustainable development. Politically, its most outspoken opposition comes from those we might call 'ultra-greens'. For them, the fuzziness of its meaning is integral to its purpose. Sustainable development is a smokescreen put up by business and development interests to obscure the conflicts between ecological integrity and economic growth, and between the interests of the rich North and poor South. Acceptance of the concept by environmental groups is a mistake, it is argued: a fatal co-option into technocratic 'global management' sideshows designed not to disturb the fundamental processes of capitalist exploitation.[6]

The third form of resistance comes from those we might call 'cultural critics', principally within academia. The argument here is that the discourse of sustainable development represents an inappropriate response to the 'environmental problematic'. It derives from the same cultural sources—modernism, scientific positivism and realism, technocratic social democracy—as the problems it is trying to address. Despite good intentions, its inability to understand or reflect recent cultural changes in industrial societies leaves its programme liable to failure.[7]

The purpose of this chapter is to illuminate the discourse and politics of sustainable development in Northern industrialized countries.[8] In doing so each of these three forms of resistance will be addressed. The present chapter explores alternative interpretations of the concept of sustainable development, responding to the claim that it is inadequately defined and therefore useless. Like other political concepts, it is argued, sustainable development has two levels of meaning. One of these is well defined; the other is the site of political contest. Answering sustainable development's opponents, the paper suggests that these two levels of meaning open up new and important possibilities for environmental politics. One of these is the development and propagation of a radical political world-view under the cloak of 'non-political' respectability. The second half of the chapter sets out a description of this emerging 'radical model' of sustainable development.

1. SUSTAINABLE DEVELOPMENT AS A CONTESTABLE CONCEPT

The 'Meaning' of Sustainable Development

Outside the field of environmental economics,[10] most of those now using the term 'sustainable development' are content to adopt one or other of the two definitions in common use. These are the so-called 'Brundtland definition' ('development which meets the needs of the present without compromising the ability of future generations to meet their own needs')[11] and the 'Caring for the Earth definition' ('improving the quality of life while living within the carrying capacity of supporting ecosystems').[12] These are generally deemed sufficient to express the concept; argument can then proceed as to what must be done to achieve it in practice.

This acquiescence in the concept of sustainable development makes many commentators and practitioners deeply uneasy, however. Such unease is particularly common among policy-makers and practitioners coming across the term for the first time. Partly because of the breadth of its endorsement—which suggests that it might have no meaning at all—there is a widespread desire to clarify more precisely the 'meaning' of the concept.

This comes from two sources. First, there is a *technocratic* view that sustainable development can only be made 'operational' in policy terms if a single and precise meaning can be agreed upon. For a start, the two common definitions are not the only ones available: of the 'gallery' of definitions quoted by the Pearce Report as long ago as 1989 (and many more have been added since), is it always clear which one we are we talking about? Are they all the same? And what exactly do these vague definitions mean anyway? What is 'development', what are 'needs', what is it that must be 'sustained', how is 'quality of life' measured? Thus Harvey Brooks: 'For the concept of sustainability . . . to be operationally useful it must be more than just an expression of social values or political preferences disguised in scientific language. Ideally it should be defined so that one could specify a set of measurable criteria such that individuals and groups with widely differing values, political preferences or assumptions about human nature could agree whether the criteria are being met in a concrete development program.'[13]

Second, there is a *political* concern among some environmentalists that the lack of clarity of the definitions allows *anything* to be claimed as 'sustainable' or as 'promoting sustainable development'. For example, does it allow economic growth or not? Does it mean a global redistribution of resources or not? At present the vagueness of the definitions, it is argued, allows business and 'development' interests (and their government supporters) to claim they are in favour of sustainable development when actually they are the perpetrators of *un*sustainability. Sharachandra Lélé's conclusion is typical: 'SD is in real danger of becoming a cliché . . . a fashionable phrase that everyone pays homage to but nobody cares to define . . . better articulation of the terms, concepts, analytical methods and policy-making principles . . . is necessary if SD is to avoid either being dismissed as another development fad or co-opted by forces opposed to changes in the status quo.'[14]

Concepts, Conceptions, and Contestation

This search for a unitary and precise meaning of sustainable development is misguided. It rests on a mistaken view of the nature and function of political concepts.[15] The crucial recognition here is that, like other political terms (democracy, liberty, social justice, and so on), sustainable development is a 'contestable concept'.[16]

Contestable concepts are complex and normative, and they have two levels of 'meaning'. The first level is unitary but vague: it can often be expressed in a short definition (for example, 'government of the people, by the people, for the people'). Often there will be a number of such definitions available; but neither this nor their vagueness makes such concepts meaningless or useless. At the first level contestable concepts are defined by a number of 'core ideas'. These are general, but substantive and non-redundant. Democracy, liberty, and social justice, for example, all have readily understood 'first level' meanings. We know what the subject is when we use these terms, there are no other terms expressing the same set of core ideas, and even people holding widely different interpretations of them can agree on the evaluation of (necessarily extreme) situations in which democracy, liberty, and social justice are *not* present.

The interesting feature of contestable concepts comes in the second level of meaning. This is where the contest occurs: political argument over how the concept should be interpreted in practice. Is representative democracy sufficient, or should it be direct? Are positive freedoms necessary for liberty, or only negative ones? Is social justice about outcomes or only opportunity? Such questions reflect alternative *conceptions* of the concept: differing ways in which it can be understood. For common political concepts, the battle is neither over the first level of meaning nor indeed whether one accepts the normative goal. Almost everyone is in favour of democracy, liberty, and social justice; the debate is over alternative conceptions of what they mean, at the second level.

Sustainable development is a contestable concept of this kind. Its first level meaning is now given: for better or worse (and as a

result of an interesting political evolution), the core ideas are fixed
and cannot now be changed through rational argument.[17] Rather,
attention needs to focus on the second level. Here there *is* a battle
for the 'meaning' of sustainable development. But there is no
point in trying to secure universal 'agreement' on a unitary meaning for the term. This will never happen, for those who use it have
different interests and political values. Such agreement is only
possible at the first level—and it now exists, coalesced around
the Brundtland and *Caring for the Earth* definitions. At the second,
there is contestation. This shouldn't be perceived as a remediable
lack of precision over what sustainable development 'means':
rather, such contestation *constitutes* the political struggle over
the direction of social and economic development. That is, disagreements over the 'meaning of sustainable development' are not
semantic disputations but *are* the substantive political arguments
with which the term is concerned.

Core Ideas and the Political Agenda

Analysis of the discourse of sustainable development reveals six
'core ideas' represented by the term. These are:[18]

(1) Environment-economy integration: ensuring that economic
    development and environmental protection are integrated
    in planning and implementation.

(2) Futurity: an explicit concern about the impact of current
    activity on future generations.

(3) Environmental protection: a commitment to reducing
    pollution and environmental degradation and to the more
    efficient use of resources

(4) Equity: a commitment to meeting at least the basic needs of
    the poor of the present generation (as well as equity
    between generations).

(5) Quality of life: a recognition that human well being is
    constituted by more than just income growth.

(6) Participation: the recognition that sustainable development

requires the political involvement of all groups or 'stake-holders' in society.

The first five of these core ideas are encompassed in the two common definitions. The sixth draws its 'textual authority' primarily from *Agenda 21* (the global action plan for sustainable development signed by 173 national governments at the Rio 'Earth Summit' in 1992),[19] rather than the Brundtland Report or *Caring for the Earth*. In those reports participation was primarily regarded as a means to the substantive ends represented by the first five core ideas. However in the consequent development of the discourse it has come to be seen as having substantive value in its own right.

Three features of these core ideas are apparent. The first is that while individually most of them have been expressed and supported before, they have not previously been put together into a single phrase or concept. Each represents a substantive value or objective. In purely conceptual terms, therefore—at the first level—sustainable development is clearly neither meaningless not redundant.

The second feature is that sustainable development is evidently *not* the path of development which has been followed by the global economy, or by most individual nations, over the past fifty years; even less over the last twenty. Environmental concerns have not been integrated into economic planning and policy; the impact of current activity on future generations has been *assumed* to be benign, not explicitly considered. Argument could no doubt be had over the extent to which environmental protection, equity, participation and quality of life (*per se*, as opposed to income growth) have been serious goals of global or individual countries' policy; the first three have certainly not been generally achieved. But in any case the important point is that in signing *Agenda 21* the majority of countries have rhetorically accepted that sustainable development *does* represent a new trajectory for development.[20]

And it is this that gives the term its political significance. The test is not whether the endorsement of sustainable development in international documents like *Agenda 21* and in national policies has actually (and already) changed the trajectory of development. Of course it hasn't (though some significant shifts are certainly apparent, such as international recognition of the importance of biodiversity, European carbon dioxide reduction policies and, in Britain, changes in transport policy). The question is whether the new discourse has changed the nature and salience of political activity and debate on these issues; and here there can be little question that it has.

In nearly every industrialized country, the period since the Brundtland Report, and then again since the Earth Summit, has seen much greater levels of activity and debate in the environmental policy field than before. In Britain, for example, we have had a White Paper, a national Sustainable Development Strategy, three accompanying strategies on climate change, forestry, and biodiversity, a forthcoming Environmental Bill setting up a new Environment Agency, a much-publicized Royal Commission report on transport and the environment, and so on. For local government, environmental management and now 'Local Agenda 21' strategies have provided a major new field of initiative. The 'greening of industry', while not as extensive as hoped for in some quarters, has seen a steady development of environmental management systems and practice. Meanwhile much of the most vibrant extra-institutional political activity has occurred over environmental issues, notably roadbuilding and animal welfare.

The relationship between this activity and the discourse of sustainable development has been three-fold. First, there can be little question that governments in democracies have felt obliged to do *something* in support of their public commitments. Once the policy arena has been opened up, particularly given the commitment to participation embedded within the sustainable development rhetoric, it has then been difficult to resist the further evolution of policy, as pressure groups and experts criticize initial proposals and demand stronger initiatives.[21] The requirement to 'do something' has infected local government and large businesses as well.

Second, government commitments to sustainable development have provided environmental pressure groups and the media with a valuable weapon, namely the apparent inconsistency between government rhetoric and action. The government's commitment to sustainable development—not least, in international agreements—is consistently used as a stick with which to beat the inadequacies of actual policy.[22] This makes NGO and media pressure considerably more effective.

Third, the sustainable development discourse has set off a process of *institutional learning*.[23] Throughout international agencies and national governments—and to a lesser extent, the business sector and other sectors—the sustainable development discourse is pushing institutions to reappraise their policies and policy-making processes. Sustainable development has provided new conceptual models for the relationship between environment and economy, and these have begun to shift the way policy-making is approached. This process is evident in all kinds of government institutions, from small district councils in England through national statutory bodies such as the Countryside Commission to international agencies like the World Bank. Of course, it has not shifted understanding or practice *enough*: a key problem (as we shall see below) is that the sustainable development 'model' has had little to say about the deeper cultural presuppositions of the institutions themselves. But it would be difficult to deny that the new discourse—to put it at its weakest—has raised awareness, and placed environmental issues and the integration of environmental and economic concerns on the table of policy debate where they were not before.

It is of course the 'not enough' claim which is made by the ultra-greens, who see sustainable development as a way for government institutions and corporations to *pretend* to act on the environment while not in fact doing so. Ultra-greens claim, not just that sustainable development has been ineffectual, but that it is positively dangerous, since it ties the environmental movement to the interests of Northern governments and multinational corporations. Yet governments would not even be pretending if it had not been for the capacity of the sustainable development discourse to generate—and then to bind them to—new commitments. Given the long period from the mid-1970s to the late 1980s in which the environment was off the political agenda, and the continued development of environmental policy now even after the initial media attention has gone, this should surely be counted as progress. The creation of a 'discourse coalition'[24] of otherwise disparate interests using the same vocabulary is a crucial component in the development of an environmental politics which has any hope of being successful. It is precisely the ability of sustainable development—a concept both substantive and challenging—to gather endorsements from states and large corporations as well as from the environmental movement which is what makes it so important.

Indeed, the extraordinary thing about sustainable development in many ways is that it *has* acquired such widespread endorsement. For the third feature of the core ideas is that they are broad in scope. Sustainable development is not, for example, simply a commitment to protect the environment; though this is without doubt the central idea, it is by no means the only one. Other political concepts encompassing as broad a range of core ideas as this rarely gain such universal acceptance; such acceptance tends to be limited to rather more basic political ideas (such as democracy or liberty). Indeed, concepts as broad as sustainable development are generally ideological in character—such as, for example, socialism or conservatism.

It is this which makes the discourse of sustainable development so interesting and significant. For as we shall show in the second half of this chapter, for its more radical proponents sustainable development *is* increasingly taking on the mantle of an ideology: a comprehensive set of values and objectives, an analysis of the operation of the political economy, and a strategy for political change. Yet at the same time the same concept is supported by a Conservative government and major corporations which would not accept the 'ideological' position at all. Sustainable development appears to have the remarkable capacity to articulate, nourish, and propagate quite radical political ideas while appearing respectably 'non-political'. Here again its advantages are apparent. We shall return to this below.

2. INTERPRETATIONS

The endorsement of the concept of sustainable development by such a wide range of interests and organizations is of course a function of its capacity for varying interpretation at the second, contested level of meaning. Observation of the discourse shows four major 'faultlines' for alternative interpretations, corresponding to the last four core ideas listed above. Each faultline yields two competing interpretations. Interpretations from each faultline can then be combined with others to generate a comprehensive *conception* of sustainable development. Again, there are two principal competing conceptions, with a continuum between them.

Environmental Protection

The first and most important faultline in the interpretation of conceptions of sustainable development lies in the *degree of environmental protection* it requires ('core idea' 3 above).

The 'weak' version of sustainable development adopts the less stringent idea of environmental conservation, i.e. a commitment where possible to protecting environmental resources and amenities. It is accepted that the environment is important and should where possible be protected, but the idea that economic activity should be confined within predetermined 'environmental limits' is rejected. In this interpretation, environment-economy integration means balancing or trading off the benefits of economic growth against those of environmental protection. No aspect or 'level' of the environment is regarded as inviolable, at least until countervailing economic benefits have been assessed. Broadly speaking this is the interpretation used by governments and business interests.[25]

The 'strong' version of sustainable development adopts the more stringent idea of 'environmental limits', i.e. a commitment to living within the limits created by the 'carrying capacities' of the biosphere. This idea comes from two sources. The ecological source is the notion of 'carrying capacity': the maximum population of a species which an ecosystem can support. In its semi-metaphorical economic sense, carrying capacity then means the amount and type of economic activity which natural ecosystems can support at tolerable levels of environmental degradation. The economic source is the concept of 'maximum sustainable yield'. This is the upper limit on the current use of environmental resources which permits the same level of use in the future. Originally derived from the economics and practice of forestry and fishing, the concept of sustainable yield—which itself is related to the non-environmental idea of 'sustainable income'— can also be more widely applied to non-renewables.

The idea of environmental limits is now one of the most powerful elements in the sustainable development discourse: a typical rhetorical expression, for example, is that 'society must learn to live within its environmental means'.[26]

These 'weak' and 'strong' versions of *sustainable development* are closely related to the 'weak' and 'strong' types of *sustainability* distinguished in the environmental economics literature. There, sustainability is defined as 'maintaining the capital stock'. The question is whether this means maintaining just the 'natural' capital stock ('strong sustainability') or the 'total' capital stock, including human-made capital ('weak sustainability'). If human-made capital can substitute for natural capital, weak sustainability need not involve maintaining natural capital *per se*. Indeed, weak sustainability is now generally presented in terms of maintaining welfare or utility over time; maintaining the capital stock is just the means.[27] Effectively, weak and strong sustainability are the same as weak and strong sustainable development. The only difference is that the debate about sustainable development (partly because it is less technical) does not concern 'capital': the trading off is between current benefits (income) provided by the environment and economic activity.

Equity

The second faultline concerns the idea (no. 4 above) of *equity*. The 'egalitarian' conception of sustainable development was that which motivated the original Brundtland Report (which brought the term into common use). 'Development' was used primarily in its Southern (Third World) sense, the point of 'sustainable development' being to emphasize that raising living standards for the poor had to include an improvement in environmental conditions and productivity. In Southern debate about sustainable development the notion of equity remains central, particularly in the demand not just that national but that *global* resources should be distributed in favour of poor countries and people.[28]

In the North, by stark contrast, equity is much the least emphasized of the core ideas, and is often ignored altogether. The dominant ('non-egalitarian') conception of sustainable development generally includes only a passing and non-committal mention of global resources distribution, and frequently fails to refer to intra-country equity at all.[29] This reflects both the 'radical' (and therefore less widely appealing) nature of the idea of equality in industrialized countries, and the uncomfortable challenge to consumption patterns and international economic relations implied by the global-egalitarian interpretation.

This difference between the Southern and Northern interpretations of sustainable development has been a major source of conflict in the international debate, particularly surrounding the Rio Earth Summit in 1992. Third World countries accuse the industrialized nations of reinterpreting the concept as simply an 'environment', not a 'development' one, which therefore implies little commitment on their part to a redistribution of global resources (and which also justifies 'imperialist' regulation of Third World resources, such as forests). This remains a source of tension not just between governments but between Southern and Northern non-governmental organizations.[30]

Partly as a result of this, global resource distribution has been receiving increasing attention among Northern NGOs recently. The two new concepts being introduced into the sustainable development discourse are the 'ecological footprint' and 'ecological space'. Both are measurements of the impact of one country's consumption on other countries' environments. They are being used to argue that Northern countries need to reduce their consumption of global resources in order to allow others access to the limited 'ecological space' they have appropriated.[31]

Participation

The third faultline concerns the idea (no. 6 above) of *participation*. Governments and businesses have tended to adopt what might be called a 'top-down' interpretation of the requirement for participation, in two senses. First, such participation is required principally in the *implementation* of sustainable development, not in deciding the *objectives* it implies. Governments decide objectives, using expert knowledge; the involvement of wider interests is mainly to carry out the policy. In these circumstances 'participation' frequently becomes a disguise for government inaction: implementation is the responsibility of everyone (businesses, individuals, voluntary organizations) *except* central government. The UK government's original policy document on climate change offered a telling example.[32] If there is any participation at the objective-setting stage, it tends to be a rather weak form of consultation.

Second, the top-down interpretation limits the participants to the major 'stakeholders' of society: businesses, local government, large non-governmental organizations. A typical mechanism is the consultative forum. The UK government, for example, convened a number of consultative 'round tables' in drawing up its National Strategy, consisting of interest groups and academics in particular fields; a number of local authorities have set up similar local bodies.[33] In this interpretation, participation is not seen as requiring a deeper or wider involvement of ordinary members of the public, except through changes in individual behaviour (energy saving, recycling).

The alternative 'bottom-up' interpretation of participation is more radical. Here objective-setting as well as implementation is subject to participative processes. In Canada, for example, 'multistakeholder' Round Tables have been set up in every province and many localities (and at national level); these are advising governments on principles and objectives for sustainable development as well as mechanisms for their achievement. Moreover, they are themselves going out to wider consultation, seeking the participation of ordinary members of the public in determining objectives.[34]

The same ideal has now been formalized in the 'Local Agenda 21' process occurring in the UK (as in other countries). While some such exercises are limited to rather top-down 'stakeholder' approaches, many are seeking innovative ways of involving the general public, both as individuals and through community organizations, in drawing up 'visions' of their localities and setting targets for key environmental and social objectives.[35]

Indeed, in some circles, this commitment to participation is coming to dominate the debate on sustainable development, even at the expense of specific environmental commitments. In the top-down interpretation the commitment to participation is essentially instrumental—it is necessary to achieve sustainable development, but has no intrinsic value, and where not required is not espoused. In the bottom-up interpretation, however, participation is a good in its own right. This leads to the fear, now occasionally being expressed, that sustainable development is losing its 'objective' relationship with carrying capacity or environmental limits. Does sustainability now mean, it is being asked, whatever emerges from appropriately participative and multi-stakeholder socio-political processes, whether or not these are ecologically sustainable?[36] We shall return to this issue below.

Scope of the Subject Area

The fourth faultline concerns the *scope of subject area* covered by the concept of sustainable development. There can be little doubt that protecting the environment is the dominant motivation for, and idea within, sustainable development. Although the Brundtland Report and Agenda 21 emphasize the importance of education, health, and other basic development needs, support the participation of poor people and women, and express commitment to indigenous practices and communities, these are essentially *derived* from the need for environmental protection; it is the latter which is their distinguishing feature and primary motivation. In most Northern countries, the debate about sustainable development is conducted entirely within the environmental field. Indeed, one of

the oddities of this debate is the extent to which it is so confined,
despite the major ramifications it has for policy in other areas,
particularly economics. The fact that the British government has
published a huge 'National Strategy' for sustainable development
went unremarked and remains unknown outside the small
environmental community. This is of course how the government
wants it: adopting a 'narrow' interpretation of sustainable development, it is happy to see the term as offering simply a new
environmental objective, nothing more.

This is not how others interpret the concept, however. Increasingly, advocates of sustainable development are using the term to
cover a much broader set of concerns. These start from the
environment, but then branch out into other fields, including
health, education, and social welfare. Consider, for example, the
provisional list of 'sustainability indicators' produced by the Local
Government Management Board (LGMB) in 1994 for piloting
among local authorities.[37] These indicators are intended to
provide measures of progress towards sustainable development
at the local level. Of the thirteen 'themes' into which the
indicators are divided, the first four and one other are environmental (resource use, pollution, biodiversity, meeting local needs
locally, minimizing environmentally damaging travel). The
remainder cover the full range of other aspects of development:
basic physical needs, work, health, freedom from fear of crime or
persecution, access to information and education, participation,
equal opportunity for culture and leisure, and beauty/'human
scale'/diversity.

This is a remarkable expansion of the concept of sustainable
development, indicating the breadth of the 'broad' interpretation.[38] Its claim to legitimacy is drawn from the notion of 'quality
of life' embodied in the *Caring for the Earth* definition of sustainable development (and from the equivalent concept of 'needs' in
the Brundtland definition). In 'narrow' formulations, the idea of
quality of life is used merely as a way of arguing that protecting
the environment is not just about safeguarding the interests of
future generations; it also has current benefits. These may not be
reflected in higher incomes or economic growth—but then (the
argument goes) man does not live by bread alone: as well as more

income we also need a better *quality of life,* and this can sometimes (as with the environment) be destroyed by income growth. The argument is usually presented in such a way that the environment appears as only one example among others of 'quality of life', but in the narrow version any others are not spelled out, and sustainable development itself is only about the environmental case.[39] In the broad interpretation, however, the connections are made explicit, and the other components of quality of life are identified and enumerated—as in the LGMB's list of indicators.

For many people this expansion of the idea of sustainable development is unacceptable, taking the concept way outside its legitimate scope. Fear is often expressed that once the concept has gone beyond the environment, it will cease to be useful, merely becoming a new term for generalized 'progress', its objectives a mere wish list of desirable social goods.[40] Yet this is precisely the aim of the advocates of the broad conception. They want to argue that sustainable development is *not* simply an environmental concept, but a general one, describing a new goal of economic and social (and, by implication, political) life.

There is an unashamed element of what we might call 'environmental imperialism' about this, since the people involved in defining and implementing the broad conception of sustainable development in local government in Britain are almost entirely drawn from the environmental field. It is not yet clear whether the enlargement of their purview to other areas of expertise will be welcomed or rejected by interest groups and professionals in those areas.

In fact, the broad conception of sustainable development goes further even than an expansion of the subject areas covered. Advocates note that the concept of 'sustainability' (something enduring into the future) is applicable not just to the environment or environmental economy, but to society itself. Surely, they ask, the aim should be to protect and maintain communities and cultures as much as the environment: both because only cohesive societies can protect nature, and because communities and cultures are valuable in their own right. This argument is made principally in relation to poorer 'indigenous' communities, particularly in the South but also in parts of the North, for example

Canadian mining communities or working-class communities in British cities. It leads to the introduction of a new form of sustainability, 'social sustainability'.[41]

The idea of social sustainability is related to both equity and participation. 'Indigenous' cultures are generally poor; a specific objective of supporting them will help to ensure that the development process is egalitarian in effect. Moreover, inequitable societies are prone to social conflict; they are therefore likely to be socially unsustainable. At the same time, indigenous communities often have their own understanding and knowledge of the natural environment. Sustainable development, it is argued, should reflect and draw on this through bottom-up participation, not destroy it in a technocratic model of progress, however 'environmental'.[42]

Alternative Conceptions

Although the four faultlines identified here are logically separate, they are in practice connected. The egalitarian, strong, bottom-up, and broad interpretations of sustainable development are frequently held at the same time by the same people. This generates what might be called the 'radical' conception of sustainable development. This is adopted not just by many greens and environmental activists, but, in Britain at least, by many advocates and practitioners within the local government world.[43] Since it is local government which is arguably at the leading edge of the debate about (and implementation of) sustainable development in Britain, this is quite significant.[44]

By the same token, the non-egalitarian, weak, top-down, and narrow interpretations are also held in common, generally by government and business interests. Together these constitute what might be called the 'conservative' conception of sustainable development. Clearly, though the core ideas are the same, the radical and conservative conceptions are very different in philosophy and practice.

3. THE RADICAL MODEL OF
SUSTAINABLE DEVELOPMENT

Environment, Ethics, Economy

The starting point for the sustainable development model is environmental degradation, at global and local levels. Such degradation is caused by economic activity; more specifically, by market forces. Such forces, governed by individual market decisions, are blind to their combined environmental impacts. They also tend towards growth. For these reasons human economic activity is exceeding the 'carrying capacity' of the biosphere, leading to degradation in its many forms.

Those who hold the sustainable development world-view tend to have four separate types of value motivating their concern about environmental degradation. Two are varieties of justice: intergenerational (concern for the impact on future generations), and intragenerational (concern for the impact that current patterns of economic activity, particularly consumption in industrialized countries, is already having on poor people, particularly in the South).

The other two might loosely be described as 'environmental ethics'. Although the argument for sustainable development is generally expressed in terms of one or both forms of justice, observation suggests that many of its strongest supporters are actually motivated more by an ethical revulsion at environmental degradation *per se*. For some, this is because the environment has 'intrinsic' value: it is wrong to destroy it. For others the value is more 'cultural': they believe that society and human nature are impoverished and diminished by the destruction of the non-human world. All these beliefs, but particularly the latter two, are in turn often expressions (and possibly sources) of a more profound belief that the values and trajectory of industrialized societies are wrong. Increasing economic expansion through the exploitation and domination of the environment denies humankind's true nature and place in the world. Whether or not this speculation about motivation is right, these four values can clearly be seen to inform environmental concern. They become expressed in the injunction that society must live within the environment's carrying capacity.

A separate argument is made at this point. The main reasons for wanting to stop environmental degradation may be concerned with future generations, people in the South, or the intrinsic or cultural value of the environment. But, it is pointed out, the environment has current benefits for all people. It contributes to health, it provides amenity and spiritual uplift, it acts as life support. Therefore environmental protection will also be of benefit to the present generation of reasonably affluent people in industrialized countries.

How can economic activity be held within the environment's carrying capacity? Market forces, it is argued, must be controlled. This requires a form of economic planning: instead of markets determining environmental impacts, these should be publicly chosen. The economy should be geared to achieving a set of environmental targets (corresponding, ideally, to carrying capacity limits). This can only be done by various kinds of state intervention in the economy, at a variety of levels, from the international to the local.

Such planning does not, it is claimed, require a cessation of economic growth. Rather, government intervention is designed to raise the 'environmental efficiency' of economic activity. That is, the aim is to reduce the impact that each unit of activity has on the environment. By such means, growth may continue even while environmental impact declines.

Growth *may* continue; while it is politically sensible to argue that it can, in practice advocates of the radical conception of sustainable development are not particularly worried about this. For they do not believe that economic growth is the ultimate objective of economic or political life. Their value motivation here is for non-economic well-being: a belief that industrialized societies (and the development process in the South) are too concerned with raising incomes, and not enough with other aspects of human well-being. These aspects do not necessarily correlate with (and cannot therefore be measured by) higher incomes; moreover, they may actually be reduced by the processes of economic growth. One such aspect is environmental quality itself. The economic goal should therefore be to raise 'quality of life', this term encompassing all the different aspects of human well-being.

Sustainability Indicators

Two further values are introduced here. Quality of life can be experienced by individuals or be an attribute of societies as a whole. In its latter form, radical advocates of sustainable development want to include the ideals of equity (interpreted as a lessening of inequality) and 'community/culture'. By the latter is meant the vibrancy of communal life, including cultural traditions and local distinctiveness, voluntary association, mutual aid, and local knowledge. It is the conservation of local cultures and communities, along with equity and a third ideal, participation, which can broadly speaking be said to make for 'social sustainability'.

If quality of life (including equity and 'community/culture') is the objective of economic policy, society will need new indicators of progress. GNP, which measures economic growth, is clearly inadequate, both because it does not take account of environmental degradation and because it fails to record non-income aspects of quality of life.

The arguments so far are now drawn together. The key idea is that of 'indicators'. An extraordinary amount of effort is currently being devoted to the design of and collection of information on 'sustainability indicators', not just in Britain but throughout the world.[45] Indicators play three roles in the sustainable development narrative. First, indicators are required for environmental-economic planning. If society is to adopt environmental planning targets (such as for CO_2 emissions or waste recycling) it will first need to identify the relevant indicators (in this case, tonnes of CO_2 emitted and, say, proportion of solid waste recycled). Similarly, indicators are required to measure social progress, such as the percentage of under-5s in pre-school education, or the number of reported racially motivated attacks. Such indicators perform a *managerial* role: they are needed by environmental, economic, and social managers to measure environmental and social impacts and the success or otherwise of policy.

Second, indicators play a *goal-defining* role. Used in political argument and in the media instead of or alongside GDP and other conventional economic indicators, they express and thereby help to define the new goals of economic and political life required by sustainable development.

Participation and Policy

Third, indicators have a *communicative* function. They help to inform the wider community about trends in the environment and wider social conditions, and thus provide a conduit for public participation. Such participation plays a crucial role in the sustainable development model. Again, the argument comes from two sides. Radical advocates of sustainability hold a normative value or ethic of participatory democracy: they think it is good for public decisions to be made through the active involvement of the public. They also recognize that participation in the process of policy-making is necessary.

Implementing sustainable development will require considerable government intervention, and this requires the consent of the governed. This is much more likely to be achieved if people have been involved in the decision-making process; it is also likely to be better policy. Moreover, governments are not all-powerful: unless the general public and the major 'stakeholders' in society are committed and involved, good intentions will fail to be implemented. Indeed, at local level, where local governments have relatively few powers, stakeholder participation may effectively *substitute* for government policy-making. The hope expressed by the Round Table movement in Canada and in similar initiatives in the UK is that these bodies will in some senses replace the policy-making role formerly reserved for government.[46] Though ultimate power must rest with democratically elected bodies, intermediate institutions with functional representation from the different sectors of society are regarded as having at least equivalent democratic legitimacy. Thus, for example, the Lancashire Environmental Action Plan in Britain is a product not of Lancashire County Council after consultation with various stakeholder groups, but of the multi-stakeholder Lancashire Environmental Forum itself.[47]

The limitations of this model of 'stakeholder democracy' are apparent to most of its proponents: it relies on the voluntary participation of the stakeholders. It is recognized that in many instances governments must make policy and enforce it, particularly at the national level. A variety of different kinds of 'instruments' are therefore advocated to influence or force others to change their behaviour. In the environmental field, these include traditional legal regulations, typically used in pollution control and in areas such as product standards, building regulations, and the land use planning system; financial incentives or so-called 'economic instruments', such as green taxes and pollution charges, tradable resource and pollution permits, subsidies and deposit-refund schemes (these have had much recent discussion but are still little used); various kinds of public expenditure, for example on infrastructure, public transport, research and development; and 'moral suasion', attempts to encourage changes in behaviour through information, publicity, and persuasion. Through these methods (and a few others, such as liability law) governments can implement sustainable development policy where pure voluntarism is not enough.

In these ways the sustainable development model seeks environmental action and changes in environmentally damaging behaviour from all sectors of society (including government itself). If sufficient, these actions and changes will raise environmental efficiency and ultimately, it is hoped, bring the impacts of economic activity within environmental limits or carrying capacity. This will safeguard the environment, along with the interests of future generations and the South. At the same time, the quality of life of the current generation in industrialized countries (as measured by the wider set of indicators) will improve.

The Politics of the Radical Model

This brief description of the radical model adds a further, interesting argument in support of the concept of sustainable development. Each of the positions taken on the contested core ideas opposes the ideologies currently dominant in British and other industrialized-country politics. The notion of environmental limits challenges the assumption implicit in conventional economic theory and practice that infinite exponential growth is possible. While the model is careful not to rule out growth altogether, the 'limits' thesis requires a fundamental reappraisal of economic priorities. So too does the idea that such growth cannot provide all the social goods required for 'quality of life'; that such goods might be better secured by changed patterns of economic activity and 'community' organization with less growth.

The redistribution of global resources towards the South, and a greater emphasis on national equity, also challenge current political priorities, certainly of Conservative governments and parties. This is true too of the commitment to participation, and the institutionalization of new forms of participatory government through Round Tables and Local Agenda 21.

In these senses, therefore, the radical model of sustainable development represents an *ideological* challenge to current politics, not just a *policy* one. Its principal target is clearly the Right, but it is by no means a simple Left programme or analysis. If anything, it could be described as 'green social democratic'. And yet—this is the interesting part—this 'ideology' is now being promoted under the auspices of a concept which has the approval (in Britain) of the British government, the Confederation of British Industry and a large number of Conservative local councils. It is being propagated at Local Agenda 21 and similar events organized on a 'non-political' basis in localities throughout Britain. There is nothing underhand about this: though contested at the second level of meaning, the radical model is drawn directly from the uncontested first level concept of sustainable development.

The 'discourse coalition' of sustainable development may therefore be having exactly the opposite effect to that worrying the ultra-greens. Far from co-opting the environmental movement into a Conservative government and business programme of non-reform, it may be allowing the articulation and dissemination of a radical world-view under the shelter of government and business approval. Of course, it is possible that both these processes are going on at the same time.[48]

2

Sustainability: Should We Start from Here?

ALAN HOLLAND

1. Introduction

The aim of this chapter is to lay bare the difficulties that surround the attempt to formulate the goal of sustainability so that it makes the difference to policy that it is supposed to make. The goal itself has emerged from a sense that we need to put a brake on economic development, as this is traditionally understood. Hence, a favoured way of characterizing sustainability is to see it as a form of constraint upon the operation of 'business as usual'. There are three concerns in particular that have pointed to the need for such constraint:

(i) First, there is a growing belief that the headlong pursuit of development does not pay *economically*. Hidden 'costs' are beginning to emerge, in the form of extensive pollution, exhausted resources and untoward impacts upon climate, life-forms, and life-sustaining systems generally. It appears, in short, that sheer economic *efficiency* requires us to take account of these previously hidden environmental costs; and this, in turn, prompts the suggestion that all policy and development proposals should be subjected to a 'sustainability' test.

(ii) Second, there is a growing belief that unrestrained development is indefensible *morally*.[1] This dimension of concern would not arise in a world in which natural resources are presumed to be

My thanks to Michael Jacobs, Wilfred Beckerman, and Bryan Norton who have kindly offered criticisms of earlier versions of this chapter.

unlimited. But as soon as the idea takes hold that there are biological and ecological limits, and that the expansion of the human niche cannot be continued indefinitely, then the question eventually arises of how, for example, we should discharge our responsibilities to our descendants. Sustainability, understood according to the classic Brundtland formulation,[2] as the requirement that we should leave future generations the wherewithal to meet their needs, is thought to supply the (morally acceptable) answer.

(iii) Finally, there is a growing belief that the costs of unrestrained development are unacceptable *ecologically*.[3] This sense of ecological loss in the face of human progress first stirred, albeit only in particular cultural settings, during the eighteenth and nineteenth centuries both as a strand in the 'romantic movement' and, more practically, in the formation of societies devoted to protecting features of the natural environment. It has culminated most recently in concerns over the loss of biodiversity, and the particular concern that rates of extinction are overtaking, and perhaps have already overtaken, rates of speciation. Once again, people have looked to sustainability, understood now to incorporate an ecological dimension, as the goal towards which social and economic policy should be directed.

Which of these several concerns has in practice been uppermost in fuelling the call for constraints is hard to say. But there is no doubting the elegant theoretical appeal of a concept—sustainability—that promises to address all three concerns at a stroke. At the same time it is as well to be aware that these are different concerns, inasmuch as each is likely to put its own particular slant on the requirements for sustainability, and is likely to issue, therefore, in different ideas about how to make that concept operational. Furthermore, the existence of these different concerns poses the question of how far it is reasonable to expect a single concept to supply the looked-for solutions.

The critical analysis that follows is offered on the premiss that pursuit of sustainability in practice is at least supposed to 'make a difference'—to constitute a departure from 'business as usual', and seeks to show that certain ways of approaching the concept that are intended to achieve this aim may not in fact do so. As it happens, not everyone believes that we *can* do any better than operate a system of 'business as usual'. Others believe that we can do better, but that sustainability is not in fact a way of doing things better. Neither of these beliefs is challenged by the analysis which follows.

2. *Sustainability as Non-Declining Welfare*

It is likely to be some combination of the economic and moral concerns referred to above that produces a version of the doctrine of sustainability expressed in terms of human welfare. According to this version, we should aim to replace current practices and institutions with ones that promise to maintain a certain level of human welfare indefinitely.

There are two initial problems with this approach:

(i) One is that the economic and the moral considerations in question might pull in different directions. For example, within a given economy it is in principle possible that gross national product, however measured, could be maximized by the introduction of a system of slavery, that would (or could) be morally unacceptable. If we transpose this idea to the inter-temporal dimension, an analogue would be the case of several generations undergoing extreme hardship for the sake of the generations to follow. This, after all, is not so unlike the ideology which is said to have informed the Stalinist regime in Russia.[4] Conversely, later generations might be the ones to undergo the hardship, being born at the fag end of a process that nevertheless delivers a higher level of welfare throughout the period in question than any alternative.

(ii) The second problem is that even if we focus on the moral dimension only, not everyone's moral sensitivities would lead them to advocate a policy designed to achieve a non-declining level of welfare over time. Wilfred Beckerman, for example, sees nothing morally commendable about such an aim, if some other pattern of distribution would in fact achieve greater overall welfare.[5] This position need not rest on a simple conviction that aggregative welfare outranks considerations of justice. It might instead rest upon a recognition that the requirements of inter-generational (diachronic) justice should not necessarily be expected to mimic those of intragenerational (synchronic) justice. Thus, it can invoke the more subtle claims that bind those who stand in asymmetrical relationships (for example, those arising from the way that future generations carry the hopes of the present, but not vice-versa), and the fact that changing circumstances can render judgements of comparative welfare inappropriate.

Even if these two problems are set on one side, there are severe and probably insuperable practical difficulties surrounding any attempt to provide for a certain level of welfare throughout a given population. These stem from the fact that actual welfare, or happiness, is a function of a number of circumstances that cannot realistically be anticipated or provided for—such as individual psychological disposition, cultural circumstances (including per-ceptions of relative levels of welfare) and unforeseeable events. These difficulties are serious enough when it is the welfare of current people which is under consideration; they are com-pounded when the attempt is being made to provide for the welfare of future people.

One response to this difficulty is to distinguish between a more, and a less, ambitious aim. The more ambitious aim would be to bring about equality of welfare over time in the most inclusive sense—that is to say, taking into account not only material welfare but also moral and 'spiritual' welfare and the satisfaction of people's ideals and aspirations, all of which contribute to their sense of whether they are living a 'worthwhile life'. The less ambitious aim would be to bring about the even-handed satisfac-tion of needs. It might be conceded that the former aim is unrealistic; but it might be claimed that the latter aim, at any rate, is no more unrealizable than is normal in human affairs.

Certainly this response would serve to mitigate the difficulty; but it is arguable that it still underestimates the extent to which even the satisfaction of needs is conditional upon the economic, social, and political conditions that obtain. The result is that any arrangement put in place that is designed to provide for the more equitable satisfaction of needs is still severely conditioned, and in particular is hostage to the institutions prevailing at the time.

3. Sustainability as Non-Declining Capacity

It is perhaps in recognition of the sorts of difficulties just outlined that one more commonly finds the goal of sustainability explained as the attempt to maintain 'capital'—by which is meant the attempt to maintain for people over time the *wherewithal*, or the means, to provide for their own welfare. So, we find Kerry Turner and David Pearce claiming that the conditions for achieving sustainability involve 'leaving the next generation with a stock of capital assets that provide them with the *capability* to generate at least as much development as is achieved by this generation'.[6] Hence sustainability comes to be elucidated as the attempt to maintain a non-declining level of *capital*.

The aggregate of the different kinds of capital is usually referred to as 'total capital'—namely the sum total of resources capable of contributing to human welfare. Included in this 'genus' are several 'species' or 'varieties'. The two main 'species' of capital are said to be 'natural capital' and 'human-made capital'. A representative view of natural capital is that it refers to 'those aspects of nature—minerals, biological yield potential, pollution absorption capacity, etc., that are utilised or are potentially utilisable in human social and economic systems'.[7] Human-made capital comprises both artefacts, such as factories, buildings, and machinery, and also human capital—the knowledge, skills, virtues, and habits needed to realize the value of both natural and other human-made capital. An important kind of capital straddling these two is 'cultivated capital' (also called 'social and economic biodiversity' by Shepherd and Gillespie[8]—roughly, the total of cultivated plants and domesticated animals, together with their very considerable concomitants, such as broad acres of grasslands. For the purpose of this discussion, therefore, we can assume the 'taxonomy' shown in Fig. 2.1.

Two versions of this approach to sustainability are commonly

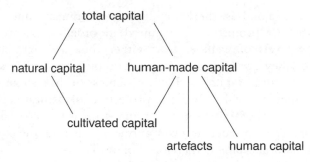

FIG. 2.1. *A taxonomy of capital*

distinguished in recent discussions—so-called 'weak' sustainability and 'strong' sustainability.[9] Whereas proponents of weak sustainability are said to advocate policies devoted to securing a non-declining level of total capital, proponents of strong sustainability are said to advocate policies devoted to securing a non-declining level of natural capital in particular. However, it cannot be assumed, without further discussion, that there really are two positions here to be distinguished. For, as long as the value yielded by the capital in question is understood in terms of its capacity to generate (present and future) human welfare, the impression which is sometimes given that 'strong' and 'weak' positions somehow differ in principle and, further, that strong sustainability has a specific and principled commitment to sustaining environmental, or 'natural', capital, is in fact quite misleading. For on one reading, the real difference between the two positions turns on what seems to be a question of fact. Proponents of strong and weak sustainability both advocate the maintenance of a non-declining capacity to generate (human) welfare; on this point of principle there is no difference between them. But whereas proponents of weak sustainability are supposed to believe that natural and human-made capital are, as a matter of fact, indefinitely substitutable, proponents of strong sustainability believe that they are not. Thus proponents of strong sustainability happen to believe that maintaining a non-declining level of natural capital is an indispensable means for achieving non-declining levels of welfare, because they happen to believe that human-made capital cannot be substituted indefinitely for natural capital. Their attachment to natural capital is therefore entirely contingent upon their belief that its protection is required in order to secure non-declining levels of welfare. Now either they are right in that belief, or they are wrong. If they are wrong, then their attachment to natural capital will cease—unless it has some other basis. If they are right, then the protection of natural capital is secured by a commitment to secure total capital—i.e. weak sustainability. Construed as a commitment to nature, the commitment to natural *capital* is therefore hollow.[10]

There appear to be three ways of rescuing strong sustainability as a distinct position. One is to have it defend natural capital even at the cost of some decline in total capital—which would mark a move towards the position referred to pejoratively as 'absurdly strong sustainability'.[11] Another is to have the distinction between weak and strong sustainability characterized as a normative disagreement—for example, over whether a section of old-growth forest, or a hospital, would most enhance total capital. But since the whole point of introducing the concept of capital is to replace value judgements with measurements, this would effectively mean abandoning the conceptual framework which pretends that these things can be measured, and therefore also the characterization of weak and strong sustainability in terms of their commitment to total and natural *capital* respectively.[12] A third way, briefly explored later in this chapter, is to sever the necessary link with human welfare, and characterize strong sustainability in terms of a commitment to the natural *world* rather than to natural *capital* (i.e. the natural world inasmuch as it is 'utilizable').

4. 'Critical' Capital

It has been argued elsewhere that the doctrine of substitutability (understood as the doctrine that human-made capital can be substituted for natural capital indefinitely) is radically indeterminate, and is by no means the straightforward empirical claim it might seem to be.[13] But suppose, for the sake of argument, that there is some straightforward sense in which it is false. What is less often observed[14] is that substitution, and failure of substitution, can *go both ways*. For, suppose that there are indeed features of the natural world for which there are no human-made substitutes. What is no doubt equally true is that there are human-made features for which there are no natural substitutes, and probably some for which there are no other human-made substitutes either. Moreover, there *are* human-made substitutes for at least some natural features. For these reasons, given that the overall goal is to maintain the capacity to secure present and future human welfare, the denial of the doctrine of substitutability does not support the protection of *all* natural capital nor does it support the protection of *only* natural capital, because it does not support the protection of natural capital in so far as it is natural, but only in so far as it is 'critical'—by which is meant, 'critical for securing future levels of human welfare'.[15] But some natural capital is not critical in this sense; and even a great deal of non-substitutable natural capital is not critical. For although 'substitutable' implies 'not essential', it does not follow, conversely, that if an item is not substitutable, then it is essential. Furthermore, because of the interdependence of natural and human-made capital, it is undoubtedly true that much natural capital is no more critical than much human-made capital, even where this capital is substitutable in the sense that it can be replicated. It has been observed, for example, that with one or two curious exceptions nature never got round to evolving wheels,[16] which happen to be critical to many a human enterprise. In fact, you would need to go back to before the time when the human race started to use tools to find a period when at least some human-made capital was not 'critical'.

But even if sustainability requires that some minimum or 'critical' level of *natural* capital be maintained, it does not follow from this that *existing* levels of natural capital should be maintained. It has in fact been argued by Turner and Pearce that there are at least four main reasons why it would not be acceptable to run down (existing) environmental assets—i.e. natural capital—in the pursuit of sustainability. They cite: uncertainty, irreversibility, life-support, and loss aversion.[17] However, none of these reasons is entirely convincing:

(i) *Uncertainty*. The argument is that we do not know the consequences for human well-being of running down natural capital, because we do not know how complex natural ecosystems work. However, uncertainty is a rather frail banner to wave in the face of those who witness human misery now, and think they see ways of alleviating that misery even though it may involve using up natural capital. (And sometimes, we can be quite certain that misery will result from not using up natural capital.) A second point is that the argument rather assumes that a world in which natural ecosystems were left to their own devices would be more secure. But if the gradual expropriation of natural ecosystems by human-made ecosystems really leads to a less secure world, it is unclear why humans have persisted in this project so tenaciously.[18] There is certainly a widespread belief that human life is made *more* secure thereby; nor is it clear that the belief is unjustified, whether one thinks in terms of the security of the average individual life, or of the human niche as a whole. It is perhaps not sufficiently appreciated how far the fears for human security that underlie the argument from uncertainty stem from the very same motivations that have led the human race to expropriate so much of the natural world in the first place.[19]

(ii) *Irreversibility*. It simply is not true, as Turner and Pearce claim, that 'only natural capital has the attribute of irreversibility'.[20] Nor is it true of all natural capital that its decrease is irreversible. In the first place, it is no more possible to replace a Norman church than to replace an ancient forest. And even if we focus on technological capital, it will often be impossible to reconstruct its *function,* even if the thing itself could be refashioned. In what sense, for example, could the 'capital' represented by a bronze spear in the bronze age be recreated? In the second place, many natural systems have remarkable powers of regeneration. All that can be claimed is that some natural systems are irreplaceable. In fact, the examples of irreversibility which Turner and Pearce suggest—species extinction and global warming— seem singularly ill-chosen. For (a) it is far from clear that global temperature could not be lowered by technological means; and (b) while it may be true that species extinction is irreversible, it is not true that the extinction of a species necessarily implies a decrease in natural capital. Natural extinctions, at any rate, have been an integral part of a process—the history of life on earth—in which natural capital may presumably be said to have 'expanded'. And since this is true, it follows that the effects of humanly induced extinctions upon the level of natural capital would each need to be judged on their merits. They do not automatically constitute a decline. The ecological effect of certain species might be to suppress possibilities of speciation which their removal could then release.[21]

(iii) *Life-support.* It cannot be denied that 'some ecological assets serve life-support functions'. But this is not true of all ecological assets, nor is it even claimed to be true (by Turner and Pearce). So consideration of their life-support functions will not constitute a defence of ecological assets (natural capital) as such. As John Lawton succinctly puts it: 'The planet can be made to work with rather few rivets'.[22]

(iv) *Loss-aversion.* It is no doubt true that people 'are highly averse to environmental losses'. But it can hardly be claimed that this is peculiarly true of *environmental* losses. If it were, why have we already lost so much? Moreover, people are *as* concerned, sometimes even more so, over the loss of a Norman church or some early cultivated variety of fruit or vegetable, as they are over the loss of many natural features.

To summarize, it turns out that the citation of natural capital in the elucidation of the position referred to as strong sustainability is something of a red herring. The pursuit of sustainability by no means entails the protection of natural capital as such. Further, although the proponents of this approach claim to capture economic, moral *and* environmental concerns, this also turns out not to be true.

5. The Relation between Natural Capital and Welfare

We have seen reason to doubt whether proponents of strong sustainability really do have grounds for maintaining the (existing) level of natural capital as such, even if there may be reason to maintain *some* level of natural capital. But let us assume, for whatever reasons, that this is thought an important component of any sustainability programme, and let us turn now to problems having to do with *measuring* the level of natural capital. Since the nature of these problems varies, depending crucially upon the *way* in which natural capital contributes to human welfare, we need first to undertake a brief analysis of the ways in which natural capital may be said to be 'used' or 'utilizable' to provide for human needs and welfare.

Natural capital may be said to contribute to welfare (a) directly, and (b) indirectly—by being transformed.

(a) Natural capital contributes to welfare directly in at least three different ways. First, it can be of value by virtue of its characteristics: for example, it can be beautiful, interesting, or symbolic. Second, it can be of value as constituting a special sphere or place of operation: for example by being a 'playground', a 'museum', a 'cathedral', or 'storehouse'.[23] Finally, it can be of value by virtue of its function: for example by being a 'sink', and by sustaining the conditions under which life is possible, with appropriate mixes of temperature, humidity, atmosphere, and suchlike.

(b) Natural capital contributes to welfare indirectly by being transformed in broadly two ways: one is by providing material for production—so-called 'raw materials'; the other is by providing material for consumption—for food, clothing, and shelter.

These direct and indirect ways of contributing to welfare are not necessarily mutually exclusive. For example, a garden results from the modification or transformation of nature, but may then be valued directly—say, for its beauty. On the other hand, these two sources of welfare can often be in competition with each other, so that the realization of the one kind of value is incompatible with the realization of the other. For example, maintaining a forest for its yield of timber may well mean sacrificing some of the interest and beauty it would otherwise have. Clearly, this fact is the source of a great many of the environmental conflicts which occur around the world.

Although the above distinction is somewhat rough and ready, it nevertheless has important implications for the question of how we go about measuring the 'level' of natural capital; for it points to an important difference in what counts as the *maintaining* of a given level of natural capital. Maintaining natural capital in so far as it is a direct source of welfare is largely a matter of *not spoiling it*. On the other hand, maintaining natural capital in so far as it delivers value by being transformed is largely a matter of *not using it in a way that involves using it up*.

6. *Some Problems of Measurement*

How, then, are we supposed to measure whether or not the level of natural capital is being maintained? Lest the idea should be entertained that we can simply equip natural scientists with a variety of measuring instruments and ask them to get on with it, let us now review some difficulties of principle that beset the whole project of 'measuring natural capital':

(i) The initial problem is that a great deal of the value of natural capital—construed as its value to the human community—is very clearly culturally specific. Consider first the kinds of value that natural capital delivers directly, such as beauty, for example. The area of the Yorkshire Dales known as the Three Peaks is today designated an area of outstanding natural beauty; whereas in 1724 Daniel Defoe found it to be a place of 'inhospitable terror'.[24] Or again, take a simple example of natural capital transformed for consumption. Certain varieties of snails, considered culinary delicacies by the French, are of no value at all in English cuisine. Parsnips, on the other hand, which are something of a delicacy in some English kitchens, are not given house room by the French chef. Such homespun examples may seem peripheral, but they point to a central problem for environmental valuation, which is how it is to deal with what philosophers know as 'Cambridge change'. A 'Cambridge change' is a change which something undergoes without changing 'in itself'. For example, if I am fully grown and my younger brother should grow to be taller than I am, then I shall have undergone a 'Cambridge change', being first taller than he is and then shorter. This is a kind of 'change' to which the value of natural capital, as we are currently understanding this term, must be constantly susceptible, and which poses formidable problems for the very idea of measurement. Far from being a simple matter of stock-taking, to be conducted by natural scientists, it must reckon with all manner of social and cultural variables.

Nor is the problem merely one of prediction. For, in the first place, the decisions we take today actually help to shape the tastes, values, and even the needs of future generations, thus changing the value that any given environmental item may have. And in the second place, we could actually decide to set about deliberately changing the tastes, values, and needs of future generations, and thus affect the amount of capital available to them in this way. Hence, 'Cambridge change' is not merely something which can happen; it is also something which our present actions can cause, or which we can seek deliberately to bring about.

(ii) The first problem turned on the fact that the value of natural capital, on this 'economic' interpretation, could fluctuate, whilst the natural items themselves underwent little change. From this it followed that maintaining the constancy of such value (or, in other words, the level of natural capital) is much more problematic than at first appears, and would certainly not be guaranteed by trying to ensure that the natural items themselves underwent little change. This problem mainly affects the value that natural capital generates directly. The second problem turns on the fact that the value of natural capital could undergo little change, whilst the natural items themselves were seriously depleted. The reason for this lies in the fact that the value which natural capital can generate by being transformed, whether for production or for consumption, is heavily dependent upon available technology and institutions—in other words, upon human-made and human capital. Thus, this is a problem that affects the second kind of value identified above, the value that natural capital generates by being transformed. Now it is important to see that the issue here is not simply that capital value could apparently be sustained despite what would normally be considered as environmental degradation, or the 'running down' of natural capital, because this would be compensated for by the buildup of human-made capital. Rather, the point is that the situation *would not properly be identified as a 'running down' of natural capital at all.* On the 'economic' view under consideration, natural capital does not consist of the actual physical items themselves, the 'physical stock', but the realized or realizable value of that stock. And if more value is realized or realizable from less physical stock, due to technological innovation, then the level of *natural* capital must be held to *remain no lower than it was before.* (This is because the economic notion of 'natural capital' is an *essentially* relational concept: it makes no sense to ask how much natural capital is represented by a grain of sand or lump of coal 'in itself'.)[25] What this implies is that, so long as the character of the human-made capital available serves to make efficient enough use of the physical stock to compensate for environmental depletion, the distinction between weak and strong sustainability will again turn out to be a sham. So long as total capital remains the same, then natural capital must be held to have remained the same also. Indeed, given that the GNP of the world economy stands higher than it has ever done before, it is hard to see how economists can believe there is such a thing as an environmental crisis at all. Some, of course, do not.

Turner and Pearce partly acknowledge these points, but decline to 'dwell' on them,[26] pointing out that the increasing capital that might result from more advanced technology will be needed to offset population growth, and that in any case not all technology is benign. (It is unclear whether they assume this is a wilful, or an unwitting, state of affairs.) However, reliance on a contingent claim about population growth, aligned with an assumption of human maleficence or incompetence, seems hardly sufficient reason to justify discounting the logical force of these points.

Herman Daly[27] might seem to have an answer to this criticism when he points out that the relation between natural and human-made capital is such that they are complementary *to* each other, not substitutes *for* each other. In outline, his argument is that in former times natural capital was plentiful, whereas human-made capital was in short supply. It therefore made economic sense to use, and even to use up, natural capital in order to build up human-made capital. Nowadays, on the other hand, whereas human-made capital is plentiful, natural capital is in short supply; it no longer makes sense to run it down. In former times, there were plenty of fish, but not enough boats; now, there are plenty of boats, but not enough fish. In short, there are now sound *economic* reasons to protect natural capital.

But according to the argument rehearsed previously, this involves a conflation of two different accounts of natural capital. There may be economic reasons to protect the fish, but the fish themselves only count as natural capital on the 'physical stock' view. On the 'economic' view, if modern boats are more efficient at catching the fish, it cannot be said that natural capital is (yet) in short supply. But against this it may be replied: (a) that whatever the fish are called, there are economic reasons to protect them which, contrary to the sense of the critique so far, would be welcomed on environmental grounds also; and (b) that natural capital in the economic sense embraces future as well as current utility and that in so far as anticipated yields are lower, there can indeed be said to have been a decline of natural capital in the economic sense. Hence, environmental concerns, and the economic conception of natural capital, are interlinked and can, after all, be seen to converge.

To assess the strength of this response, we need to face up to the question of the status of 'cultivated' capital. The threat to the fish stocks has prompted further technological innovation, specifically the enhancing of fish through genetic manipulation. If cultivated capital counts as natural capital (for genetically engineered fish can reasonably be viewed as genetic capital), then in the light of these developments, it is not clear we *can* say that anticipated yields are lower. Perhaps we have reason to think they will keep pace, and in this sense to be confident that, from an economic point of view, natural capital is being maintained. At the same time, it is far from clear that environmental concerns are met by the assurance that the seas can be stocked with genetically engineered fish and the lands with artificial forests. At the very least, what becomes clear is that an undifferentiated concept of natural capital is unhelpful. It may be that the overall level of natural capital is being maintained by virtue of the new transforming agency, but this will be at the cost, say, of the inspirational value conferred directly by wild nature. If the environmental interest were correctly represented by the economic conception of natural capital, this ought not to be disturbing; but it is. An even more disturbing reflection is that the newly transformed capital will actually require protection *from*, and therefore possibly the destruction of, the wild nature that competes for the use of the fish stocks or the forests, or competes with them.[28] It seems reasonable to conclude that the adoption of the economic conception of natural capital will lead to a way of measuring sustainability which is very far from satisfying environmentalist concerns.

(iii) A third problem is posed by the question of which natural items are to be counted as 'utilizable'. For example, suppose that a use for uranium never had been and never was going to be found. Would this substance nevertheless count as contributing to the level of natural capital? Perhaps *any* natural item is capable of delivering welfare to humankind if we take into account technology that is at present unimaginable. But clearly, if we understand capital in this very broad sense, it would not provide us with a usable criterion. In *that* sense, the level of natural capital could be said to be maintained for more or less as long as the principle of the conservation of matter was in operation. Therefore, in order for there to be a usable measure of the level of natural capital, a judgement needs to be made as to what counts as natural capital— that is, relative to available knowledge, or at least to predictions about what kinds of knowledge and technology are likely to become available. Thus it turns out that, amongst other complications, the concept of natural capital contains an epistemological variable: changes in the level of natural capital are contingent, not upon changes in the natural world, nor simply on its actual utility, but upon changes in assumptions about its utility. (We are faced, in other words, with a further dimension of 'Cambridge change'.) Referring back to the example of uranium, this century would seem to reckon it a considerable addition to the store of natural capital. If the next century judges the nuclear experiment to have been an unmitigated disaster, judgements as to the state of our current natural assets would need to be seriously revised.

(iv) A fourth problem is posed by the question whether we consider natural capital as providing the capacity to maintain *aggregate* welfare, or the *average* welfare per individual. The first point to notice is that these would generate different judgements over whether or not the level of natural capital was being maintained. The second point is that either option would have somewhat counterintuitive consequences. If we take first the option of supposing that a policy of sustainability should be aimed at maintaining the capacity for a non-declining aggregate of welfare, then it would be possible to increase the value that natural capital provides *directly,* by *increasing* the human population—not normally something which environmentalists advocate. If, on the other hand, we suppose that the aim should be to maintain the capacity for non-declining welfare per individual, then it would be possible to increase the value produced from the *transformation* of natural capital, by *decreasing* the human population. We could increase the value of natural capital dramatically, for example, by painlessly poisoning half the world's population— much more so if we chose the richest half!

(v) Even supposing that we can somehow find ways of measuring these ups and downs in the level of natural capital, a final problem is posed by the question of *what* level of natural capital should be aimed for in the first place. Is it enough that people should have the wherewithal to enjoy the level of welfare enjoyed by the ancient Egyptians, or by our Neanderthal ancestors? An obvious response is that the question is an unreasonable one and that we can do no other than start from where we are. But the question is not so unreasonable as might first appear. For the fact is that it *costs* something to set out on a sustainability path; we have to forgo things. But then it is perfectly proper to press the question of why we should forgo things, if it turns out that the present level of welfare, resulting from a burst of industrial activity, is higher than could be sustained over the long term anyway. In that event we might as well sit back and enjoy what may now be construed as a windfall. As with a lottery win, there is no general perception that justice requires any one to give up a windfall.

7. A Response

One response to these various problems is to say: 'These so-called problems should come as no surprise; they do no more than spell out the contextual character of measurements in the economic domain. Even scientific measurements admit relativity: length is measured to within a certain degree of accuracy, the freezing point of water is 32°F at sea-level, and so forth.'

This much may be conceded; but two significant points remain:

(i) Measurement was introduced as a way of bringing some independence and objectivity to bear on the business of decision-making. But the more that sensitivity to context has to be recognized, the more is this alleged benefit undermined.

(ii) The choice of relevant context is either arbitrary or a matter of judgement. If it is arbitrary, then the resulting measurements will carry no normative force. If it is a matter of judgement, then we should recognize the role of judgement at the outset and abandon the pretence that levels of natural capital can simply be 'measured'.

8. The 'Physical Stock' Approach

So far, discussion has focused on natural capital in the sense of the actual and potential economic value residing in natural items. There is, however, another possible approach to the problem of measurement, which is to attempt an inventory of the natural items themselves, and simply rely on 'informed' judgements to decide whether and in what sense there has been any depletion. An attraction of such an approach is that it might enable us to avoid some of the entanglements that we have shown to surround the attempt to measure economic value, especially those which arise from the fact that economic value is inevitably a function of the relation between the natural world and prevailing cultural and technological institutions.

An initial point to notice is that to adopt such an approach is to do more than adopt a different system of measurement; it is to lay stress on a different kind of value. So far as the measure of economic value is concerned, the transformation of a natural item must be seen as enhancing or even creating the natural capital; for it would have no value if it was not utilized or utilizable. This seems to be borne out in actual markets, where one pays far more for meat or for kindling than for the animal 'on the hoof', or for the tree. (Of course, the transformation might at the same time destroy other kinds of value that it has, but that is a different point.) To focus on the natural items themselves, on the other hand, would seem to involve laying stress on their *potential* value; and this is not an unreasonable thing. Natural items in their original state might be thought of, on the analogy of the cells that constitute living things at the very outset of their development, as 'totipotential'. To transform them is, arguably, to limit the possible range of uses to which they may be put, just as differentiation in the case of the cells limits their developmental role. The 'paradox' of natural capital is that the realization of its potential is at one and the same time the limitation of its potential.

So far as particular kinds of natural item are concerned, making an inventory seems to present few problems. There are ways of estimating stocks of coal and oil, and ways of judging whether there are fewer or more bullfinches this year. In this way, perhaps, each 'resource' might be itemized and some estimate of the 'amount' of the given item arrived at. The major question that arises, however, is how far an *aggregation* of natural items is possible, or even makes sense. If all else remains the same, and a couple of lesser spotted woodpeckers go missing, then no doubt we can judge that the stocks of natural capital have been slightly depleted. But consider even so simple an example as that provided by the 'twelve days of Christmas'. 'Four colley birds, three French hens, two turtle doves': what is the total capital here? Well, nine birds, perhaps. But suppose there were three colley birds and four French hens. Would the total be the same? Now throw in nine lords-a-leaping. What is the total here? Eighteen animals perhaps? But what if we now add in the five gold rings?[29] Or an ozone layer, perhaps? One begins to see the difficulties.

They may not be insuperable, since there are more sophisticated ways of making an inventory. One way is to look for indicators rather than to count numbers. The decline of a particular species can tell us that all is not as it should be. Conversely, the presence of otters and dippers along a stretch of a river can testify to its state of 'health'. Plants, in particular, can function like the canaries that in former days were taken down mines, as harbingers of climatic and other adverse kinds of change which threaten to deplete natural capital. Indeed, it seems that there must be signs of this sort available; otherwise it is hard to see how there can have been the awareness of environmental degradation that fuelled calls for sustainability in the first place. Another way is the use of more comprehensive indicators such as biodiversity, which, because of ecosystemic dependencies, can reveal the state of organic/inorganic compounds such as soil and water, as well as the state of biotic communities. Finally, from a more managerial perspective comes the idea that natural capital might be treated along the lines of the portfolios of investment companies. The particular point here is that a comparison of portfolios may not require the impossible calculation of the total assets of each, but judgement, that takes in a range of factors such as stability, range of options, and so forth.

9. Sustainability and Justice

A tentative conclusion to be drawn from the foregoing discussion of sustainability is that the 'physical stock' view of natural capital, often discarded as impossible to operate, may be found to have fewer methodological drawbacks than the 'economic' view, usually more favoured because it seems to offer a single criterion by which to measure the total amount of natural capital. What also seems to be true is that the objective of maintaining natural capital when this is understood in the 'physical stock' sense is more likely to do justice to specifically environmental concerns. But this may well be at the cost of both economic and moral considerations and shows up a real disagreement about fundamental values. Natural capital will only be sustained at a certain cost. The question might be and has been raised what possible point there can be in making economic sacrifices to secure the continued existence of obscure species of beetles. Even more pressing is the question whether we could be morally justified in diverting resources into environmental projects that might otherwise be used, say, to provide clean drinking water; unless, of course, it could be demonstrated that the one is a means of securing the other. Strong reasons can be given for at least qualifying the 'physical stock' approach by reference to economic value, and for limiting attention in some degree to natural capital that is 'used or utilizable'. Thus, economic value may need to play a part in determining *which* items should count, even if we have found reason to doubt that it provides a satisfactory way of counting them.

If the attempt to track levels of natural capital is as problematic as is argued here, the question arises whether the notion of intergenerational justice is equally problematic. For many see maintaining natural capital as the key to securing justice across generations. If intergenerational justice is conceived along the lines of intragenerational justice, this view is indeed a natural one to take. Just as intragenerational (distributive) justice is seen as a matter of ensuring the equal distribution of goods among the members of the same generation—unless there are reasonable grounds for unequal distribution—so, holding capital constant across generations is seen as tantamount to distributing equal amounts of good (or access to good) across successive generations.

However, a moment's reflection will suggest that this analogy is hard to sustain. Within a single generation, the outcome of a system of distribution can be coupled to the process so that the justice of the process can in principle be assessed with reference to the outcomes it produces. Over time, and across generations, however, the link between process and outcome is severed. Just outcomes can only be identified after the event, and there is no clear way of identifying the processes that will produce these outcomes in advance. The point is perhaps clearest if we compare the case of 'paths' that are sometimes presented as alternatives to the pursuit of sustainability. One such 'path' is mapped out by the instruction to 'maximize present value'.[30] This instruction is at least one that we can follow 'now'—whenever 'now' may be. A different 'path' seemed to be mapped out by Wilfred Beckerman in his contribution to the seminar series from which these papers are drawn (see Chapter 3) when he spoke of a path that would 'maximize social welfare over the time period in question'.[31] This appears to refer to the result of aggregating the 'sequence of welfares' enjoyed by each generation. Concerning the former 'path', economists have been quick to point out that it might easily generate miserable conditions for later generations.[32] The latter 'path', while allowing for inequalities of welfare between generations, is unlikely to sanction prolonged periods of misery. But it faces a difficulty of a different kind. The difficulty is that, armed with the instruction to follow the path that 'maximizes social welfare *over time*', there is simply no way of telling what one should do next—what process should be put in place to secure the desired outcome. Because the link between process and outcome is severed, knowing what outcome is being sought provides no guide at all to the process that will secure it. There is no instruction that we can follow 'now'—whenever 'now' may be. Precisely the same difficulty arises in attempting to secure intergenerational justice by maintaining the level of capital—i.e. essentially the attempt to produce, as outcome, a 'sequence of *equal* welfare'. Although we may know that certain actions, if taken now, would frustrate such a sequence, we have little idea what action, taken now, would constitute the first step to achieving it. Nor, in particular, do we know if we should 'start from here', in the sense of maintaining present levels of capital.

The lesson to be drawn is that we should abandon the pursuit of intergenerational justice where this is understood as the attempt to bring about a certain long-term outcome, and settle instead for a 'procedural' understanding of our responsibilities regarding future generations. This would mean acting today in ways that take account of likely future needs, where we are seen as discharging our responsibilities to future generations in terms of the principles upon which we act, rather than in terms of the outcomes we bring about. On this view, for instance, it is unlikely that a policy of maximizing present value could be construed as just from a procedural point of view, which would require that we

be far more attentive to a whole range of distributional considerations.[33] It would not mean that we should have to abandon some
of the common articulations of the goal of 'sustainability', such as
the requirement not to act in ways that compromise the ability of
future generations to meet their needs. But it would mean reinterpreting what counts as achieving that goal.

10. Conclusion

In sum, the project of maintaining total, or natural, capital is not a
practicable one; and even if it were practicable, it would not be
desirable. For the 'economic' reading of sustainability in terms of
the maintenance of capital, natural or otherwise, has enormous
potential for frustrating not only environmental but also moral
objectives. It has just been argued that the project of maintaining
capital is not necessary for securing intergenerational justice, in
the only sense in which this objective is also feasible. But worse
than this, if the level of natural capital is measured economically,
in terms of the strength of concern abroad in some given society[34]
and the impact on welfare, and if that society provides unequal
opportunity for the voicing of concern and exhibits manifest
inequalities of welfare, then the project of maintaining capital,
far from being a means to securing intergenerational justice, is
simply a way of translating present injustices into the future.

PART II

PART II

3

Sustainable Development and our Obligations to Future Generations

WILFRED BECKERMAN

1. Introduction

In the last decade or so, increasing attention has been paid to the question of intergenerational distributive justice. This has been largely the result of increasing concern with environmental hazards. The fear that we may use up finite resources (including clean air and water or biodiversity) so that future generations will be condemned to lower standards of living is very widespread, with the attendant concern that this conflicts with some principles of intergenerational equity. But whereas the analysis of equity within any given society is an ancient topic, the problem of equity across generations is relatively very new.

Furthermore, the problem of intergenerational equity raises exceptional logical problems to which there may be no solution. Consequently, there is no attempt in this paper to provide any original contribution to the ethics of intergenerational justice. The purpose of this paper is partly to show that there is nothing particularly equitable about one of the main solutions that is widely proclaimed, namely the concept of 'sustainable development', and

I have been helped by discussing some of the issues in this chapter with Joseph Raz and (via e-mail) with John Broome, as well as by comments from participants in seminars on sustainable development at the University of Keele. The usual disclaimer applies. An earlier version appeared as W. Beckerman, 'Intergenerational Equity and the Environment', *Journal of Political Philosophy*, 5 (1997), 392–405.

partly to propose that priority among our obligations to future generations should be given, instead, to the goal of bequeathing a more just and decent society than that in which most people today live.

2. The Sustainable Development Solution and Intergenerational Equity

The relatively late appearance on the philosophical scene of the issue of intergenerational justice and the particularly intractable problems to which it gives rise have left a gap in ethical theory. It is not surprising, therefore, that 'stop-gap' solutions should be eagerly received. The most important one today is the concept of 'sustainable development', for which one of the main justifications usually given is its concern with intergenerational equity.[1] Now 'equity' is not, of course, the same as 'equality' since egalitarian principles are not the only possible kind of principles of equity. Nevertheless, most—if not all—theories of equity or distributive justice contain, as a crucial ingredient, some appeal to the desirability of equality of something or other.[2]

The precise role that intergenerational egalitarianism plays in the concept of sustainable development depends, of course, on which of a very wide variety of definitions of this concept one adopts. Advocates of different concepts of sustainable development often disagree with each other even more than they disagree with me.[3] Nevertheless, in his authoritative and extensive survey John Pezzey (1992) concluded that most definitions still 'understand sustainability to mean sustaining an improvement (or at least maintenance) in the quality of life, rather than just sustaining the existence of life'. He went on to adopt as a 'standard definition of sustainable development' one according to which welfare per head of population must never decline.[4] The same definition is adopted in the editorial introduction to a more recent extensive collection of articles on sustainable development, where it is stated that 'Consequently, non-negative change in economic welfare per capita becomes the inter-temporal equity objective.'[5]

Sustainable development is also sometimes interpreted as meaning that per capita welfare must never fall below that enjoyed by the current generation. But it is difficult to see why one should attach crucial normative significance to the current level of welfare. It cannot be argued that, by some extraordinary coincidence, the present average standard of living constitutes some minimum subsistence level below which future generations must not be allowed to fall. For past generations seem to have survived with far less, as do about half the people in the world today (depending on which precise concept of the average one adopts). And if the rule is to be interpreted, instead, as one that needed to be adjusted over time—i.e. each generation to ensure that successor generations did not fall below the level of welfare that they had reached, however high that may be—then it is really transforming into the rule that precludes any decline in welfare in any period.

But this rule is not intergenerationally egalitarian at all. For it permits welfare to rise continuously, which, over time, would obviously lead to great inequality between generations—*as has happened in the past up to the present time.* If welfare started at a relatively low level and rose continuously, the subsequent distribution of welfare over time could be just as unequal, or even more unequal, than a path that started at a high level and fell continuously. However, it may be argued that, whilst it is glaringly obvious that a rising path of welfare is not, *per se,* necessarily more egalitarian than a falling path, a comparison between hypothetical time paths that do not start from the same level of welfare is irrelevant. At this point in time we are not choosing, it would be argued, between two world histories starting at different levels, but between two future feasible development paths starting from the same present level. But this argument gives the game away.

For it is, of course, true that, *starting from any particular level,* if we want to maximize something 'good', like 'welfare', it is better for it to go up—or even remain stable—than to go down. But that is only because, and in so far as, we expect that this will lead to total welfare over the future being greater than it would otherwise be. So in the end all that one is really concerned with is the total welfare over some future time period, and the purely technical characteristic of 'going up' or 'going down' is irrelevant.

This means that, faced with the choice between two technically feasible development paths over some given future time period, if one path includes a period of declining welfare and the other does not, but the former leads to higher total welfare over the whole period, then that is the one that should be chosen. If, instead, we reject it on (perhaps mistaken) egalitarian grounds we must have forgotten why we tend to prefer periods of rising rather than falling welfare and we are making a choice that is inconsistent with our underlying objective of maximizing welfare.

And it is perfectly feasible, even starting from the same level, for a path that did not contain any periods of declining welfare to lead not only to greater intergenerational inequality but also to lower total welfare than does a path containing a period of declining welfare but that would fulfill the usual economists' objective of maximizing social welfare over whatever time period is regarded as relevant. For example, in Figure 3.1 the sustainable development path, SD, represents both lower total welfare over the whole period and greater intergenerational inequality than does the path, MSW, that maximizes social welfare over the period. It seems unlikely that any ethical principle to justify this would be easy to find.

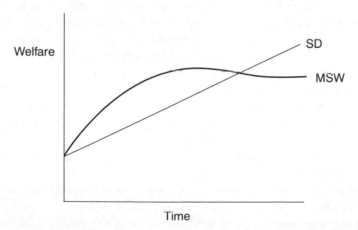

FIG. 3.1. *Sustainable development versus maximum social welfare*

3. The Unjustified Significance of Rising Welfare

The notion that—quite apart from its relationship to intergenerational equality, which we have seen is non-existent—rising (or constant) welfare is somehow or other better than falling welfare *even if it may imply a cumulative lower total welfare over time* is too widespread to ignore, although it is not central to the main theme of this paper. No less an authority than Nozick has defended this position at some length.[6] He writes that

even if happiness were the only thing we cared about, we would not care solely about its total amount. . . . We would care also about how that happiness was distributed within a lifetime. Imagine graphing someone's total happiness through life; the amount of happiness is represented on the vertical axis, time on the horizontal one. . . . If only the total amount of happiness mattered, we would be indifferent between a life of constantly increasing happiness and one of constant decrease, between an upward—and a downward-sloping curve, provided that the total amount of happiness, the total area under the curve, was the same in the two cases. Most of us, however, would prefer the upward-sloping line to the downward; we would prefer a life of increasing happiness to one of decrease. Part of the reason, but only a part, may be that since it makes us happy to look forward to greater happiness, doing so makes our current happiness score even higher. (Yet the person on the downward-sloping curve alternatively can have the current Proustian pleasure of remembering past happiness.) Take the pleasure of anticipation into account, though, by building it into the curve whose height is therefore increased at certain places; still most of us would not care merely about the area under *this* enhanced curve, but about the curve's direction also. (Which life would you prefer your children to have, one of decline or of advance?)[7]

With two minor modifications that are not, I believe, relevant to the argument, the situation described by Nozick can be represented in the Figure 3.2 model. The modifications are that (i) successive generations replace successive stages in the lifetime of a single person; (ii) the term 'welfare' replaces 'happiness' (solely in order to preserve continuity with the preceding argument of this chapter, not to indicate any intentional difference in their meanings). I shall also assume, as does Nozick, that all the welfare

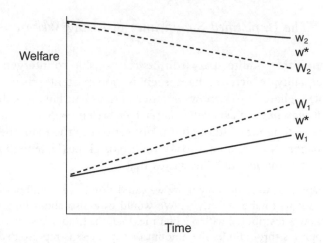

FIG. 3.2. *Instantaneous welfare paths adjusted for direction of path*

(happiness) that we would derive from anticipating a future increase in welfare (not necessarily our own) would be incorporated into the welfare at the moment of time when the anticipation is experienced. Conversely, the loss of welfare resulting from expectations of decreasing welfare (again, not necessarily our own) would be subtracted from the welfare experienced at the time the expectation is held. Cumulative welfare over the whole period, under these assumptions, therefore, will incorporate these expectational additions or subtractions.

Let the welfare, W, of any unit (in this case a generation), be composed of two elements, w and w*. w is a vector of all variables, such as income, status, family life, and so on, that determine its welfare other than its relationship to the w of other units. w* is the effect on its total welfare of the relationship between its own w and that of other units. The Σ sign indicates the summation over the time period in question of the 'instantaneous' welfare experienced at any moment in time. Since, in this model, the units are generations, we can make the extremely plausible psychological assumptions that each generation's w* is positively related to:

(i) the excess of its own w over that of the previous generation's (since it will not feel guilty about having failed to transfer wealth to earlier generations, and will be pleased that, for example, the incidence of infant mortality has decreased, literacy has risen, and so on); and

(ii) the expected excess of the next generation's w over its own (since it will be proud of being able to hand on a better world to the descendants).

Consider now the two life paths shown in Figure 3.2. In one scenario w_1 is rising, so that w^*_1 is positive and hence W_1 rises even more. In the other w_2 is falling, so w^*_2 is negative, and W_2 must fall even more. But clearly this does not imply that the ΣW_1 (which is identically equal to $\Sigma w_1 + \Sigma w^*_1$) is greater than ΣW_2. It only implies this if the arithmetic sum of the two Σw^* (remember that one is negative) is greater than the difference between the two Σw. Obviously this is not logically implied by the assumptions.

However, for Nozick this is clearly not the end of the matter, since he goes on to say that, even under the key assumptions of the model (i.e. incorporating the anticipation and recollection effects), one may still prefer a life represented by the rising path to the life with the declining path even when the cumulative welfare (happiness) in the former life is less than under the latter. This may be because in the situation where we are evaluating alternative life profiles for, say, our children, we would evaluate '. . . the life as a whole from a point outside it',[8] and it would be we, not the children, who would prefer their lives to follow the rising welfare/happiness paths. Transposing to the intergenerational context, it would amount to this generation having a preference for a rising path for future generations even though, in terms of the above model, total welfare was no greater—and possibly even smaller—than under the falling path.

But in both cases—i.e. of evaluating the life path of individuals (e.g. our children) or of future generations—it is *our* preferences that are being satisfied, not those of the subjects in question (our children or the future generations). This rather reduces the moral force of such preferences. Neither our children nor future generations may thank us for choosing a rising path to a falling path if cumulative welfare under the former were smaller than under the latter, particularly if they had very good memories of their pasts and gave little thought to their futures. Furthermore, Nozick does accept that if the downward sloping path '. . . encompassed vastly greater area, the choice might be different.'[9] In other words, there appears to be some trade-off between the direction of the time path of welfare and the total cumulative welfare. But it is difficult to see how this can be the case while the intrinsic value of 'rising' (as distinct from 'falling') cannot be incorporated into the value of the welfare experienced at any point of time and hence incorporated into the height of the curves.

Of course, it may well be that a limitation on the above model is that the particular satisfaction derived from the prospect of future increases or the dismay caused by decreases is that these two types of experience (incorporated in w*) are incommensurate with the welfare that is represented by w (or on the vertical axis in the above Figures). If that were the case it would not be possible to combine them with the other sources of welfare (incorporated in w) to arrive at a total W. But most subjective experiences and mental states differ from each other in one way or another and it is difficult to see why those arising from increases or decreases in welfare over time (or differences in one's welfare compared to that of other people) should be singled out as being any more incommensurate than the innumerable other forms of satisfaction that contribute to one's welfare. And if one believes that most satisfactions are, indeed, incommensurate with each other and cannot be combined together into some aggregate concept of 'welfare' then the whole exercise is futile anyway and the analysis of changes in welfare between generations should be abandoned.[10]

A possible variant of this objection to the above model is not so much that some 'goods' are incommensurate with the welfare variable represented in the above model but that they cannot be allocated to any particular time. For example, it may be thought that an increasing welfare life path is a feature of the whole time path and its desirability cannot be allocated to any particular point in time as is done in the above model. Although I have difficulty in accepting the notion of a satisfaction, or 'good', or source of happiness or welfare, that does not ultimately accrue to somebody at any particular time, I recognize that this is another complex philosophical problem on which I do not feel competent to comment.[11]

Whether or not I am justified in rejecting the priority—or even the weight—accorded to 'going up' in sustainable development doctrine, I suspect that for most people the preference given to upward sloping welfare paths is not based on deep philosophical considerations but arises from the natural tendency to prefer going up to going down when we are dealing with some 'good' (such as welfare) and when it is assumed *that we are starting from the same level*. For example, the psychological satisfaction that one would derive from the prospect of one's childrens' progress throughout their lives suggests that this is because we envisage them as starting from some given level of happiness. But, as shown above in connection with Figure 3.1, in the context of choices affecting many future generations, in which the degree to which some generations use up the environment can—at least theoretically—lead to some periods of declining welfare for subsequent generations, the usual assumption of the superiority of constantly rising paths of welfare does not apply.

4. Is there a Case for Intergenerational Equality Anyway?

Thus it seems that sustainable development does not help in providing guidance as to our obligations to future generations, either because it is not intergenerationally egalitarian after all or because its emphasis on the 'no decline in welfare' rule cannot be justified. But this does not necessarily imply that its egalitarian concern should be abandoned. This might be a case of throwing the baby away with the bath water. Could intergenerational egalitarianism still be a valid objective freed from the constraints of the 'no decline in welfare' rule? In this section it will be argued that the answer is 'No'.

The Instrumental Value of Intergenerational Egalitarianism

Since the most common grounds put forward for egalitarianism within any generation are instrumental grounds we shall begin by considering the difficulties of applying such egalitarian arguments to the intergenerational context.

For example, one common argument in defence of egalitarianism in dimensions such as income, or status, or opportunity, is that it might promote a greater sense of social cohesion, or greater productive efficiency, and so on, all of which may promote welfare. But it is difficult to transpose such instrumental advantages of egalitarianism intergenerationally. It cannot be argued, for example, that greater intergenerational equality of, say, incomes, would promote intergenerational harmony. Another common egalitarian instrumental argument is that great disparities of wealth or income eventually enable the rich to exercise undue power over the poor, leading, perhaps, to unacceptable inequalities of liberty. Clearly this, too, would not be feasible intergenerationally.

In the same way, the type of benefit of greater equality in certain aspects of life that are eloquently set out by Tawney—reduction in envy, a greater sense of social solidarity and sense of community, and so on brought about by greater equality '. . . not equality of capacity or attainment, but of circumstances, institutions, and manner of life,'[12] are clearly inapplicable between generations. Even within any generation Raz is surely right in saying—in connection with the view that greater equality would reduce envy and hostility between groups—that '. . . to the extent that some of these attitudes are deeply rooted in the human psyche, and social conditions only channel their expression, egalitarian devices are a wild good chase after the unachievable.'[13] Those who advocate equality on grounds of its instrumental value in reducing envy may be merely providing moral authority for the envy that they are seeking to eliminate.

Furthermore, if one makes the very plausible psychological assumptions adopted in the model set out above concerning the effect on the welfare of any generation of its relationship to the welfare of preceding and subsequent generations, it is obvious that total welfare, over time, will be greater the faster is the growth in the non-relational component of each generation's welfare, although this will also imply greater inequality over time in both the non-relational component of welfare and total welfare.[14]

The Intrinsic Value of Intergenerational Egalitarianism

But, it might be argued, criticism of the intergenerational relevance of *instrumental* arguments for egalitarianism misses the point. For, as we have seen, the standard definitions of sustainable development are in terms of welfare itself, not of some variable that contributes to it. In that case what matters is the *intrinsic* value of intergenerational equality of *welfare*.

It would be out of place here to embark on the very complex issue of how exactly one should interpret the concept of an *intrinsic* value.[15] In common parlance people often use the term to refer to a value that is held to be so important to them that the valued object is 'irreplaceable'. In such cases, it would be argued, acceptable trade-offs against other values cannot be envisaged and rational choices—such as those formalized in cost-benefit analysis— are inadmissible. Sometimes, however, although choices in such situations may be extremely painful, to refuse to make them may be a form of moral cowardice, however understandable under the circumstances.[16]

But the term *intrinsic* value is also often used simply in the context of an exhaustive and mutually exclusive twofold classifica- tion of values into those that are instrumental—i.e. are required in order to promote some higher order value—and the intrinsic values which are valued for their own sake. And the latter class of values is also sometimes interpreted in different ways. For example, sometimes it includes what are known as 'inherent values'—which are values that an entity possess on account of being valued for its own sake rather than for any utility it yields (works of art being the most common example). And sometimes intrinsic values are limited to those that do not depend on the existence of any valuer—i.e. they possess some form of *objective* value.[17]

Obviously, all instrumental values must, in the end, finish up being justified in terms of some top-level intrinsic value that is required for its own sake. Whether there is only one such top-level intrinsic value—such as one's pleasure or welfare or some other concept of an all-embracing prudential value—or whether, instead, there may be a whole set of independent intrinsic values, such as integrity, compassion, justice, and so on, which may conflict with prudential values, is an old issue in philosophy to which I would not presume to be able to make any contribution. My own position is that there may well be a plurality of top level intrinsic values, but no values can exist if they are not held by somebody. That is to say, I take the position that 'value' is a relational concept referring to the status that some X has in the eyes of some valuer, Y. If there is no Y to attach value to X then X has no value.[18]

In the present context, then, the question we have to ask is who is the valuer who attaches value to intergenerational equality of welfare? Some generations will lose, and others may gain. But in so far as the latter value the greater equality on account of their gain they are attaching instrumental value to it, not intrinsic value.

For a given society it is conceivable (though not necessarily valid) that one can subscribe to some communal egalitarianism— i.e. that '. . . the ownership of the good of equality is communal; it is not the good of any individual or individuals', and Broome contrasts this with individualist egalitarianism, which '. . . takes the good of equality to be owned by individuals.'[19] But for a succession of different generations it is difficult to see what could be *the* community that values one distribution as morally superior to another. There is no one unique state of affairs or community for which the degree of inequality between successive generations can have more or less value. To appeal to some transcendental unique community comprising groups of people who have no contact with each other in order to provide an entity that values greater equality over generations seems to be stretching the concept of community beyond reasonable limits. There would be something paradoxical about claiming that intrinsic values are held by a community that does not even have an intrinsic identity.

Of course, one could fall back on the position that the valuer in question is not some metaphysical entity consisting of a succession of future generations, but is us, here and now. One could claim that it is the present generation that attaches intrinsic value to intergenerational equality of welfare. Leaving aside the important and difficult question of how far a whole generation, containing people with conflicting views, can be regarded as a 'valuer', it is difficult to believe that *any* members of the present generation would seriously attach intrinsic value to greater equality of welfare among generations *per se,* and hence want to promote it even at the possible cost of a loss of welfare for some of them and even if total cumulative welfare was lower. It would hardly make sense retrospectively.

It would be ludicrous to say, for example, that, because of the great inequality between the welfare levels of the different generations covered, we regard the state of the world over the past thousand years as having been morally inferior to what it would have been had we made much less progress over this period! Anybody believing this would presumably want to reduce the inequality by reducing current levels of welfare, even though this cannot add to the welfare of past generations and hence reduces overall cumulative welfare up to this point in time.[20] But such a proposal is unlikely to be supported even by the most die-hard intergenerational egalitarians. Yet if one attaches some intrinsic value to intergenerational equality in any society over time one ought to be ready to sacrifice *some* current welfare, however small, in the interests of reducing the intergenerational inequality to which the relative prosperity of current society contributes. The trade-off may not be definable in any precise manner and the intrinsic value ascribed to intergenerational equality may be incommensurate with total cumulative welfare. Nevertheless, some sacrifice of current welfare, however small, should be acceptable in the interests of greater intergenerational equality. If not then the claim that equality has some intrinsic value is humbug. Some environmentalists like to claim that certain environmental objects have intrinsic value, which they interpret to mean that they cannot be sacrificed for any compensation, however great. It would be ironic if environmentalists were to claim that intergenerational equality also has intrinsic value but is not worth acquiring if there is price for doing so, however small.

5. *Intergenerational Egalitarianism*
or Humanitarianism?

Thus it appears that intergenerational egalitarianism is difficult to defend on grounds of either its instrumental or its intrinsic value. It should be discarded, therefore, as a guide to those of our policies that may affect future generations. Indeed, it may not be possible to appeal to any theory of distributive justice or even to any 'theory' of anything. How then should we formulate our intuitions concerning our obligations to future generations?

As usual there are different moral intuitions and they tend to be mixed up. The underlying ones are probably not necessarily egalitarian at all. They reflect the fact that most people are distressed by the sight of, or knowledge of, the various manifestations of poverty, suffering, sickness, and so on. In any given society it is natural to resent the co-existence of such conditions together with the affluence enjoyed by other sections of the population. This leads to the intuitive feeling that what is ethically indefensible is the inequality *per se*. But in fact what really offends us is not so much the inequality as its assumed consequences in the particular society in which we live, namely the poverty and suffering that exist.

As Harry Frankfurt has succinctly put it: 'Inequality is a purely formal relationship, from which nothing whatever follows as to the desirability or value of any of the unequal terms. The egalitarian condemnation of inequality as inherently bad loses much of its force, I believe, when we recognize that those who are doing considerably worse than others may nonetheless be doing rather well. Surely what is of genuine moral concern is whether people have good lives, and not how their lives compare with the lives of others.'[21] In similar vein, Raz writes that '. . . wherever one turns it is revealed that what makes us care about various inequalities is not the inequality but the concern identified by the underlying principle. It is the hunger of the hungry, the need of the needy, the suffering of the ill, and so on.'[22]

This argument is also, of course, an argument against egalitarianism at any moment of time (in which context it was being used by Frankfurt and Raz). But at any moment of time the appeal of egalitarian doctrines faced with the obvious suffering of the very poor is—even if misplaced—understandable and possibly justifiable from a policy-oriented point of view. For egalitarian rhetoric may be instrumentally useful, at any moment of time, in order to promote policies designed to attack the real enemy, poverty. It is then natural for those who are accustomed to believing that egalitarianism has ethical value within any society (even if really only for instrumental reasons) to take the further step and assume that intergenerational egalitarianism is also ethically justified.

But this involves two errors. The first is the concentration on egalitarianism when what we really need to be concerned with is the avoidance of policies that will impoverish future generations. Differences between future generations who may be well-off to different degrees should be of no moral significance. The second error is the failure to give priority to people living today over those alive in the future in spite of the fact that future people are very likely to be far better off materially than those alive today.[23] For example, there is something paradoxical about the current willingness in environmental circles to impose constraints on the extent to which the current generation of Chinese can increase their carbon emissions, which would reduce their income levels, in order to add a few percentage points to the GNP of Chinese alive in, say, 100 years' time when their income levels are likely to be ten or twenty times as high as they are now. This would be inverted ancestor worship that is not likely to appeal to the Chinese of any generation.

This suggests that one should abandon egalitarianism in favour of what Temkin calls 'extended humanitarianism', and of which he says that 'People are drawn to extended humanitarianism not as a position expressing what the egalitarian *does* care about, but rather as a position expressing what the egalitarian *should* care about. More accurately, it may seem the reflective egalitarian is forced to extended humanitarianism—that is, that it is the closest thing to an egalitarian position one can plausibly adopt.'[24] This relieves us of any obligation to worry about the welfare of some group whose welfare could still be high even if it is below that of some other group.[25]

If then we abandon intergenerational egalitarianism altogether, much of the current debate between proponents of various equilisands—welfare, opportunities, capabilities, resources, 'midfare' and so on—is irrelevant.[26] The debate has thrown up many important insights into what variables should be taken into account in deciding how far somebody has, or is lacking, something, 'G', that is valuable to him (or her) in his (or her) pursuit of his (or her) aims in life. Hence the debate has thrown light on what sort of policies will give people more G. And the question of what exactly is the G that we have a moral obligation to provide to as many people as possible (ignoring their location in time) is an important issue in moral philosophy. But this discussion can be constructive without having to revolve around the issue of what G, if any, should be distributed equally.[27] It is important to clarify our ideas as to what constitutes G without searching for a 'theory' to demonstrate that, whatever it is, people ought to be provided with equal amounts of it.

6. Priorities in our Obligations to Future Generations

What, then, should be the order of priorities among our moral obligations to future generations? If egalitarianism is not at the top of the list, the derived claims of environmental considerations also look less compelling. A far more compelling starting point, surely, should be concern to bequeath to future generations greater basic liberties and the conditions of what Margalit calls a 'decent society'.[28] For Margalit, the chief characteristic of such a society is that 'institutions do not humiliate people'.[29] As Margalit points out, this means that a Rawlsian 'just' society must be a 'decent society', for one of the conditions of Rawls's just society is that there is a just distribution of primary goods, the most important of which is self-respect.[30]

But Margalit's concept of the decent society encompasses considerations that lie outside the domain of the Rawlsian theory of justice and that are very relevant here. First, a decent society should also treat decently people who are not members of that

society. In the present context that would include future generations. Secondly, concern for beings who are not members of our
society in the normal sense of the term would also include non-
human sentient creatures. Thus, compassionate treatment of
animals would also be a feature of a decent society and would
not need to be defended only on the usual Kantian lines.

Nevertheless, in so far as a decent society gives priority to the
need for human institutions to treat human beings with respect
and compassion it is a useful antidote to the excessive concern with
the natural world that characterizes some of the 'deep ecology'
sections of the environmentalist movement. Most environmentalists are no doubt motivated chiefly by highly commendable
compassion for animals, aesthetic appreciation of nature, and
altruistic concern for future generations. But there is a danger
that, to some people, a love of nature is a counterpart of a
disregard—if not worse—for human beings. And some environmentalists distrust the priority accorded by human-rights activists
to human beings relative to other species.[31]

It is not totally coincidental that the most detailed legislation
regarding the protection of nature and animals in the history of
humanity was introduced by the Nazi regime and Hitler personally in the 1930s,[32] or that the project to draft the World Charter
for Nature was originally proposed by President Mobutu.[33]
Indeed, some of the mystical reverence for the environment and
the appeal to a return to pre-modern conditions of life that is
encountered in much deep ecology literature seems to be an
appeal to renounce the rational, scientific, and humanist tradition
that has largely dominated human thought throughout the last
century or more.[34]

A further reason for giving priority, among our obligations to
future generations, to bequeathing to them a more decent society
is that the existing body of internationally accepted human
rights—at least on paper—which usually include rights to association, political expression and participation, legal redress, and so on
would, if implemented everywhere, go a long way to enable weak
groups in many countries to improve and protect their environments and hence their living conditions. It is no accident that the
countries of the ex-Soviet bloc were characterized by some of the

worst environmental devastation that has been witnessed. More recently, the much-publicized disregard of the environmental interests of the Ogoni tribe in Nigeria and the intolerable treatment of those who protested at this treatment could not have taken place in the context of a decent and just society. (It is striking that, until this case brought to light the environmental aspects of the situation, it did not get much international and media attention. People's basic rights, it seems, can sometimes be trampled on without much outcry as long as the environment is not harmed!). Even more recently, commenting on the social weaknesses responsible for the air pollution originating in the burning of forests in Indonesia, *The Economist* writes that 'Political systems are often too rigid or underdeveloped for large expressions of popular feeling that might make such widespread vandalism impracticable.'[35]

One particular environmental benefit that would flow from greater respect for human rights would be the voluntary reduction in the birth rate in countries where this is required if women's rights to equal education and social status were respected far more than they are today.

According priority among our obligations to future generations to bequeathing a more decent and just society does not mean that we would ignore environmental obligations to future generations. We can agree with Margalit that a society is not a decent one '. . . in so far as its living conditions of grinding poverty are perceived as humiliating.'[36] Thus a 'decent society' should avoid policies that might condemn future generations to acute poverty on account of their being deprived of what is known as 'critical natural capital'.

If one has to justify this concern in the context of a theory of justice it could be done so in terms of the traditional 'impartiality' approach to theories of justice. For it can be argued that it would be *unfair* of any generation to take advantage of the fact that it happened to arrive earlier in time in order to use up supplies of critical natural capital to the point that future generations would be reduced to dire poverty.[37] But this is not a strictly egalitarian injunction such as 'the available supply of X has to be shared out equally among all the n people who will ever inhabit the Earth, including those who are alive today.' For we have no idea of the size of n or the supply of any X. And, even if we did know that there was some finite resource that the operation of the price mechanism and the incentives to technical progress in the face of increasing scarcity will not succeed in conserving for ever, humanitarianism would only require that we leave enough for future generations to meet their basic needs. The principle would be that 'no generation should use up so much X that future generations would not have enough X to meet their basic needs.' Even in theory, therefore, this injunction does not specify that present or near-future generations should not consume more of any resource than the minimum resources that need to be left for future generations.[38]

In any case, both economic theory and overwhelming empirical evidence suggest that there is no need to fear that we shall one day exhaust supplies of some product or that, if we did, human civilization as we know it would come to an end.[39] As I pointed out a long time ago we have managed very well without any supplies at all of Beckermonium, the product named after my great-grandfather who failed to discover it in the nineteenth century.[40]

Furthermore, what horrifies most of us about the past is not so much the acute poverty in which earlier societies lived on account of the low level of development, but the needless atrocities, persecution, humiliation, and suffering inflicted by some sections of the world population on others—as is still too often the case today. There is every reason, therefore, to give priority to ensuring that similar human-induced suffering not be allowed to persist in the future, particularly when its widespread existence today is indisputable, whereas the predictions of future poverty on account of resource scarcities are no more likely to be fulfilled than they have been during the last two thousand years. In other words we should be much more concerned with the political and social institutions, the social norms, and the degree of personal liberty and respect for human rights, than with the number of species or supplies of minerals that should be bequeathed to posterity. In spite of many internationally accepted conventions and declarations that enumerate in some detail certain basic human rights that are accepted by almost all nations *in principle,* in practice they are violated all over the world. Even in some large countries where certain universal human rights such as freedom of assembly or of political representation are respected, basic women's rights are still violated.

If it is accepted that our prior obligation to future generations is to bequeath to them a more decent society than the one in which many—and probably most—of them live today, there is much that could be done in the world already to move in the right direction. Unlike the alleged conflict between present and future needs conjured up by the doctrine of sustainable development there is not some finite quantity of justice and decent behaviour between people that has be shared out between generations, like a finite amount of some allegedly non-renewable resource.

Concern with future generations should thus take the same form as concern with people alive today, namely give priority to providing them with the three components of what I am tempted to call 'Wilfare'. The precise content of this cannot be laid down for all time (or space), but it should comprise *minimum* levels of both (i) personal and publicly provided goods and services, and (ii) human rights and liberties, as well as (iii) *minimum* standards of institutional and personal behaviour towards other sentient beings, that are essential to the self-respect and opportunities for personal fulfillment that characterize a decent and civilised society. This would be a principle of entitlement, not an egalitarian principle specifying an equal share-out over time of some allegedly finite resource.

7. Conclusion

Intergenerational egalitarianism has nothing to recommend it. The importance attached to intergenerational equity in environmental discourse is thus unwarranted. Furthermore, there is nothing particularly intergenerationally equitable about the objective of sustainable development that plays such a predominant role in environmental thinking and policy. None of this relieves us of the need to consider our moral obligations to future generations.

But we should do so unconstrained by any concern with the welfare of some distant generation whose welfare could still be high even if it has fallen below that of some of the preceding generation that was even higher.

Among our obligations priority should be given to the relatively simple humanitarian objective of moving towards just institutions and a 'decent' society. This objective should replace egalitarianism or 'sustainable development' as our major obligation to future generations for various reasons.

First, moves in this direction can begin today. For the very widespread institutionalized hardship and violation of basic human rights in the world today are indisputable facts, not matters of speculation about distant futures based on assertions that run counter to both economic theory and historical fact. The worst problems facing future generations are those that have existed already for millennia. Hence, the best way to provide decent societies for future generations is to improve the institutions that are partly or largely responsible for the humiliating circumstances in which many people live today. Such an objective calls for no constraint on present living standards or continued economic growth. There is thus no conflict of interest between generations and hence no need for any theory of intergenerational justice to resolve such conflicts.

Secondly, the concept of a decent society encompasses decent treatment of entities that are not members of contemporary human society, including future generations and non-human species. Although, Rawls's insistence on the importance of self-respect among the 'primary goods' that should be distributed equally at any point of time means that, in spirit, his just society would also be a decent society, it is well-known that justice sometimes conflicts with compassion.

Thirdly, greater respect for the basic human rights that are enshrined on paper in many international conventions would, in fact, help to protect the environmental conditions of large sections of the world's population. At present these interests—along with others—are too easily trampled on by despotic governments. And a reduction in the discrimination against women that persists in one form or another in most countries of the world would also help reduce the high birth rates that are a cause of poverty and environmental degradation in many parts of the world.

Fourthly, according priority to the treatment of human beings by other human beings is a valuable antidote to the danger that excessive concern with the environment leads to opposition to scientific and technical progress and to the rational and humanist tradition that has made such progress over the last century or so but that is now open to attack from various fundamentalist quarters, including ecological fundamentalism. Disillusion with the benefits of modern civilization is too easily channelled, by some environmentalist groups, into an attack on rising standards of living and humanistic values, sometimes with the aid of violent and anti-democratic practices. Societies that have confidence in the ability of their own institutions to resolve fairly their own internal conflicts in a peaceful and democratic manner do not have to conjure up melodramatic apocalyptic environmental scenarios involving artificial conflicts between generations in order to escape from their problems.

4

Sustainability and Intergenerational Justice

BRIAN BARRY

1. *The Question*

As temporary custodians of the planet, those who are alive at any given time can do a better or worse job of handing it on to their successors. I take that simple thought to animate concerns about what we ought to be doing to preserve conditions that will make life worth living (or indeed liveable at all) in the future, and especially in the time after those currently alive will have died ('future generations'). There are widespread suspicions that we are not doing enough for future generations, but how do we determine what is enough? Putting the question in that way leads us, I suggest, towards a formulation of it in terms of intergenerational justice.

A methodological principle to which I shall appeal more systematically in section 2 is that we shall make most headway in asking ethical questions about the future if we start by asking them about the present and then see how the results can be extended to apply to the future. The rationale for this procedure is that we are accustomed to thinking about relations among contemporaries and have developed a quite sophisticated apparatus to help us in doing so. We have no similar apparatus to aid our thoughts about relations between people living at different times. Rather than starting from scratch, then, my proposal is that we

This chapter was first published in *Theoria*, Vol 45 No 89 (June, 1997), pp. 43–65.

should move from the familiar to the unfamiliar, making whatever adaptations seem necessary along the way.

If we follow this precept, and start from relations among contemporaries, we shall immediately run into a contrast that virtually all moral systems draw, though they derive it differently and use different vocabularies, between what it would be desirable (virtuous, benevolent, supererogatory) to do for others and what it would be wrong not to do for them. We may be said to have a duty or an obligation to do things that it is wrong to do, though this entails taking the words outside their natural homes in, respectively, institutionally generated roles and constraints imposed within rule-governed activities (e.g. legal obligations or promissory obligations).

Another family of terms that fits in somewhere here is the one made up of 'just', 'unjust', 'justice', and 'injustice'. A broad conception would make 'unjust' roughly equivalent to 'wrong' or 'morally impermissible'. John Stuart Mill proposed a broad use in chapter 5 of *Utilitarianism,*[1] and I have myself employed a similarly broad conception of justice in a recent book.[2] However, we would not in normal usage describe murder or assault as unjust, even though they are paradigmatically wrong. Rather, we reserve terms from the 'justice' family for cases in which some distributive consideration comes into play. For the present purpose, it will make little difference whether we choose the broader or the narrower conception of justice. This is because the questions about intergenerational justice that are liable to create distinctive moral problems are very likely to be issues of justice in the narrow sense: cases where there is (or is believed to be) an intergenerational conflict of interest. Thus, suppose we could provide a benefit or avoid a loss to people in the future at some cost to ourselves, are we morally required to do it? This inter-temporal distributive question falls within the scope of justice in the narrow sense. It is quite true that we can also damage people in the future without benefiting ourselves. But such actions will normally be wrong in relation to contemporaries or at the very least recklessly imprudent. Thus, if the people living at a certain time devastate a large part of the world by fighting a nuclear war, that will obviously be bad for later generations (assuming that human life is not entirely wiped out). But its inflicting immense evils on subsequent people is of a piece, as it were, with its devastating effect on those alive at the time.

I qualified my equation of injustice and wrongness in the broad sense by saying only that they are roughly equivalent. I had in mind two ways in which we can behave wrongly but not unjustly. First, I take it to be uncontroversial that we can act wrongly in relation to non-human animals. It is, of course, controversial whether or not certain practices such as using them in medical experiments or raising them for food are wrong. But scarcely anybody would deny that some acts (e.g. torturing them for fun) are wrong. We can, I think, stretch 'duty' and 'obligation' further beyond their core applications to enable us to talk about duties or obligations to non-human animals. (Even here, though, the core applications exert a pull: we are especially liable to use the vocabulary of duty where a role-related responsibility is at issue.) In contrast, it does not seem to me that the concept of justice can be deployed intelligibly outside the context of relations between human beings. The reason for this is, I suggest, that justice and injustice can be predicated only of relations among creatures who are regarded as moral equals in the sense that they weigh equally in the moral scales.

The second way in which wrongness and injustice come apart is that it is possible to behave wrongly even where the interests of sentient beings are not involved. Here, it is controversial that there are really any cases in which we can treat 'nature' wrongly unless the interests of sentient beings are somehow affected. I shall defend the claim below (section 5) though I shall there argue that the common move of appealing to the 'independent value of nature' is a mistaken one. For the present purpose, however, I can bracket the validity of the claim. Let me simply say that *if* it is in some circumstances wrong to behave in a certain way in relation to 'nature', there is no entity that can properly be described as a victim of injustice.[3] I also believe, incidentally, that talking about duties or obligations to 'nature' is misguided. My reason for holding this will, I hope, become apparent when I explain the sense in which I think we can behave wrongly in relation to 'nature'.

To sum up the discussion this far, behaving unjustly to future generations is wrong but (even in the broad conception of justice) it is not the only thing that those currently alive can do in relation to the distant future that is wrong. Injustice is, however, such a manifestly important aspect of wrongness that it is well worth the amount of attention it gets from political philosophers. Further, if we define 'distributive justice' to correspond to the narrow conception of justice, which focuses on conflicts of interest, we may say that questions about intergenerational justice are characteristically questions about intergenerational distributive justice.

With that by way of preamble, I can now set out very quickly what I see as the question to be asked about the ethical status of sustainability. This is as follows: Is sustainability (however we understand the term) either a necessary or a sufficient condition of intergenerational distributive justice?

2. Distributive Justice

In accordance with the methodological maxim that I laid down at the beginning, I shall approach the question of the demands of intergenerational justice via the question of the demands of distributive justice among contemporaries. The premiss from which I start is one of the fundamental equality of human beings. (It is precisely because this premiss does not make moral standing depend on the time at which people live that principles of justice valid for contemporaries are *prima facie* valid for intergenerational justice too.) Fundamental equality is, as John Stuart Mill said, 'the first principle of morals'. 'Bentham's dictum, "everybody to count for one, nobody for more than one"' is, as he noted, a specific application of it to the utilitarian calculus, telling us that pains and pleasures of equal intensity are to be given the same value in the calculus, regardless of the identity of the person to whom they belong.[4] An application that is not tied to utilitarianism is that different treatments of different people must be justified by adducing some morally relevant ground for different treatment. This is, of course, not saying a great deal until we know what are to count as morally relevant reasons. But even if we simply say that they are grounds which we ought reasonably to expect the person affected to accept freely, we shall rule out many historically prominent forms of domination and systematic inequality of rights, which have rested on nothing but the power of the beneficiaries to impose them.[5]

I do not know of any way of providing a justification for the premiss of fundamental equality: its status is that of an axiom. I will point out, however, that it is very widely accepted, at least in theory, and attempts to provide a rationale for unequal treatment at least pay lip service to the obligation to square it with the premiss of fundamental equality. Moreover, it seems to me that there is a good reason for this in that it is very hard to imagine any remotely plausible basis for rejecting the premiss. In any case, it is presupposed in what follows.

In brief compass, then, I shall propose four principles which are, I claim, theorems of the premiss of fundamental equality. These are as follows:

1. *Equal rights*. Prima facie, civil and political rights must be equal. Exceptions can be justified only if they would receive the well-informed assent of those who would be allocated diminished rights compared with others.

2. *Responsibility*. A legitimate origin of different outcomes for different people is that they have made different voluntary choices. (However, this principle comes into operation fully only against a background of a just system of rights, resources and opportunities.) The obverse of the principle is that bad outcomes for which somebody is not responsible provide a prima-facie case for compensation.

3. *Vital interests*. There are certain objective requirements for human beings to be able to live healthy lives, raise families, work at full capacity, and take a part in social and political life. Justice requires that a higher priority should be given to ensuring that all human beings have the means to satisfy these vital interest than to satisfying other desires.

4. *Mutual advantage.* A secondary principle of justice is that, if everyone stands *ex ante* to gain from a departure from a state of affairs produced by the implementation of the above three principles, it is compatible with justice to make the change. (However, it is not unjust not to.)

What implications do these principles of justice have for justice between generations? Let me take them in turn.

1. *Equal rights.* I cannot see that this principle has any *direct* intergenerational application. For it would seem to me absurd to say, e.g. that it is unfair for a woman to have more rights in Britain now than a century ago, or unfair that a woman had fewer rights then. Surely, the principle of equal rights applies to contemporaries and only to contemporaries. However, the present generation may be able to affect the likelihood that there will be equal rights in the future. Thus, it seems to be a robust generalization that rights suffer at times when large challenges to a system demand rapid and co-ordinated responses. (To offer a relatively modest example, I would guess that all individual university teachers and departments have lost autonomy in the last twenty years.) The more environmental stress we leave our successors to cope with, therefore, the poorer prospects for equal rights.

2. *Responsibility.* This principle will clearly apply among people who are contemporaries in the future, as it does among people who are contemporaries today, to justify inequalities of outcome that arise from choice. But what place, if any, does it have in relations between different generations? People in the future can scarcely be held responsible for the physical conditions they inherit, so it would seem that it is unjust if people in future are worse off in this respect than we are. (This, of course, leaves open the question of what is the relevant criterion of being well off, and I shall take that up in the next section.) What future people may be held responsible for, however, is how many of them there are at any given time.

Clearly, if we take the view that the principle of responsibility applies to population size, it will have highly significant implications for the requirements of intergenerational justice. I shall pursue this further in section 4.

3. *Vital interests.* The fundamental idea that location in space and time do not in themselves affect legitimate claims has the immediate implication that the vital interests of people in the future have the same priority as the vital interests of people in the present. I shall take up the implications of this in section 4.

4. *Mutual advantage.* In theory, it would be possible for the principle of mutual advantage to have cross-generational implications. That is to say, it could be that there are intertemporally Paretian improvements to be made in comparison with a baseline constituted by the outcomes of the other principles working together. However, I think it quite implausible that there are. The scope of the principle in relation to the distant future is particularly limited because it is explicitly stated in terms of preferences, and the further into the future we look the less confidence we can have about the preferences that people will have.

An objection commonly made against a universalist theory of justice such as this one is that it does not provide an adequate account of motivation to conform to its demands. It is certainly true that it leaves a gap in a way that 'communitarian' accounts do not. Consider, for example, Avner de-Shalit's book *Why Posterity Matters.*[6] It seems to me that his account closes the gap only too successfully. For in essence what he is saying is that concern for people in the future is something we naturally have, to the extent that we see them as carrying on with projects that are dear to us, because that gives depth and meaning to our own lives. This is doubtless true to some degree, though it would seem more for some than for others, but (except to the extent that it can generate intragenerational obligations arising from the 'principle of fair play') it does not tell people that they have to do what they are not inclined to do anyway. Moreover, because it is a cross-generational form of communitarianism, it cannot offer any reason for people in rich countries to cut back so as to improve the prospects of future people in other communities. Yet that is, as it seems to me, the most important thing for a conception of intergenerational justice to deliver.

In almost all the world, there is discrimination against women: they have fewer legal rights than men, are poorly protected by the law, and even more by its administration, against domestic violence, they have restricted educational and occupational opportunities, and so on. In most countries there are (*de facto* or *de jure*) different grades of membership based on race, ethnicity, language, religion, or some other characteristic. Such practices have powerful beneficiaries and it might be said (and is by so-called communitarian political philosophers) that it is 'no use' applying universalistic criteria of justice and pointing out that according to these criteria practices such as these are unjust. The only 'useful' criticism is 'connected' criticism, which deploys already accepted ideas. But this means that criticism cannot get a foothold so long as those who discriminate on the basis of gender or ethnicity have an internally coherent rationale. Meanwhile, it remains none the less true that such practices are unjust. And even if that thought does not have any motivating effect on those within a country who are in a position to change things, it may motivate people outside to organize boycotts and lead international organizations to exclude such countries from the benefits of international trade and aid.

I believe that the core idea of universalism—that place and time do not provide a morally relevant basis on which to differentiate the weight to be given to the interests of different people—has an immense rational appeal. Its corollaries—the illegitimacy of slavery and the impermissibility of assigning women an inferior legal status, for example—have been acted on for the past two centuries in a significant part of the world, despite strongly entrenched interests and beliefs in opposition to them. In the past fifty years, concern for people who are distant in place and time has grown in a quite unprecedented way. The great question for the future is whether or not that concern will grow sufficiently to induce action of the kind called for by the demands of justice. But I can see no reason for supposing that those demands should be scaled back to match pessimistic predictions about the way in which that question will be answered, even if we believe pessimism to be a reasonable response to the evidence so far.

3. *Sustainability*

Many people who have thought seriously about the matter have reached the conclusion that the concept of sustainability is inherently incapable of carrying the burden it would have to bear if it were to constitute a basic building block in a theory of intergenerational justice. With due diffidence, as a non-expert, I should like to make two observations on the literature that I have read. I first note a tendency to elide an important distinction. I have in mind here on the one hand the problem of producing a definition of sustainability that is coherent and comprehensible, and on the other hand the problem of drawing out concrete policy implications from any such definition. It seems to me that the problem of application is undeniably enormous, but that this should not be allowed too readily to impugn the possibility of achieving a definition of the concept.

The other point that occurs to me about the pessimists is their propensity to cite disagreement about the concept of sustainability as a basis for dismissing it. But we need not despair so long as the disagreements reflect substantive differences of viewpoint. Thus, let us suppose that concern about sustainability takes its origins from the suspicion that I articulated at the beginning: the suspicion that we are shortchanging our successors. If we then take this to mean that we should not act in such a way as to leave them with less of what matters than we enjoy, and call that sustainability, it is clear that the content of sustainability will depend crucially on what we think matters. For example, one writer may assume that what matters is utility, understood as want-satisfaction. (Such a writer is unlikely to be anything other than an economist, but economists loom quite large in the literature of sustainability.) Others will disagree and propose some alternative. There is nothing either mysterious or discreditable about this. It is, in fact, exactly what we should expect.

The core concept of sustainability is, I suggest, that there is some X whose value should be maintained, in as far as it lies within our power to do so, into the indefinite future. This leaves it open for dispute what the content of X should be. I have already mentioned one candidate: utility, understood (as is orthodox in economics) as the satisfaction of wants or, as they are usually called, preferences. The obvious objection to this criterion is that wants are (quite reasonably) dependent on what is, or is expected to be, available. Perhaps people in the future might learn to find satisfaction in totally artificial landscapes, walking on the astroturf amid the plastic trees while the electronic birds sing overhead. But we cannot but believe that something horrible would have happened to human beings if they did not miss real grass, trees, and birds.

The want-satisfaction criterion does not enable us to explain what would be wrong with such a world. This sheds light on the oft-noted tendency of economists to be disproportionately located at the 'brown' end of the spectrum on environmental issues. For economists are also, as I have already noted, the most significant adherents of the want-satisfaction criterion. Combine that criterion with a faith in the adaptability of human preferences and you have a formula that can easily generate optimism about the future. For it will seem plausible that almost any environmental degradation that does not actually undermine productive capacity will be compensable by advances in technology that we can safely assume will continue to occur.

If I am right that substantive disputes about the concept of sustainability reflect disagreements about what matters, we can begin to see why what appear superficially to be technical questions of definition are so intractable. Consider especially the arguments in the literature about the status of 'natural capital'. For someone who adopts want-satisfaction as a criterion, all resources are in principle fungible: if plastic trees are as satisfying as real ones, there is no reason for worrying about the destruction of the world's trees so long as the resources exist to enable plastic replacements to be manufactured in sufficient numbers. Those who insist that 'natural capital' must be preserved are in effect denying the complete fungibility of all capital. But what is this disagreement actually about? On the interpretation I wish to offer, this is not a disagreement that turns on some matter of fact. It would be quite possible to agree with everything that might be said in favour of fungibility and still deny that it amounts to a case against the special status of 'natural capital'. For the case in favour of giving the preservation of nature an independent value is that it is important in its own right. If future people are to have access to what matters, and unspoilt nature is an essential part of what matters, then it follows that loss of 'natural capital' cannot be traded off against any amount of additional productive capacity. (I leave until section 5 the idea that nature might have value independently of its contribution to human interests, broadly conceived.)

What helps to obscure the point at issue is the terminology of 'capital' itself. For this naturally suggests that what is going on is a technical dispute about the conditions of production. On this understanding of the matter, the proponents of 'natural capital' are insisting that production has a natural base that cannot be run down beyond a certain point without putting future production in jeopardy. But the 'fungibility' school are not committed to denying this. They insist on fungibility *in principle;* whether or not everything can be substituted for *in practice* is a matter of fact on which they do not have to be dogmatic. But if I am right the real dispute is at the level of principle, and is not perspicuously represented in terms of the properties of different kinds of capital.

'Capital' is a term that is inherently located within economic discourse. A mountain is, in the first instance, just a mountain. To bring it under the category of 'capital'—of any kind—is to look at it in a certain light, as an economic asset of some description. But if I want to insist that we should leave future generations mountains that have not been strip-mined, quarried, despoiled by ski-slopes, or otherwise tampered with to make somebody a profit, my point will be better made by eschewing talk about 'capital' altogether.

Let us dismiss the hypothesis that X is want-satisfaction. What, then, is it? On the strength of the objection urged against want-satisfaction, it might appear that what should be maintained for future generations is their chance to live a good life as we conceive it. But even if 'we' agreed on what that is (which is manifestly not the case), this would surely be an objectionable criterion for 'what matters'. For one of the defining characteristics of human beings is their ability to form their own conceptions of the good life. It would be presumptuous—and unfair—of us to pre-empt their choices in the future. (This is what is wrong with all utopias). We must respect the creativity of people in the future. What this suggests is that the requirement is to provide future generations with the opportunity to live good lives according to their conception of what constitutes a good life. This should surely include their being able to live good lives according to our conception but should leave other options open to them.

This thought leads me to the suggestion (for which I claim no originality) that X needs to be read as some notion of equal opportunity across generations. Unfortunately, however, the concept of equal opportunity is notoriously treacherous. Although, therefore, I do believe this to be the right answer, I have to confess that saying this is not doing a lot more than set out an agenda for further study.

To summarize an extensive and in places technical literature with desperate brevity, there are two natural approaches to the measurement of opportunity, both of which rapidly turn out to be dead ends. One is to count opportunities. This has the obvious drawback that three options that are very similar (three apples of the same variety) will have to be said to give more opportunity than two more dissimilar options (an apple and an orange). But why is a greater range more valuable? A natural response might be that a choice between a number of apples is fine if you are an apple-lover but leaves you out of luck otherwise, whereas a choice between an apple and an orange gives you two shots at getting something you like. We might be tempted to move from this to the conclusion that what makes a range of options valuable is the want-satisfying property of the most preferred item in it. From there it is a short step to identifying the value of a set of opportunities with the utility of the most preferred option in it.

Notice, however, that if we follow this path we shall have insensibly changed the subject. We began by asking for a measure of the *amount* of opportunity provided by a set of options. What we have now done is come up with a measure of the value of the opportunities provided by a set of options. Even if we concede that the value of the most preferred element is for certain purposes an appropriate measure of the value of a set of options, it is strikingly counterintuitive as a measure of the amount of opportunity offered by a set of options. Thus, for example, it entails that opportunity is not increased by adding any number of desirable options to a singleton choice set, so long as none of those added comes as far up the agent's preference scale as the one option with which we began.

Another way of seeing the inadequacy of this measure of opportunity is to note that it takes preferences as given. But the whole reason for our taking opportunities to be constitutive of X was that we could not accept utility based on given preferences as the criterion of X. If preferences in the future are such that plastic trees (the only kind, let us suppose, that are available) give as much satisfaction to people then as real trees do now to us, the amount of opportunity in the future is not diminished. Thus, if we embrace the measure of opportunity that equates it with the utility of the most preferred item in the choice set, we shall simply be back at utility as the criterion of X. All that will have happened is that it will have been relabelled 'opportunity'.

The notion of a range of opportunity cannot be reduced either to the sheer number of opportunities or to the utility of the most preferred option. We must define it in a way that tracks our reasons for wishing to make it our criterion of X in the first place. That means taking seriously the idea that conditions must be such as to sustain a range of possible conceptions of the good life. In the nature of the case, we cannot imagine in any detail what may be thought of a good life in the future. But we can be quite confident that it will not include the violation of what I have called vital interests: adequate nutrition, clean drinking-water, clothing and housing, health care and education, for example. We can, in addition, at the very least leave open to people in the future the possibility of living in a world in which nature is not utterly subordinated to the pursuit of consumer satisfaction.

More work, as they say, needs to be done, but I cannot hope to undertake it within the bounds of this chapter. The most important contention that I have tried to establish in this section is that the concept of sustainability is irreducibly normative, so that disputes about its definition will inevitably reflect differing values.

If, as I maintain, the root idea of sustainability is the conservation of what matters for future generations, its definition is inescapably bound up with one's conception of what matters.

4. Sustainability and Intergenerational Justice

Having said something about intergenerational justice and something about sustainability, it is time to bring them together. We can be encouraged about the prospect of a connection if I am correct in my contention that sustainability is as much a normative concept as is justice. And I believe that there is indeed a close connection. It may be recalled that the question that I formulated at the end of section 1 asked if sustainability was either a necessary or a sufficient condition of intergenerational justice. It appears that sustainability is at least a necessary condition of justice. For the principle of responsibility says that, unless people in the future can be held responsible for the situation that they find themselves in, they should not be worse off than we are. And no generation can be held responsible for the state of the planet it inherits.

This suggests that we should at any rate leave people in the future with the possibility of not falling below our level. We cannot, of course, guarantee that our doing this will actually provide people in the further future with what we make possible. The next generation may, for all we can know, go on a gigantic spree and leave their successors relatively impoverished. The potential for sustaining the same level of X as we enjoy depends on each successive generation playing its part. All we can do is leave open the possibility, and that is what we are obliged by justice to do.

An objection sometimes raised to the notion that it would be unjust to let future generations fall below our standard (of whatever is to count as X) is that there is something arbitrary about taking the current position as the baseline (see Beckerman Ch. 3 in this volume). We are, it is argued, better off materially than our ancestors. Suppose we were to pursue policies that ran down resources to such an extent that people in future would be no better off than our ancestors were a hundred years (or two hundred years) ago. Why would that be unjust? What is so special about the present as the point of comparison? In reply, it must be conceded that the expression 'intergenerational justice' is potentially misleading—though perhaps it actually misleads only those who are determined to be misled. It is a sort of shorthand for 'justice between the present generation and future generations'. Because of time's arrow, we cannot do anything to make people in the past better off than they actually were, so it is absurd to say that our relations to them could be either just or unjust. 'Ought' implies 'can', and the only people whose fate we can affect are those living now and in the future. Taking the present as our reference point is arbitrary only in some cosmic sense in which it might be said to be arbitrary that now is now and not some other time. It is important, however, to understand that 'now' means 'now' in the timeless sense, not '1998'. Wilfred Beckerman suggested in a presentation to the seminar from which this chapter arose (see Beckerman in this volume) that there was something arbitrary in privileging 1998 from all dates in history as the benchmark of sustainability. So there would be. But in 1999 the benchmark will be 1999, and in 2099 it will be 2099. There are, as I have explained, excellent reasons for starting from now, whenever 'now' may be. But just as 'here' does not mean my flat (though that is where I am as I write this) so in the sentence 'We start from now' the meaning of 'now' is not rigidly designated.

We now have to face a question of interpretation so far left aside. This is: How are we to deal with population size? On one quite natural interpretation of the concept of sustainability, the X whose value is to be maintained is to be defined over individuals. The demands of justice will then be more stringent the larger we predict the future population to be. Suppose we were simply to extrapolate into the indefinite future growth rates of the order of those seen in past decades. On the hypothesis that numbers double every forty years or so, we shall have a world population after two centuries of around a hundred and fifty billion and in a further two centuries a population of five thousand billion. If the increase were spread evenly round the world, this would imply a population for the UK more than ten times the size of the whole current world population.

It is surely obvious that no degree of self-immiseration that those currently alive could engage in would be capable of providing the possibility of an equal level of X per head even that far inside the future. This would be so on any remotely plausible definition of X. (Indeed, we can be certain that some cataclysm would have occurred long before these numbers were reached.) But even far more modest increases in population would make it impossible to maintain X, if X is taken to include the preservation of so-called 'natural capital'.

This is worth emphasizing because the 'cornucopian' school of optimists about population, such as Julian Simon, cite in support of their ideas the alleged failures of early neo-Malthusians (from the mid-nineteenth century onward) to predict correctly the course of events. But I believe that the pessimists have already been proved right on a central point: the deleterious impact on the quality of life of sheer numbers. Thus, John Stuart Mill's forebodings a century and a half ago (in 1848 to be precise) have, it seems to me, proved quite uncannily prescient. All that he feared has already in large measure come to pass, and every bit of future population increase will make things that much worse.

Mill was quite prepared to grant the 'cornucopian' premiss that material conditions might be able to keep up with a greatly expanded population (or even more than keep up with it). But he still insisted that the population increase should be regretted. 'A population may be crowded, though all be amply supplied with food and raiment . . . A world from which solitude is extirpated, is a very poor ideal . . . Nor is there much satisfaction in contemplating the world with nothing left to the spontaneous activity of nature; with every rood of land brought into cultivation, which is capable of growing food for human beings; every flowery waste or natural pasture ploughed up, all quadrupeds or birds which are not domesticated for man's use exterminated as his rivals for food, every hedgerow or superfluous tree rooted out, and scarcely a place left where a wild shrub or flower could grow without being eradicated as a weed in the name of improved agriculture.'[7]

Treating future population as parametric is in effect assuming it to be beyond human control. But any such assumption is obviously false. I suggest, therefore, that the size of future population should be brought within the scope of the principle of responsibility. We must define intergenerational justice on the assumption that 'the increase of mankind shall be under the guidance of judicious foresight', as Mill put it.[8] If future people choose to let population increase, or by default permit it to increase, that is to be at their own cost. There is no reason in justice for our having any obligation to accommodate their profligacy. Concretely, then, the conception of sustainability that makes it appropriate as a necessary condition of intergenerational justice may be formulated as follows: Sustainability requires at any point in time that the value of some X per head of population should be capable of being maintained into the indefinite future, on the assumption that the size of the future population is no greater than the size of the present population.

It is worth emphasizing again that we always start from now, and ask what sustainability requires. The question is: What amount of X could be maintained into the indefinite future, given things as they are now, on the assumption that future population will be the same then as now? The way in which 'now' is always moving would not matter if (a) the demands of sustainability were correctly assessed in 1998; (b) sustainability were achieved in 1998 and maintained thereafter; and (c) the assumption of stable population control were in fact accurate. If all these conditions were met, we could substitute '1998' for 'now', but not otherwise.

We know that stabilization of population is perfectly possible as a result of voluntary choices made by individuals because a number of Western countries have already arrived at the position at which the (non-immigrant) population is only barely replacing itself, if that. Although they stumbled into it without any particular foresight, the formula is now known and can be applied elsewhere. Women have to be educated and to have a possibility of pursuing rewarding occupations outside the home while at the same time compulsory full-time education and stringent child-labour laws make children an economic burden rather than a benefit.

Unfortunately, however, many countries have such a large proportion of their population below the age of fifteen that their numbers would double before stabilizing even if every female now alive had only two children. Stabilizing population at its current level in these countries can be achieved only if women have only one child. So long as a policy restricting women to one child is operated consistently across the board, it does not contravene any principle of intragenerational justice, and is a requirement of intragenerational justice. Combined, as it has been in China, with a focus on medical care and education for children, there can be no question that it offers the next generation the best chance of living satisfactory lives, and removes a huge burden on future generations.

At this point, however, we must expect the response, already anticipated in general terms, that whether or not this is just it simply conflicts too strongly with religious objections to contraception and abortion and to powerful pronatalist norms, especially in many parts of the world where great importance is attached to having a male heir. If we are impressed by this, we shall have to say that justice demands more of people than they can reasonably be expected to perform. But what follows from that? At this point, it seems to me unavoidable to enter into the question that I have so far left on one side: the concrete implications of any criterion of sustainability. Suppose we believed that it would be fairly easy to provide the conditions in which X (e.g. some conception of equal opportunity) could be maintained into the indefinite future for a population twice the existing one. We might then treat as parametric the predicted doubling of world population and redefine sustainability accordingly. But my own conjecture is that the criterion of sustainability already proposed is extremely stringent, and that there is little chance of its demands being met. If I am right about this, all we can do is get as close to that as we can, which means doing everything possible to reduce population growth as well as everything possible to conserve resources and reduce depletion.

What then about the future? Suppose that the demographers' (relatively optimistic) projection for world population is correct, so that it stabilizes some time in the next century at double its current size. If we stick to the proposition that intragenerational justice is always a problem for the current generation (because they are the only people in a position to do anything about it), the implication is that sustainability should be redefined by each generation as the indefinite continuation of the level of X over the existing population, whatever it is. Whether people in the past have behaved justly or not is irrelevant. But if I am right in thinking that we are going to fall short of maintaining sustainability even on the basis of the continuation of current population size, it seems highly unlikely that people in the future will achieve it on the basis of a population twice as large. The only ray of light is that getting from a stable population to a gently declining one would not be difficult (nothing like as difficult as stabilizing a rapidly expanding population), and that the power of compound interest means that even a gradual decline in numbers would suffice to bring world population back well below current levels over a matter of a few centuries.

My conclusion, after this vertiginous speculation, is that we would be doing very well to meet the criterion of sustainability that I originally proposed. The more we fail, and the more that world population is not checked in coming decades, the worse things will be in the future and the smaller the population at which it will be possible to maintain tolerable living conditions. Perhaps the right way to look at the matter is to think of population and resources (in the largest sense) as the two variables that enter into sustainability: we might then say that sustainability is a function of both. Realistically, any given generation can make only a limited impact on either. But what can at least then be said is that if some generation is failing to meet the condition of sustainability (defined in the standard way over a fixed population), it can at least be more just than otherwise towards its successors by ensuring that the dwindling resources will have to spread around over fewer people.

Interpreted on some such lines as these, sustainability is, I suggest, adequate as a necessary condition of intergenerational justice. Is it also a sufficient condition? I feel strongly inclined to say that it is: if we were to satisfy it, we would be doing very well, and it is hard to see that we could reasonably be expected to do more. My only hesitation arises from the application of the vital interests. (I noted in section 2 that this needed later discussion.) Obviously, if we give the principle of vital interests priority over the principle of responsibility, we are liable to be back at a version of the absurd idea that we are obliged to immiserate ourselves to a level capable of sustaining a hugely larger population if we predict there will be one. For if we predict an enormously greater number of people in the future, meeting their vital interests trumps any objective we might have. I have not specified priority relations among the principles, and I do not think this can be done across the board. The principles are guides to thinking, not a piece of machinery that can be cranked to grind out conclusions. However, in this case it seems to me that giving the principle of vital interests priority produces such absurd results that this cannot possibly be the right thing to do.

Even if we make the principle of vital interests subordinate to the principle of responsibility, there is still a feature of the principle of vital interests that is worth attention. So far 'generations' have been treated as collective entities: the question has been posed as one of justice between the present generation as a whole and future generations as wholes. But the principle of vital interests forces us to focus on the fates of individuals. Suppose we leave future generations as collectivities with 'enough' between them to satisfy the criterion of sustainability, but it is distributed in such a way that the vital interests of many will predictably fail to be met? Does this possibility suggest that the criterion of sustainability has to be supplemented in order to count as a sufficient condition of intergenerational justice?

What I think it shows is that the distinction between intergenerational and intragenerational justice cannot be made absolute. I pointed out in section 1 that some things that would be wrong in relation to people in the future (e.g. fighting a nuclear war) would in the first instance be wrong among those alive at the time. Similarly, the primary reason for our being able to predict that the vital interests of many people in the world will not be met in the future is that they are not being met in the present. Formally, I suggest we have to say that maldistribution in the future is intragenerational injustice in the future. But we must recognize that intragenerational injustice in the future is the almost inevitable consequence of intragenerational injustice in the present.

5. *Beyond Justice*

If the current generation meets the demands of justice, is that enough? In the broad sense of justice, we would not be doing wrong in relation to human beings if we met the demands of justice. But we can (as I said in section 1) behave wrongly in relation to non-human animals even though this does not fall within the scope of justice. If we factor this in, what difference does it make? As far as I can see, its main effect is to reinforce the importance of keeping the lid on population, since the pressure on the habitats of the remaining wild non-human animals are already being encroached on at an alarming rate as a consequence of the growth of population that has already occurred.

The remaining question is the one that divides environmentalists into those for whom the significance of the environment lies solely in its contribution to human (or if you like animal) welfare from those for whom the environment has some significance beyond that. (Perhaps talking about 'the environment' is itself prejudicial since it suggests something in the background to another thing that is more important. But I take it that the distinction is familiar enough in a variety of descriptions.) I have to confess that I cannot quite decide what I think about this question because I find it hard to focus on the question when it is put, as it often is, as one about the 'independent value of nature'. Let me explain.

In *Principia Ethica,* G. E. Moore sought to discredit Sidgwick's claim that nothing can be said to be good 'out of relation to human existence, or at least to some consciousness or feeling'.[9] To this end, he asked his reader to consider

the following case. Let us imagine one world exceedingly beautiful. Imagine it as beautiful as you can; put into it whatever on this earth you most admire—mountains, rivers, the sea, trees, and sunsets, stars and moon. Imagine these all combined in the most exquisite proportions so that no one thing jars against another but each contributes to increase the beauty of the whole. And then imagine the ugliest world you can possibly conceive. Imagine it simply one heap of filth, containing everything that is most disgusting to us, for whatever reason, and the whole, as far as maybe, without one redeeming feature. Such a pair of worlds we are entitled to compare: they fall within Prof. Sidgwick's meaning, and the comparison is highly relevant to it. The only thing we are not entitled to imagine is that any human being ever has or ever, by any possibility, *can,* live in either, can ever see and enjoy the beauty of the one or hate the foulness of the other. Well, even so, supposing them quite apart from any possible contemplation by human beings; still, is it irrational to hold that it is better that the beautiful world should exist, than the one that is ugly?[10]

It is surely obvious that the question is loaded, because the two worlds are already unavoidably being visited by us, at least in imagination. It requires a self-conscious effort to avoid being affected by that. But if I make that effort conscientiously, I have to say that the whole question strikes me as ridiculous. In what possible sense could the universe be a better or a worse place on one supposition rather than the other? It seems to me an abuse of our language to assume that the word 'good' still has application when applied to such a context.

If adherence to the 'deep ecological' or 'dark green' position entails giving Moore the answer he wanted about the two worlds, I have to be counted out. But I wonder if all (or even many) of those who wish to endorse such a position feel thereby committed to attaching an intrinsic value to nature in the sense suggested by Moore. And, quite apart from that biographical question, there is the philosophical question: is there any way of being 'dark green' that does not entail being committed to Moore's preferred answer about the two worlds?

I am inclined to think that there is an attitude (which I share) that is distinguishable from the first position but is perhaps misleadingly expressed in terms of the intrinsic value of nature. This is that it is inappropriate—cosmically unfitting, in some sense—to regard nature as nothing more than something to be exploited for the benefit of human beings—or other sentient creatures, if it comes to that. There is an obvious sense in which this is still somehow human-centred, because it is about the right way for human beings to think about nature. But the content of that thought could be expressed by talking about the intrinsic value of nature.

It is important to observe that what I am saying here is not to be equated with the kind of environmental utilitarianism put forward by Robert Goodin in his *Green Political Theory*.[11] According to this, we do as a matter of fact care about unspoilt nature— for example, even the most carefully restored site of open-cast mining is 'not the same' as the original, any more than a perfect copy of a statue is 'the same' as the original. A sophisticated utilitarianism will therefore take our concerns about nature into account and set more stringent limits on the exploitation of the environment than would be set by our merely regarding the environment as a factor of production. This enables us to press 'green' concerns but still within a framework that makes human interests the measure of all things.

What I am saying is quite different from this. For it is a purely contingent matter whether or not people have the attitude to nature attributed to them by Goodin or, if they do, how far it weighs in their utility function compared with, say, cheap hamburgers from the cattle raised on pasture created from the ravaged Brazilian rain forest. The view that I am proposing says bluntly that people behave wrongly if they act out of a wrong attitude to nature. Although this is in a sense a human-centred proposition, it cannot be captured in any utilitarian calculus, however extensive its conception of human well-being.

6. Conclusion

I want to conclude by saying that I can understand and indeed sympathize with the impatience that will undoubtedly be felt by any environmental activist into whose hands this might fall. (Jonathon Porritt eloquently expressed such sentiments—and not only in relation to my contribution—during the final session of the Keele seminars on social justice and sustainability.) What the activist wants is ammunition that can be used in the fight for greater ecological awareness and responsibility. Fine-drawn analyses of sustainability such as those offered here are hardly the stuff to give the troops. But is it reasonable to expect them to be?

Let me make what may at first sight seem an eccentric suggestion. This is that it is not terribly difficult to know what needs to be done, though it is of course immensely difficult to get the relevant actors (governmental and other) to do it. I do not deny that there are large areas of scientific uncertainty, and probably always will be (e.g. about global warming), since the interacting processes involved are so complex. But what I am claiming is that virtually everybody who has made a serious study of the situation and whose objectivity is not compromised by either religious beliefs or being in the pay of some multinational corporation has reached the conclusion that the most elementary concern for people in the future demands big changes in the way we do things. These could start with the implementation by all signatories of what was agreed on at the Rio Conference.

Moreover, whatever is actually going to get done in, say, the next decade, to move towards a sustainable balance of population and resources is going to be so pathetically inadequate that it really does not matter how far it falls short. We know the direction in which change is required, and we know that there is absolutely no risk that we shall find ourselves doing more than required. It really does not make any practical difference whether we think a certain given effort represents 10 per cent of what needs to be done, or whether we think it is as much as 20 per cent. Either way, we have good reason to push for more. If I am right about this, it explains the feeling among practitioners that philosophical analyses have little relevance to their concerns. For whether we make the demands of justice more or less stringent, it is going to demand more than is likely to get done in the foreseeable future. What then is the use of pursuing these questions?

One obvious answer is that as political philosophers we are concerned to discover the truth, and that is an adequate justification for our work. The agenda of a scholarly discipline has its own integrity, which is worthy of respect. Distributive justice among contemporaries and within the boundaries of a state has been at the centre of the dramatic revival of political philosophy in the last quarter century. Extending the inquiry into the nature of distributive justice beyond these limits is a natural and inevitable development. But I think that there is also something to offer to those who are not interested in pursuing these questions for their own sake. It is surely at least something to be able to assure those who spend their days trying to gain support for measures intended to improve the prospects of future generations that such measures do not represent optional benevolence on our part but are demanded by elementary considerations of justice. What I have aimed to do here is show that the application of ideas about justice that are quite familiar in other contexts have radical implications when applied to intergenerational justice, and that there is no reason why they should not be.

5

Ecology and Opportunity: Intergenerational Equity and Sustainable Options

BRYAN NORTON

1. Introduction: Two Strategies to Achieve a Sustainability Metric

Freedom is about choices; choices require options. So options are a prerequisite of true freedom; if I control the options you choose among, I control the range—and the substance—of your free choice. The purpose of this chapter is to explore whether this intimate conceptual connection between the range of options and opportunities[1] available and an unquestioned value—freedom of choice—might support a new approach to long-term environmental valuation and management. In particular, I propose to explore whether this connection might shed light on the theoretical and practical problem of stating the requirements for sustainability and for sustainable development. The core idea of sustainability is best captured, I will argue, as an expression of an obligation to maintain options and opportunities for the future; if I am correct in this conclusion, and if my analysis of what would be necessary in order to express that obligation operationally is right, it will be necessary to rethink the role of economic analysis in the search for environmental sustainability. Accordingly, in this chapter it is assumed that some obligations to future generations exist, and the task accepted is to clarify and explain these obligations.

The sustainability question, put crudely, is: What should we save for future generations? Answers to the question, thus crudely put, might come in two, broad varieties. One might, first, say that what we owe the future should be an opportunity for undiminished utility; and so the question of fairness across generations will be formulated as a comparison of aggregated welfare opportunities available to individuals living at different times. We will have been fair to the future, on this view, provided we do not reduce the opportunity of persons in future generations to be as well off as prior generations have been. We can refer to this general type of approach, which comes in several varieties, and includes most of the extant theories of intergenerational fairness, as the 'utility comparison' (UC) approach. A second type of answer would proceed not by comparisons of individual well-being, but by listing 'stuff' that should be saved for future generations (the LS approach). By 'stuff' I mean any aspect of the natural world that is physically describable, including important sites, biological taxonomic groups, standing stocks of resources, and important ecological processes. Examples of stuff would include: adequate supplies of fresh, clean water; the Grand Canyon, grizzly bears (or, more generally, 'biological diversity'); an undiminished ozone shield in the upper atmosphere; and also perhaps landscape features, such as a predominantly forested landscape. Explicators of sustainability concepts apparently must pursue one or the other of these two broad strategies: either one compares welfare across generations and defines sustainability as, in some sense, the sustainability of human welfare, or one specifies stuff—aspects of the natural, physical world, which we should not allow to disappear or be degraded if we want the future to be as well off as we are.[2]

In order to make explicit this important divergence in strategies more explicit, let us distinguish (a) comparative assessments of 'well-being' across time, from (b) comparisons of measurable economic welfare across time. In this paper we will use the term 'well-being' as a general term, referring to how well off a person or group of people are, but leaving open how well-being will be characterized or measured, while we will use 'welfare' to refer to well-being as it is measured within the technical apparatus of mainstream welfare economists. Thus we can compare well-being of time-cohorts of people in general terms, and assert that fairness to future generations requires that there be no decline in well-being from one generation to the next, without committing ourselves to the specific view that maintenance or decline of well-being should be characterized and modelled using the techniques of welfare economics. Accordingly, we can agree with the general assertion that sustainable living requires that present people do nothing to reduce the opportunities for well-being of future generations, without accepting the similar-sounding—but much more specific, on our definitions—claim that acting sustainably is to avoid causing a reduction in the opportunities of future persons to achieve a level of economic welfare equal to their predecessors. References to comparative well-being of generations, in other words, mark no commitment to either the UC or the LS approaches, while references to welfare comparisons imply a commitment to a specific economic version of the UC approach.

Given this clarification, it is possible to identify a common, shared definition of sustainability, as long as we state that consensus in terms of 'opportunities for well-being'. Robert Solow, who will appear in section 3 as the champion of 'weak sustainability'—a version of the narrower, welfare-comparison approach—says, 'I will assume that a sustainable path for the national economy is one that allows every future generation the option of being as well off as its predecessors.'[3] Richard Howarth, on the other hand, a critic of weak sustainability and an advocate of a 'deontological' approach to constraining economic choices with intergenerational impact, similarly refers to the following as an 'axiom' of sustainability discussions: 'The sustainability principle is rooted in the view that each generation holds a duty to ensure that the life opportunities of its offspring are no less satisfactory than its own.'[4] This general idea has also found favour with leading philosophers and moral theorists. For example, the moral philosopher Brian Barry says: 'In the absence of any powerful argument to the contrary, there would seem to be a strong presumption in favour of arranging things so that, as far as possible, each generation faces the same range of opportunities with respect to natural resources.'[5] At first glance, this broad consensus might appear to provide a firm foundation for moving toward a consensually accepted approach to defining our sustainability obligations to the future.

The broad consensus just highlighted, however, does not resolve the strategic question of how to proceed to compare intergenerational well-being, nor does it point unambiguously to one or the other of the two general strategies. A physical scientist, for example, might proceed to list certain physical features of the world that are essential to human well-being, such as the existence of at least a minimal amount of fresh water. In doing so, the scientist is implying that, if we fail to protect supplies of fresh water, we would be harming the future and violating the sustainability obligation. Such an LS approach, it must be admitted at the outset, is quite limited: it refers to just one type of thing, fresh water, and this approach is also based on a variety of important assumptions regarding the likely effects of diminishing water supplies on human life and also concerning the range of possible technological responses to shortages of fresh water, etc. But in principle it is possible to specify a set of features that are arguably essential for future well-being, and then devise the best indicators possible to track those features.

Economists, enthusiastic utilitarians for the most part, are more likely to eschew physical measures and explain and define opportunity by adopting the theoretical principles, conceptual models, and technical devices that economists have developed to measure and compare welfare. This specific application of a UC approach promises to provide models and data by which to measure and compare opportunities to enjoy welfare of individuals existing at different times and in different generations. It is undeniable that the economists' approach is attractive because it holds some hope of being *both* comprehensive *and* quantitative, provided one can measure aggregated individual welfare at different times, and provided these measures can be expressed in terms that are commensurable across time. In the next section we will explore one such attempt at a comprehensive and potentially measurable criterion, based in the economic theory of savings and growth.

Philosophers and political theorists, it turns out, while not necessarily endorsing welfare economics as their guide to comparisons of well-being, do mostly assume the problem of specifying inter-generational obligations is to be addressed, in some sense, by comparing aggregated well-being of individuals existing at different times.[6] What these various UC approaches share is a commitment to measuring or comparing aggregated welfare of individuals, *qua* individuals, across generations. Although my argument will be addressed, for specificity and precision, at the economic models designed to measure sustainability, I believe my arguments apply equally to all UC approaches, including philosophical ones.

In this introduction we have posed a question that is simple in form, but exceedingly difficult to answer: What do present people owe to people of the future? We have noted that there are two practical strategies for addressing this question, the UC approach and the LS approach, both of which are consistent with the insight that what we owe the future is not to destroy their opportunities for well-being. They differ in that one seeks an operationalization of the UC idea, while the other approach attempts to specify aspects of the physical environment, perhaps represented by physical indicators that will be essential to future well-being. Because the economic model promises a quantitative *and* potentially comprehensive system of valuation, it justifiably demands considerable attention in public policy discussions. While there is much discussion of important physical features that should be protected, on the other hand, the scientists and environmentalists developing these ideas do not, as do economists, have a shared way of understanding and computing values, so LS proposals often seem disjointed and lacking in coherence. It is possible to specify measurable physical characteristics of the environment and to hypothesize that these characteristics track features that are essential to save if future people are to have opportunity equal to ours, and to choose precisely and easily measurable characteristics as indicators to represent those features. What the LS approach lacks, then, is not so much methods of quantification, but a unifying theory and concepts for expressing, as well as an associated method for measuring and comparing, values. Proposals by advocates of the LS approach, since they are not based on a unifying theory of intertemporal value, often seem arbitrary and incomplete by comparison to economists' measurements of welfare. If there were a unifying theory to explain what stuff we owe the future, and why, that theory would guide LS advocates to operationalize key physical indicators that they believe to be essential to future well-being. This paper sets out to explore the LS approach by seeking a theory relating well-being of generations to the range of options or choices available to its members, and to further explore the possibility that this theory could be made operational by specifying physical features as indicators of future well-being. This theory would then play the same role within the LS approach that the theory of economic welfare plays in the UC approach. It will turn out, as the analysis proceeds, that both the strategy of specifying stuff and the strategy of comparing utilities must—if they are to progress to measurable indicators—do so on the basis of powerful, and controversial, assumptions. A choice between the LS approach and the UC approach must therefore be based on the justifiability and appropriateness of the assumptions they embody for the task at hand. This task is to determine reasonable and morally acceptable sustainability requirements.

2. Intergenerational Fairness:
An Analysis of the Problem

In this section, the complexity of the problem of intergenerational fairness is explored, in order to provide some intellectual background for a discussion of the appropriateness of the assumptions of the UC and LS approaches to intertemporal comparisons of human well-being. The philosophical problem of what we owe the future is not a single, monolithic problem, but rather an interrelated cluster of sub-problems. For convenience, we group these sub-problems into three categories and give them somewhat descriptive names.[7] They are: (1) *the distance problem*—how far into the future do our moral obligations extend? One might argue that our current approaches to environmental valuation, which treat all future values as discounted functions of present values, are 'present'—they do not adequately consider the interests of people who will exist in the future. Is it possible to develop a theory of value that helps us to determine what is fair to the present *and* fair to successive generations in the future? (2) *the ignorance problem*—who will future people be and how can we identify them? And, how can we know what they will want or need, or what rights they will insist upon? Since individuals who will live in the future cannot express their concerns and interests, and since we are reluctant to impose a particular version of 'the good' upon them, it is difficult even to begin to evaluate policies that will affect them. And (3) *the typology of effects problem*—how can we determine which of our actions truly have moral implications for the future?[8] If I cut down a mature tree and plant a seedling of the same species, it seems unlikely that I have significantly harmed people of the future, though there will be a period of 'recovery' in which that 'resource' is unavailable. If, on the other hand, I clear-cut a whole watershed, thereby setting in motion severe and irreversible erosion, siltation of streams, etc., it is arguable that I have significantly harmed the future, having irreversibly limited the resources and options available to them; and that I have restricted their options for pursuing their own well-being in their own time. However intuitive this distinction seems in particular cases such as this, however, it is extremely difficult to provide a general definition for characterizing, and to offer a theoretically justifiable practical criterion for separating, cases of these two types.

Interestingly, these three philosophical problems intersect in key arguments that separate advocates of 'weak sustainability' from 'strong sustainability', a debate which roughly parallels the disciplinary debate between mainstream and 'ecological' economists.[9] To summarize a very complex argument, mainstream economists believe that, provided we maintain a non-declining stock of aggregated capital (monetary, technological, natural), we will have fulfilled our obligation to ensure that the future is as well off as we are. Ecological economists, on the other hand, believe that an adequate bequest package for the future must protect an adequate supply of 'natural capital'. This dispute turns mainly on the extent of substitutability among resources.[10]

3. Solow and Weak Sustainability

Robert Solow's work[11] exemplifies weak sustainability theory. Solow's basic idea is that the obligation to sustainability 'is an obligation to conduct ourselves so that we leave to the future the option or the capacity to be as well off as we are'. He doubts that 'one can be more precise than that'. A central implication of Solow's view is that 'there is no specific object that the goal of sustainability, the obligation of sustainability, requires us to leave untouched'.[12] Solow thus argues that all we need avoid is passing on a smaller stock of generalized capital to the future than we inherited. He bases his argument on a strong premiss asserting our total ignorance regarding what we can know about the preferences of future people: 'We realize that the tastes, the preferences, of future generations are something that we don't know about.'[13] So, he argues, the best that we can do is to maintain a non-diminishing stock of capital in the form of wealth for investment and in the form of productive capacity and technological knowledge. Solow continues: 'Resources are, to use a favorite word of economists, fungible in a certain sense. They can take the place of each other.'[14]

In this argument, ignorance problems completely dominate the other two sets of problems—the distance problem and the typology of effects problem. The Grand Simplification is so Grand because it apparently resolves the seemingly perplexing distance question, subsuming concern for distant generations within a simple obligation to save and to maintain a non-declining stock of capital for the next generation.[15] And, it sidesteps the typology of effects problem by assuming the fungibility of resources across uses and across time. We need only maintain an adequate savings rate in order to rule out spending down the general stock of capital, and that will take care of our obligations to the future. As long as the future is richer, the future will have no right to complain that they have been treated unfairly.[16]

Ecological economists, recognizing that these assumptions greatly restrict our ability to analyse impacts of specific policies on the future, have challenged Solow's principle of unlimited fungibility, arguing that certain elements, relationships, or processes of nature represent irreplaceable resources, and that these resources constitute a scientifically separable and normatively significant category of capital—natural capital. This position apparently contradicts Solow's central conclusion—that sustainability is achieved, provided simply that the *total* stock of capital is not declining.

4. Stronger Sustainability?

Ecological economists such as Herman Daly argue that human-created capital and natural capital are complements, and that they are imperfect substitutes for one another.[17] Daly and Cobb[18] propose that, having identified certain resources as natural capital, these particular assets should be set aside because they are essential to the welfare of future generations. We can say, then, that whereas the weak sustainability theorists believe we owe to the future an *unstructured bequest package,* the strong economic sustainability theorists *structure their bequest package,* differentiating special elements of capital-in-general that must be included in the capital base passed forward to coming generations. While they insist on structuring the bequest package, the strong sustainability theorists never question the comparability of natural and other forms of capital with respect to their impacts on welfare as experienced at different times. They never, that is, question the UC approach.

To see this, consider the accounting system proposed by Daly and Cobb,[19] who propose corrections to national income accounts (similar to depreciation of factories and infrastructure, etc.), to national accounts for 'depreciation of natural capital', to ensure that we recognize and measure impacts of currently unsustainable consumption and other environmentally damaging activities on the income of future people.[20] Therefore, in an extensive Appendix, they operationalize an 'Index of Sustainable Economic Welfare'. Arguing that resource depletion is already affecting income and that it will continue to do so,[21] they say:

'We have thus deducted an estimate of the amount that we would
need to set aside in a perpetual income stream to compensate
future generations for the loss of services from nonrenewable . . .
resources. In addition, we have deducted for the loss of resources
such as wetlands and croplands . . . This may be thought of as an
accounting device for the depreciation of "natural capital . . ."''[22]
Resources necessary for the future are thus equated with an
'income stream' from a trust fund that will compensate their
loss of resource availability.

Even though ecological economists have criticized the methods
and approaches of mainstream economists regarding natural and
human-built capital, they still operate on the same set of assumptions and beliefs that support the Grand Simplification. If we
destroy natural capital, a trust fund must be set up to compensate
the future—implying that the present dollars invested in the trust
are, if not a *substitute* for natural capital, at least acceptable *compensation* for the loss of opportunities suffered in the future. And,
while Daly and Cobb do not endorse presentism, it is difficult to
see how their insistence on trust-fund compensation for future
people in perpetuity provides protection beyond Solow's admon-
ition to maintain a fair savings rate so as not to impoverish the
future. Strong sustainability, for all practical purposes, collapses
into weak sustainability.[23] While Solow explicitly endorses the
Grand Simplification, Daly and Cobb 'back into' it by allowing
compensation for any type of loss.

What is remarkable, nevertheless, is that the Grand Simplification is achieved on no better foundation than a simple declaration
of an implausibly strong, even extreme, statement of the ignorance problem,[24] coupled with the unargued assertion of the fungibility assumption. I have argued elsewhere that the Grand
Simplification has apparently implausible practical implications.[25]
Here, my point is not to argue that the Grand Simplification is
certainly wrong, but to show that it rests on a set of questionable
and inappropriate assumptions about our intergenerational
obligations. These simplifying assumptions obscure legitimate
questions of distance and of how to specify effects.

While the Grand Simplification rests on shaky assumptions, it is
attractive to such a variety of theorists because it plugs a crucial

hole in the UC approach. It is reasonable to expect proponents of the UC approach, which turns on making comparisons of opportunities to enjoy welfare as experienced at different times, to provide some way to measure and compare cross-time welfare effects of various sustainability requirements we might live by. The Grand Simplification accomplishes a reduction of concern for the future to aspects of welfare that are amenable to treatment within the paradigm of economic growth theory, Solow's professional specialization within welfare economics. But the Grand Simplification—toggled together from an unargued commitment to technological optimism (the total fungibility assumption) and an exaggeration of the ignorance problem—is really only attractive as an account of intergenerational obligations to someone who has already opted for UC, and who is desperate for a quantified model by which to compare intergenerational opportunity.

It is important to realize what is at stake in this argument. Since welfare economics, and more specifically the growth-theory model, are proposed as the basis for comparison of intergenerational opportunities, then the concept of opportunity takes on, in practice, the weight of the implausible assumptions and beliefs that are required to make the metric operational. Efforts at quantitative comparison—apparently essential to UC approaches—will be helpful only if one can quantitatively measure and aggregate opportunity to enjoy welfare at given, but significantly different, times, and to express these in terms that are commensurable across those times. Actual dollars earned and spent, which might serve as a useful measure of exchange value, of course, do not themselves have this commensurability across time. Unless one develops a model, based on a set of empirical and conceptual assumptions, it is impossible simply to compare income dollars across decades or generations. Economists address this problem by choosing present dollars as the 'currency' of the analysis, and by 'correcting' future values back to present values. For example, anyone would probably accept adjustments in future values that correct for inflation.

So far, so good. But correction for inflation is not the only assumption the economists make to gain commensurability across longer temporal durations. There is also the issue of the 'discount rate'. It is well known, based on masses of virtually unquestionable empirical data, that individual consumers tend to discount future values, at least because of uncertainty and because of the constant possibility that mortality will preclude enjoyment, and perhaps for other reasons. So, in standard economic analysis, future values are also 'corrected' by a percentage that attempts to represent this discounting behaviour. It is therefore accepted and standard practice to discount future values by the rate of real interest; the reasoning is that time preference of an individual for sooner rather than later consumption corresponds roughly to the 'price of money'—the rate at which the individual could enhance his money by loaning it out at the going rate of interest.[26] Even if it is justified when analysing individual decisions in markets of exchange, however, the discounting adjustment is more controversial when applied to public goods, to multi-generational goods and, especially, to inter-generational harms, however.[27]

The practice of discounting values across generations, which can be thought of as a technical device for operationalizing presentism, can be questioned on at least two significant grounds. First, the possibility of early death and associated uncertainties with deferred consumption should drop out of the picture. If we assume, as seems reasonable, that *someone* will be alive to enjoy the welfare in the future, the death or misfortune of individuals should not affect economic/utilitarian reasoning, which is based on aggregated welfare. Discounting therefore loses its core justification when applied in intergenerational contexts.[28] Secondly, and this is the most important moral consideration, using present dollars to evaluate future well-being requires reducing future values and welfare to what present consumers are willing to pay to support it.[29] Comparisons of welfare across generations, when expressed as present values in Solow's model, are based on assumptions of fungibility of all resources, and simply represent the altruistic commitment of present people to set aside capital for future generations. Whereas in the individual case, the same person who favours the present over the future must eventually live with the consequences of earlier choices; applying discounting to multiple generations represents only the discounters' sense of altruism toward future people.

It is now possible to define an alternative to both weak and strong sustainability. This proposed approach follows strong economic sustainability theorists in insisting that the bequest package from earlier to later generations must be structured, but the structuring would be accomplished through an LS strategy, rather than by creating a present-value accounting system for comparing welfare opportunities across time. The goal of the LS approach is to specify features and processes constituting the environment as essential for future well-being, claiming that these features and processes are so important that any bequest to the future which does not protect them will inevitably leave the future worse off than they would have been had these features been protected. While it would be possible to make this third approach seem superficially similar to strong economic sustainability by designating these features and processes as 'natural capital', I avoid this move because designation of anything as 'capital' encourages consideration of it as a broadly 'economic good', and it is my intention to sharpen, not blur, the distinction between strong economic sustainability and ecological sustainability. Further, the specification of features that are essential to the well-being of the future should not be confused with compensatable losses in the sense introduced by Daly and Cobb—these features are such that their loss cannot be repaired by setting up trust funds or other devices to monetarily compensate or repay the future for their destruction. The loss of these features would be understood to result in the diminution of the quality of future lives, *regardless of the amount of compensation/wealth that is provided as a substitute for the lost features.*[30] Individuals in the future could, if these features are lost, justifiably blame present people for failing to protect these features, no matter how wealthy they turn out to be.

5. Options and Opportunities: A New Look

We are left, at this point in the argument, with a sort of informal 'draw' between the UC and LS approaches to specifying what we owe the future. While the UC approach is often put forward as if its advocates are well on their way to having a quantified model for comparing welfare across generations, the model that is invoked involves a hopelessly simplified account of intergenerational impacts. The conceptual assumptions necessary to create even the semblance of commensurability of welfare measures across generations are so unattractive as to cry out for an alternative approach. In the interest of formulating an alternative, let us return to the idea, mentioned at the outset of this chapter, that living sustainably and caring for the future have something to do with maintaining an undiminished range of free choices open to people of the future; the outstanding disagreement regards how to understand opportunity comparisons across time and what metric to use to capture and operationalize that understanding. We saw that there is a shared commitment, by all sides, to the idea that we owe undiminished opportunity to the future. Advocates of the UC approach, insofar as they have adopted the growth theory / shallow sustainability model, have linked opportunity to income and to the ability of people in the future to consume. But, while we no doubt do have an obligation to avoid impoverishing the future economically, there may also be an obligation not to unduly narrow the range of options and opportunities open to future people. Can we make sense of the notion, then, that one might reduce the options available to another person, and thereby harm that person, even while one has protected that person from economic impoverishment?

Apparently, this complex judgement does make sense, at least in some cases. Consider, for example, a very wealthy widower who, being a well-intentioned despot and also a hopeless chauvinist, refuses to allow his daughters to pursue an education, and instead places their inheritance in a productive and secure trust, ensuring that they will have a more-than-adequate income for life (provided they never go to college under pain of disinheritance). In this case, which of course differs from our sustainability cases in some perhaps important ways, I think it could be said that, if any of the daughters wanted to attend college, they would have been made worse off than they would have been had their father not forbidden them to do so. Further, it rings far truer—given that the daughters are lavishly cared for financially—to explain the harm done the daughters not in terms of economic impoverishment, but in terms of a narrowed range of options and life choices.

If that case makes sense, it is not a much further step to an environmental case: suppose that our generation converts all wilderness areas and natural communities into productive mines, farmland, production forests, or shopping centres, and suppose that we do so efficiently, and that we are careful to save a portion of the profits, and invest them wisely, leaving the future far more wealthy than we are. Does it not make sense to claim that, in doing so, we harmed future people, not economically, but in the sense that we seriously and irreversibly narrowed their range of choices and experiences? A whole range of human experience would have been obliterated; the future will have been—at least given the values of many environmentalists— impoverished.

One confusing aspect of these cases has to do with the nature of judgements about future well-being. To carry on the above case, at least two quite different outcomes might occur. First, suppose it turns out that, once wilderness and natural places are destroyed, people of the future, lacking an opportunity to develop a 'wilderness sensibility', simply do not miss it. In this case, they will not feel their loss of this whole range of experience, or at least they will not regret it, finding adequate fulfilment in human-dominated landscapes. Alternatively, however, suppose wilderness enthusiasts, despite their failure to protect wilderness areas from conversion to intense use, retain their love of wilderness, maintain wilderness clubs, etc., and insist that they have been materially and spiritually impaired by our economic choices. In a diverse society, of course, it may turn out that both of these outcomes will occur, creating a society including some people who feel a great loss at their inability to experience wilderness and some who do not. Having noted these cases, it is still reasonable to say, whether they recognize their loss or not, that future people who are deprived of the opportunity to experience wilderness are simply worse off than they would have been if that option had been held open. When thinking along these lines, it seems reasonable to think of our obligation to the future as including, in addition to maintaining a fair savings rate, an obligation to maintain a non-diminishing range of choices and opportunities to pursue certain valued interests and activities.

To further clarify these concepts, we must first explore the meaning of the terms 'option' and 'opportunity' more carefully and, in the next Part, introduce a conceptual model for thinking about intergenerational fairness in terms of maintaining options. The task—and I cannot deny it is a daunting one—becomes to correlate, in some policy-relevant way, options and opportunities—not with dollars or with present values at all—but rather directly with a physically describable feature of systems. The problem, under this conception, becomes one of specifying those ecological features and processes that support valued future options. On this view, the problem of defining a fair path to the future requires creating a clear articulation of a specific community's long-term values, and of identifying features of the ecosystem and landscape that are essential to maintain these locally important values into the future.

Most authors who discuss our obligations to future generations have used the terms, 'options' and 'opportunities' virtually interchangeably (see note 1, above), although the usual meanings and the Latin roots of these terms are very different. The term 'option' simply means 'the power, right, or liberty of choosing'–quite simply, a choice. Its Latin root is *'optare'*, 'to desire'. In one quite specific meaning–the economic one–it has come to mean an acquired right to buy or sell something at an established price at some time in the future. 'Opportunity', on the other hand, takes its root from 'port'–door–and the prefix, 'ob'–literally 'at the door'–with the clear emphasis on temporal appropriateness, the implication that a propitious time has come to step across a threshold. An opportunity, then, refers to a hospitable time for a particular action or choice.[31]

It is possible to speculate that the tendency to use these rather different terms interchangeably may result from the popularity of the UC model and the economic metric often associated with it. To the extent that 'opportunities' are viewed in the specialist terms of economics, which presuppose fungibility of all forms of capital and wealth, opportunities are reducible to the present value of an option. Because dollars are necessarily present dollars, the temporal contingency so important to the connotation of an opportunity simply disappears—it is 'reduced away' by our decision to count all values as present values. In a timeless system of value such as contemporary welfare economics, to save someone an opportunity at some time in the future can be understood as purchasing for them an option in the present. And if they would like to exercise that option at some time in the future, and that option is not available at the time needed, then no opportunity will be missed, provided the person is properly 'compensated' for the loss of that option. The collapse of opportunities into options, if this linguistic speculation is correct, is therefore a symptom—a conceptual fall-out—of the tendency of UC theorists to treat all future values as exchangeable and fungible—as economic values.[32] As we shift our attention from the possibilities for human production and consumption at different times, toward an ecophysical characterization of systems that maintain a rich range of options, it is possible to think of options as 'standing resources'— available for use at any time—and 'opportunities' as temporally indexed options that exist at choice-points in the future. Once options are linked to ecological systems that are understood as ongoing, dynamic, and physical processes, it may be possible to recover the temporal connotation of opportunities as time-relative, and re-establish a distinction between options and opportunities.

Aside from this temporal aspect, I think there is another problem with the collapse of 'opportunities' into 'options'. An option is a 'right, power, or liberty' to take some action or to enjoy some state. But having the right to some thing is not the same as having the power to act to use or enjoy that thing. To understand this difference, suppose our generation succeeds, against all odds, in instituting strong controls on resource over-exploitation, and furthermore institutes successful restoration of existing damage. We would then have succeeded, in some sense, in having protected an option—understood as a standing resource available for use. But suppose also that, in the meantime, democratic institutions are replaced by a centralized, totalitarian government that doles out existing resources mainly to a power elite, while most people live in abject poverty without access to existing resources. Future people would, we might argue, have a right to those resources, and our generation would in some sense have succeeded in holding open choices to use key standing resources. Under this supposition, we would have protected, physically, the birthright of future generations—we have maintained options insofar as having options depend on ecophysical resources—and yet most people would not have the power to exercise those options. It would be a sad cynicism to claim, in this situation, that the 'opportunities' of these future people have been protected.

Employing these two clues—that 'opportunity' adds to 'options' both a time-sensitivity and a recognition of the importance of the power to actually choose—I propose the following set of definitions. An *option* is a natural resource available for human use. Options are in this sense the 'stock' of usable resources available at a time. I am using the term 'resource' extremely broadly, to include all uses, and enjoyments, and also the 'character' and distinctiveness of the area itself, as will become clear. Options exist for long or short durations—they are, so to speak, 'enjoyments waiting to happen'—they are potential uses and delights. In this sense, the ancient forests have presented many options for human inhabitants for many generations, but new technologies open new options over time, and sometimes close off traditionally existing options. Some of those options for use— sustainable harvest of natural products, for example, would retain the basic ecological character and range of options, while the clear-cutting over large areas cancels virtually all options for a period extending until the resource recovers. Note, then, that options have a duration—they provide the raw material of opportunities for as long as the options are held open. Options can have long or short durations, and the exercise of some options leads to irreplaceable loss of other options, while others leave the range of options intact. An *opportunity*—a more complex concept that includes options as one aspect—is a situation in which all the conditions are right to allow the choice to use the resource at that time. One of these conditions is that the option be available at the time a choice is faced, but an opportunity requires also the power to act to use or enjoy that option at a particular time. For a resource option to truly present an opportunity, the resource must continue to exist in a non-degraded and usable form at the time the person faces the choice, and the person must have the power, both physical and political, to gain access to that option.

Interestingly, it is now possible to incorporate weak sustainability within our model. The weak sustainability requirement represents one important aspect of the accessibility component of sustainability. Being fair to the future requires ensuring, to the extent possible, access of future people to those options that are protected. Access therefore breaks down into *political* access, which requires the development of politically open and responsive institutions to distribute resources, and *economic* access, which involves maintaining adequate wealth/income (represented by Solow's non-declining stock of general capital). The first requirement is institutional in the broad sense—it requires the development of a political culture and a participatory process to ensure equal access to decision making and, in turn, to resources.[33] Speaking generally, this aspect of sustainability has intergenerational fairness—especially fair access and distribution of political powers within generations—as its main purview. This is a much-neglected aspect of the sustainability debate, but it is beyond the scope of this general and conceptual chapter. The second requirement of access—the problem of maintaining income so that future persons can acquire the necessities of a happy life—may well be represented by weak sustainability. If this is the conceptual outcome, then Solow will have been vindicated to the extent that his model, or a successor to his model, will represent one of the necessary (but not sufficient) conditions of sustainable living. In the remainder of this chapter, I will concentrate on the analysis of options, since this is the newest and least understood aspect of the proposed intergenerational model.

Having an option, given the model being developed here, is a necessary but not sufficient condition of having an opportunity. So an opportunity can only be protected if the option is protected. Deciding what the current generation owes to future generations thereby becomes a matter of determining which set of current options our generation can exercise without unfairly blocking options that should be held open to present future opportunities. It seems clear that some of the options we actually choose narrow the range of resource options available, at least on a local basis.

Subsequent to clear-cutting, the option of sustainable cropping of the forest is a foreclosed option for the period required for forest regeneration. If the clear-cut occurs on steep slopes with erodible soils, the period of regeneration may be extended radically. The problem of charting a strongly sustainable path to the future now becomes the problem of determining which of the future resource-use options open to the present are consistent with maintaining the fullest range of options, and what are adequate trade-offs when an option is chosen that will significantly narrow future options, and hence opportunities for many generations.

Using this conceptual model, it is possible, therefore, to introduce some structure into the decision space which we use for evaluating policy options. I have elsewhere represented this structure as a 'Risk Decision Square',[34] which plots irreversibility against physical scale, and treats policies that risk irreversible changes over ecosystem scales as being especially significant risks for calculating our obligations to future generations. In general, the higher the degree of irreversibility and the greater the physical scale of an impact, the larger the likelihood that that impact will significantly narrow future human opportunities. It is therefore possible to, at least roughly, quantify the temporal and the physical aspects of the problem. Temporal scale—or 'horizon'—of a risk to an environmental value will be a function of the time it takes to recover those options lost, once they are lost. Losses that can be restored in one generation or less are practically renewable, in that each generation can choose what to do about those resources, while choices with impacts requiring longer recovery times will involve the pre-emption of significant options that future generations may value highly. Spatial scale is somewhat more complex to define, if I am correct in believing that we must consider environmental values within a socially constructed space.[35]

6. Adaptive Evaluation

The task now faced—that of specifying a concept of *options* that is both operational in physical terms and also useful as an indicator of human well-being—remains a daunting one. The goal is to provide a general theory of resource distribution; this theory must, on the one hand, help us to identify precisely quantifiable and easily measured physical indicators. And on the other hand, it must explain why those indicators are worthy of representing important social values, including obligations to future generations.

Fortunately, C. S. Holling and his colleagues in the tradition of adaptive management[36] have provided much of the basic theory necessary to explore an alternative approach to modelling inter-generational impacts. Holling refers to the multi-levelled system of nature as a 'panarchy', which refers to the Greek god, Pan, god of field, forests, and wild animals, and also evokes, through the prefix 'pan' meaning 'all-embracing', the important idea that dynamism and information flow pervades the entire system.[37] Holling describes a panarchy as a self-organizing system viewed from the inside, and requires a different paradigm than that of Newtonian, objective and detached science. It also requires a departure from mechanistic models in favour of dynamic, non-linear models of reality. Holling's idea of a panarchy incorporates the formal rules of hierarchy to characterize, from the inside, the scaled environment as it is encountered by human perceivers/ actors. Speaking formally, hierarchy theory is characterized by two central assumptions: (1) all system descriptions must be formulated and measured from within a complex, dynamic system; and (2) spatial relationships can be represented as embedded subsystems with larger systems, changing more slowly and providing the environment against which smaller subsystems adapt.[38]

In a panarchy, free choices by level-one individuals respond and adapt to patterns and processes at level two, a larger, slower-scaled dynamic—the environment—that encompasses individuals in a system of nested subsystems. These individuals encounter their environment as a complex presentation of options and constraints. They must make 'choices', gathering what information they can about how to exploit the options and avoid the constraints. These choices and activities are analogous to one sense of individual freedom—the freedom to choose between available options, to adapt in an effort to survive, prosper, and leave successors. While

Holling's adaptive model recognizes pervasive information-flow, time is necessarily asymmetrical in a dynamic, irreversible system, as is expressed in the second axiom of hierarchy theory. Constraints flow down the hierarchy, but information flows upward in the system as well—the aggregated choices of level-one individuals are component processes in the larger, landscape-scale environment. Individual, 'free' choices are made against a stable backdrop, or environment, which appears to individual choosers as a mix of options and constraints. In essence, individuals appear both as individuals on one level and also as parts in a larger dynamic system.

In a longer frame of time, the cumulative impacts of individual choices reverberate as changes in the environment—and alter the ratio of options to constraints faced by future persons. The intergenerational impacts of a culture on the landscape can therefore be understood in terms of cross-generational exchanges in which the operative currency is freedom, options, expressed as a ratio of options to constraints. These options are stored in the structure of an ecological system. If growth in human impacts erode these essential processes embodied in ecological systems on larger and slower time scales, future generations will face more constraints and fewer options as cumulative impacts of many human individual actions skim off options (such as capital stored in ancient forests) and leave constraints (poor and eroding soils exposed by clear-cuts). Alternatively, if resources are protected and if important and productive ecosystem processes are maintained, the people of the future will, as we have, face an abundance of options.

Ecological systems are thus modelled as dynamic, open systems that are organized asymmetrically in space and time. Economic systems are understood as dynamics driven by choices of individuals who live, choose, and die on relatively rapid cycles by comparison to the rate of change in the surrounding environment. The economic system, then, is represented as a dominant subsystem within a natural environment. Regularities and predictable patterns on these larger levels provide the opportunity for biological and cultural evolution. Human individuals interact with their environment, usually through the mediation of an economic system. Individual perception, accordingly, is geared to short-term changes that occur in economic time. Large-scale ecological impacts of human activities must be understood both as results of cumulative individual actions on level one, and also as having spill-over impacts on the larger scale of environmental systems, systems that would normally change so slowly that their dynamic is unnoticed by short-sighted humans. One requirement of acting sustainably is to analyse our impacts on these normally slower scales, because accelerated change at these scales may affect the context in which future members of our society will face choices and adapt.

Holling[39] argues that human activities, when they simplify processes by concentrating productivity into a few crops or species, can make large-scale systems more 'brittle', ecologically. Because this style of management reduces the redundancy of pathways fulfilling such essential functions as energy transfer, the system becomes more prone to shift into a new steady, functional state, one that is less likely to be supportive of the cultural and economic behaviours/adaptations that have emerged in response to the opportunities available in local environments. Accordingly, Holling[40] has proposed that we must recognize two concepts of 'resilience'.[41] One concept, which operates at the economic/engineering level of the system, assumes a single stable point to which the system, once disturbed, will return. This concept is appropriate for individuals to apply in making day-to-day economic decisions—it assumes system organization and behaviour will be unaffected by an individual decision, and develops equilibrium models to understand human behaviour on the individual level. On this level, we expect economic, partial equilibrium models to function reasonably well, and, as noted above, it is possible to incorporate weak sustainability as a necessary condition of sustainability in the short run. The other concept of resilience—ecological resilience—becomes relevant when the concern is to understand cumulative impacts of individual decisions on the larger, ecosystem scale, where the concern is that the larger system will shift into a new stable state of functioning. Since such new stable states are almost always less desirable for humans, it is important that environmental management be for-

mulated and evaluated on both the short-term, single-state model
and on the longer-term model that monitors whether cumulative
impacts are threatening to exceed a threshold and cause a flip into a
new system state. The concept of resilience may turn out, if it can
be made precisely measurable, to be applicable to many local
systems, and hence to be a general characterization of one indicator of the maintenance of ecologically based options.[42] If
resilience can be characterized so that it is clearly associated
with important, socially valued ecological processes and services
based on them, then it might be an important element in a
measurable indicator of whether an ecosystem is maintaining
options, and to the extent that options support them, opportunities. Again, this would be an area for further exploration and
discussion.

7. Evaluating Development Paths

The Panarchical Model focuses attention clearly on the problem of
defining a sustainable development path—any community that
intends to act sustainably must find a path toward development
that, over time, protects and expands, rather than contracts,
options of intertemporal social importance. What is needed is
an index of options and constraints (OCI), which can be observed
and measured from many particular perspectives. Such an index
would track the balance of constraints to options that are presented to individuals, firms, and governments across time, and in
places, as a means to evaluate current and proposed policies that
affect the future of their communities. More conceptual and
empirical advances will be required here, because it is almost
certainly not possible to understand the OCI as a simple count
and comparison of the whole range of options and constraints
available at a time. This stipulation follows from the fact that all
possibilities provided by nature ('options') cannot be treated as
equal in the face of prevailing human values. For example, it is
reasonable to assume that people of the future will not blame us
for 'destroying their option' to die of the smallpox virus, if we

extinguish it. The valuation of options must, therefore, be under-taken in conjunction with an articulation of both the fears and the aspirations of the relevant community. To operationalize the notion of an OCI, it is necessary to identify key community values and associated options as ones that should be sustained. It could be argued that sustainable paths are ones in which, at each point in the future, the range of choices for investment and development include those options that express the character—the sense of place—of a locally based community. Thinking in terms of adapt-ability, a high OCI implies that the range of possibilities for paths that allow persistence of individuals and of local cultures/communities, is constant or broadening. Since, on the approach sketched here, the OCI is to be linked to physical indicators, it is an LS approach. The contrast between this LS approach and UC approaches, and the challenges they face, now becomes clearer. Because the UC approach apparently requires a comprehensive accounting of human welfare in order to compare well-being across generations, it is saddled with the need for adjustments, many of them *ad hoc,* to maintain commensurability in inter-generational accounts. The LS approach, while faced with difficult hurdles, need not count units of welfare but can simply evaluate trends and changes as likely to protect certain options or not. Deciding which options are most important, and most worthy of protection, becomes (in a democratic society) an exercise (hope-fully participatory) in community self-definition.

My method in this section will be to explore several 'develop-ment pathways', which are actual or hypothetical ways that a culture can develop or grow through time. If these explorations succeed in communicating the difference between paths of development that protect, and those that fail to protect, options for the future, this success gives me hope that we might be able to choose some observable characteristic(s) that mark developmental and landscape trends that preserve rather than eliminate valued options. My idea is that, provided a community can articulate a core sense of values that unite them as a culture with their physical environment, then it may be possible to identify some 'indicator' characteristic, or characteristics, that can be expected to correlate with the protection of these especially valued options within that environment.

The method envisaged can be understood more clearly by applying it to choices faced in the development of the US Pacific Northwest since about 1800. This is a useful example, historically, because the economy of that region has been highly dependent on natural resources, and the case is reasonably well known. It is also a place where development has proceeded far enough to realize where successes have occurred, and where mistakes were made. Consider three possible development paths, one of them actual and two of them hypothetical.

Path 1: The Actual Development Path

One describable development path is the one that was actually followed. I will characterize the present outcome in the most sketchy terms, because it is my intention to avoid controversies about specific factual statements regarding the actual situation; but it helps to be as concrete as possible. The development of the Pacific Northwest since 1800 has been characterized by (1) rapid development of resources such as old-growth forests, fisheries, and of water-power resources; (2) relative independence of planning and development across sectors (for example, the power resource was developed without much thought regarding impact on the salmon fishery); (3) rapidly escalating exhaustion of resources, and conflicts among resource users across sectors and within sectors in the late twentieth century, resulting in serious political conflict; (4) overall acceptable rates of regional economic growth, as the economy makes up for losses in timber and fishery jobs with high-tech development in the larger cities, but localized pockets of extreme hardship emerge as resource-dependent industries shut down in areas where resources are exhausted or no longer economically exploitable.

There is no question that there are job losses and a general decline in the importance of the resource-exploitation sector in the Pacific Northwest, but there are several important differences in the analyses offered to characterize these changes. For example, one analysis says that there is a real shortage of timber, and that the timber industry is entering an inevitable decline, becoming a less productive sector in the economy. Many economists, however, deny that there is a real shortage of timber. There is plenty of harvestable new growth, they argue, but it is not in the right place to provide jobs for existing timber-based communities, and because it is much smaller in stem size, it does not provide appropriate inputs for the technologies developed to exploit old growth. Because my goal is not to become embroiled in empirical and analytic controversies, but rather to contrast alternative development paths, I here offer two idealized alternative paths, leaving open the question of whether, and to what degree, these idealized paths coincide with what actually happened over the last two centuries.

Path 2: The Maximal Economic Growth Path

Another possible path toward development would be one in which early profits are generated from the most rapid possible development and use of natural resources, with optimal levels of saving and investment generated by the profits of this exploitation. On this path, the economy would go through a maturation process in which natural resources are depleted to generate profits that will be invested in industries that are less dependent on regional natural resources.[43] According to this growth model, it is appropriate for early development to be wasteful of resources, provided resource development on the whole maximizes profit for reinvestment.[44]

Note that the Economic Development Path is designed to correspond to the ideal that would emerge from an economy that is functioning according to growth models in mainstream welfare economics. One feature of this model is that it treats resources and other forms of capital as essentially interchange-able—'fungible'. Clark[45] has shown that, as long as the opportunity cost of money is high—if there are adequate alternative investment opportunities available—it may be economically efficient to exploit renewable resources to extinction.

Further, economic performance is measured in monetary terms; success—profits—are place-independent and there is no guarantee that locally derived profits will be reinvested in the region. One consequence of these by-now familiar assumptions, is that the investment side of the model has no place orientation; there is no built-in preference for local investment.[46] Consequently the region must compete on the international market for investments that will actually cause growth and development in the post-exploitational phase of regional growth. On this model, the only criterion for resource use is the profit motive. If one can generate higher profits by specializing in extraction and sale of whole logs, this will be the best development policy, even if this leads to rapid reduction in the available resource base, and even if the profits so gained are invested in another part of the world. The theory behind this path is that maximizing profits also maximizes savings and investment in other sectors, and hastens the transformation of the economy to a mature, natural-resource-independent state.

Path 3: The Integrated Regional Development Path

Consider another possible path toward growth in the Pacific Northwest. Suppose (contrary to historical fact) that, 50 to 100 years ago a political movement and political leadership emerged that was willing to invest public resources in shaping the path of growth in the region and that public funds were devoted to shaping investment patterns to favour economic diversification based on existing resources. For example, a state or regional authority might have instituted a tax on the extraction of resources and used the funds generated by this tax to subsidize start-up loans for co-operatives and other locally based businesses that form to mill timber, or industries that use locally grown and milled lumber to make furniture or components of houses for construction. The development ideal that is sought, here, is to maximize the amount of locally recoverable value added per unit of resources extracted.

On this idealized model, one would expect the development of a more diversified economy in which many local communities will have, in addition to extractive industries, other local industries that depend upon natural resources less directly, such as timber milling and furniture making. Unlike the idealized growth model of the Economic Growth Path, a special value is placed on development that leads to this kind of vertical integration of the economy, as development that is built upon responsible management of the local, natural resource base. Vertical integration, in turn, maximizes jobs supported in the geographic location of resource extraction over longer periods of time. These intertemporal values would be manifest in a place-based economy and in decisions that are place-conscious and organized around key resources of the region. Resources and capital are on this path not fully fungible. Some resources, such as timber or salmon runs, are seen as 'keystone resources' in economic and community development. These resources become keystones in the local economy in that maintenance of jobs in the region, in extraction, in transportation, in tourism, and in manufacturing, all depend upon protecting those resources. If families hope, for example, to remain in the region for generations, they will value these keystone resources as essential to maintain the same range of opportunities for the next generation. When they think about their community in the long run—as a multi-generational, ongoing project, they will therefore see careful use of these primary, keystone resources as an investment that protects the core values of the community. And, if more economic development is generated per log cut or per fish caught, presumably it is possible to have development that does not use up these keystone resources as quickly as does the exhaust-and-invest strategy of Path 2. If these keystone resources are over-exploited and exhausted, however, their loss will have many times the effect on the economy of a simple loss of income (as, for example, when an employer closes a local factory or moves it out of the region). Keystone natural resources, on this model, are not interchangeable with other forms of capital. These are the resources that form the foundation of place-based regional development. Their loss erodes the distinctiveness of the landscape and the diversity of available habitats in the region.

Just as importantly, these keystone natural resources form the basis for an enduring and place-based cultural identity, based both on the distinctive resource mix that greeted early settlers and on the distinctive cultural practices and institutions that have been built to use those resources. They are basic to any strategy of regional development that recognizes the importance of natural resources to the comparative advantage of the region. The Integrated Regional Development Path, therefore, emphasizes place-relative development, which in turn links the economy and local residents in a more and more integrated system of economic and cultural links and institutions. These links are place-based and intergenerational in nature.

Of these three 'models', one is actual and therefore subject to many controversial judgements regarding the empirical situation, while the other two, defined as idealizations, can be understood as theory-driven. The idealized, theory-driven models can be used as sorts of hypothetical laboratories to illustrate and address the central problem of identifying socially valued options. For example, we would expect that, following decades of development that is based on the ideal expressed in Path 2, individuals will face a variety of opportunities that have been generated by investment in industries, but there will be no reason to believe these industries will be integrally related to the original resource base. As local natural resources become less important to the economy of the region, new growth will increasingly be based on fungible assets such as infrastructure, the wage rate in local areas, etc. Simultaneously, the competition for investment will become more and more place-independent over time, as standing natural resources are transformed into investments in infrastructure and education. To compete for investors, the region must out-compete other regions for 'place-independent' industries, which will locate where costs of labour or taxes are lowest. Communities compete, that is, by impoverishing themselves, and often by sacrificing the distinctive features of the life-style their ancestors have developed in their local place in order to attract this place-independent development.[47] Investment and other economic choices are more and more driven by interregional competition and less and less by the natural resource foundation in keystone resources. The region therefore has less and less reason to protect its distinct natural resources, as these are viewed as expendable.

We would expect this model to lock into a self-replicating, spiralling effect of less and less motivation to protect local resources, and a corresponding kickback that further fuels its underlying cause: the tendency to transfer assets from the natural resource sector into human capital. This spiralling effect creates a positive feedback loop and a classical lock-in situation. By treating investments in extraction and investments in protection of capital as interchangeable goods, a society locked into this feedback loop must compete for 'investments' by reducing the value of its residents' labour and by reducing tax revenues for schools and infrastructure. This exhaust-and-invest, growth model might be expected to lead to a general deterioration of ecological conditions as options for amenities and enjoyment of collateral values are lost, as local natural resources approach exhaustion. Cities devoted to a local resource, treated as exhaustible, become ephemeral. More mobility creates more reasons to be mobile, as individuals and communities compete for jobs and investors, and the competition drifts further and further from any anchoring identity based on the natural history of the region.[48] This model therefore suggests a pessimistic outcome with respect to protecting regional diversity and characteristic ecological processes; the policy responses it embodies are predictably too little and too late, as investors and firms—free to go wherever they can get the highest return—call the shots in a progressive impoverishment of natural resources through a competition for investment in place-independent industry accelerates.

In contrast to this exhaust-and-invest path toward development, Path 3—the Integrated Regional Development Path—attempts to build upon, and at the same time protect, central defining features and sources of value in each particular place. Policies that encourage vertically oriented economies (with competition on each level) should result in investments that strengthen and integrate levels of the economy. These same policies should result in the protection of the distinctiveness and local identity of communities, perhaps helping to build a sense of place and a better understanding of the role of the natural history of the place in generating this distinctive economy and culture.[49] A regional culture will be distinctive to the extent that it is organized around the distinctive, keystone resources of an area. Developed along this path, the region will change, but it will grow upon a more constant foundation; the economy and the ecology of the region will co-evolve, but there will be a cross-generational link, a character that reflects the original opportunities that the region offered its pioneers. Current action grows out of natural history and cultural history. Human communities, on this path, are more connected to their place and more continuous in values, aspirations, and character across time.

But perhaps this is about as far as we can go, given the abstract and general nature of this paper. One consequence of the theory developed here is that sustainable opportunities—which are in turn defined in terms of socially valued options—can only be specified more precisely on a local and regional basis.

8. Conclusion

The obligation to live sustainably can be stated generically as an obligation not to diminish the opportunities of future generations to achieve well-being at least equal to their predecessors. There is, however, no shared understanding of how to compare opportunities for well-being across time and across generations. It has been shown that both weak sustainability—the idea that prior generations have fulfilled their obligation to the future as long as they maintain a non-declining stock of general capital—and strong sustainability—which requires also that natural capital be protected for future generations—ultimately allow the future to be *compensated* for any and all irreversible alterations of the resource base. This paper suggests an alternative to these approaches, which share a commitment to the moral completeness of the economic methodology and to the underlying idea that measuring fairness across generations is ultimately a matter of comparing opportunities to consume (comparing capital accumulated or income). I have argued that the best way to achieve a stronger form of sustainability is to specify certain aspects or features of the world, to associate these with physically measurable 'indicators', and to insist that these features be protected. Loss of these features would then be considered noncompensable harms to the future: people of future generations will be worse off, if these features are lost, than they would have been had the features been protected, *regardless of the economic wealth of future people*.

This alternative approach to comparing well-being across time was then explored by requiring that certain options (which are prerequisites for true opportunities) be held open for future generations. An abstract model, based on the idea of adaptive management, was introduced for comparing the range of opportunities—opportunities based in the availability of crucial resources and options they present—available to people in communities at different times. Pursuit of this approach to a sustainability metric, then, suggests that environmental values and valuation processes (in addition to maintaining weak sustainability) should also evaluate possible 'development paths' with respect to the impact of those paths on the range of choices, options, and opportunities available to people at different times. According to this approach, a truly strong version of sustainability will require both that earlier generations protect the accumulated capital and the income possibilities of future generations (weak sustainability), and also that the earlier generations choose a development path that holds open options and opportunities for the future.

6

Social Justice and
Environmental Goods[1]

DAVID MILLER

The question I address in this chapter is how (if at all) environmental goods can be integrated into the theory of social justice.
This is not a question that is frequently asked, at least not in the
form in which I have put it. Those who have thought most deeply
about social justice, as I shall illustrate shortly, have usually taken
its domain to be the distribution of rights, opportunities, and
resources among human beings, with environmental issues being
placed in a separate region 'beyond justice'. Environmental philosophers, on the other hand, while often expressing themselves in
favour of policies of social justice, fail to ask precisely how
environmental concerns and social justice are supposed to mesh
together. Either they focus on potentially cataclysmic environmental disasters, concluding that unless we adopt the right environmental policy there will be no human beings left among whom
to practise justice. Or they point out, quite relevantly, that it is
very often the poorest members of society who bear the brunt of
pollution and other forms of environmental degradation, and pass
easily to the conclusion that good environmental policies must
also serve the cause of social justice.

As I shall try to show in this chapter, matters are far more
complex than this. If we want to pursue social justice and safeguard

I should like to thank the participants in the ESRC seminar on Social Justice and
Environmental Sustainability at the University of Keele for their comments on an
earlier version of this chapter, and especially Avner de-Shalit, Michael Jacobs, and
Albert Weale for writing to me with helpful criticisms and suggestions.

and enrich our environment at one and the same time, we have some hard thinking to do about both the principles that should guide us and the institutions we should utilize for this purpose. I come at the question from the social justice side, and I suspect with different assumptions about how practically speaking we should value the environment from many of those working in the fields of environmental ethics or green political theory. But I hope that even green aficionados will find some merit in the investigation that follows.

Let me begin by explaining briefly how I understand the two ideas contained in my title. The problem of social justice I understand as one of finding principles to govern the basic structure of a society, meaning the set of institutions that directly or indirectly allocate liberties, rights, resources and other advantages to its members.[1] More concretely, social justice comprises principles to regulate the legal system, the structure of the economy, welfare policy, and so on and so forth, looking at these in terms of the distribution of benefits and burdens to individual people that finally results. (This characterization implies that social justice must be understood in the first place as applying within a self-determining political community, though there may be extensions to international and intergenerational justice; in what follows I shall make a parallel assumption about environmental policies, leaving aside at this point the complex issues that arise when cross-national collaboration is needed in order to resolve environmental problems, as of course is frequently the case.) 'Environmental goods' is to be understood in as wide and loose a sense as possible, to include any aspect of the environment to which a positive value may be attached, whether a natural feature, a species of animal, a habitat, an ecosystem, or whatever (it will turn out later to be important to my argument that the set of environmental goods is radically heterogeneous). Thus the maintenance of the ozone layer, having rivers free of pollution, the continued existence of the Siberian tiger, the availability of open uplands for hikers, and the preservation of ancient monuments would all count potentially as environmental goods in my sense. As the list is meant to suggest, environmental goods may be valued in different ways—as having value in their own right, for example, the Siberian tiger, as instrumental to human welfare (the ozone layer), and so forth. Although for some purposes the question of how we are to understand the value of different aspects of our environment is a central one, I shall try as far as possible to bracket it off in the discussion that follows.

Against my claim that theories of justice have largely ignored environmental issues it might be said that the environment has featured largely in discussions of intergenerational justice, where it has frequently been argued that policies of resource depletion and environmental degradation destroy the fair balance of benefits and burdens between the present generation and its successors. There is something curious about this argument, however. We attempt to show that policies to protect the environment are just by appealing to the claims of members of future generations. But how can these future persons have claims of justice to environmental goods unless some at least of our contemporaries have such claims too?[2] For I take it that the argument is not simply that by pursuing resource-depleting and polluting policies we are creating an unjust inequality between this generation in the aggregate and its successors in the aggregate, the argument must be that individual members of future generations have claims of justice to resources and environmental features that will be denied if existing policies are allowed to continue. But it seems that whatever gives members of future generations claims to environmental goods must also endow members of the present generation with such claims. So the argument from intergenerational justice to environmental justice seems to be back to front. We ought first to show that people in general (whichever generation they belong to) have claims of justice to environmental goods, and then having established the general principle we would move on to consider justice between generations in respect of such goods. But to do this we would need to integrate environmental values into the theory of social justice as it applies to contemporaries.

At first glance it may seem obvious why theories of justice have tended to ignore the environment. These theories are theories about the proper distribution of advantages to individuals: they are about A's share of liberty, or opportunity, or material resources, or welfare compared to B's, C's, and D's. They ask, for instance, whether economic institutions should be arranged so that each person gets an equal share of resources, or so that the share going to the worst-off group is maximized. Environmental goods, in contrast, are not distributed to individuals. Nobody gets a particular share of the ozone layer or the Siberian tiger. If the ozone layer is preserved and the tiger saved from extinction, these goods are made available to everyone. So whatever questions we may want to ask about the promotion of environmental goods are not properly speaking questions of justice. To say this is not necessarily to say anything about priorities. You may believe that environmental concerns have nothing to do with justice and yet think that some of these concerns should take precedence: it's more important to protect the ozone layer than to rectify the income distribution in a country like the UK. So to say that environmental goods shouldn't feature in our understanding of social justice is not to downgrade the importance of these goods.

But on closer inspection the issue is far less straightforward. Consider what happens when a government enacts some policy on environmental grounds. Very often it will reduce people's liberty in some respects, or transfer resources from private to public use. A policy to control the pollution caused by cars may involve requiring people to use cleaner fuels, to fit catalytic convertors, or more radically to reduce their use of cars in one way or another. Protecting an endangered species or an ecological system will in nearly every case require public expenditure, and this must either increase the tax burden on individuals or be financed by cuts in other expenditure programmes, for instance education or social security. We should not expect the impact of these measures to be neutral across persons, for two reasons: the cost will fall more heavily on some people than on others, and the environmental good will benefit some more than others. If my job requires me to make frequent use of a car, then restrictions on car use will be correspondingly more burdensome than on someone who rarely drives or has no car at all. If tax revenues are used to buy areas of heathland which contain the last remaining breeding sites of the Dartford Warbler, this may benefit on balance those who like bird-watching or simply like to know that the

Warblers will carry on breeding, but it may harm those who are indifferent or those who would like to use the heath for bike scrambling.

Almost every environmental measure will have distributive implications of this kind. Moreover it would be rash to assume that the impact will be random, in the sense that people will gain from one measure but lose from the next, so that overall the distribution of benefits and burdens will be unaffected. We cannot say *a priori* whether the redistributive impact will favour the better-off or the worse-off. I noted earlier that it is sometimes taken for granted that the costs of environmental degradation are borne mainly by the poor, because inequalities in political power mean, for example, that polluting factories and other such hazards get sited close to lower-class residential areas. On the other hand in the case of environmental goods that are provided equally to everyone (such as the preservation of animal species or eco-systems), standard economic analysis leads us to expect that the rich will gain more from their provision than the poor, so that unless the tax regime that funds these policies is strongly progressive, their net impact is likely to be regressive.[3] So it seems that we cannot after all place environmental goods outside the scope of our theories of justice. We should regard them as potential benefits, often accompanied by restrictions, that need to go into the distributive calculus alongside goods like opportunity, income, and wealth.

Eagle-eyed readers may think that the argument of the last two paragraphs goes through only if we make certain assumptions about how environmental goods are to be valued: by treating such goods as benefits going to individuals or classes of individuals, I am presupposing an anthropocentric, or even more narrowly an instrumental, understanding of environmental value. This is an issue that will turn out to be important later in the paper. But before getting to it, I want to look more closely at how, if at all, contemporary theories of justice deal with environmental questions, to see whether it might be possible to build out from these theories to construct a more systematic treatment. I focus on the theories of John Rawls and Ronald Dworkin as arguably the most influential accounts of social justice in the mainstream liberal tradition.

In his two books, *A Theory of Justice* and *Political Liberalism,* Rawls devotes only a few paragraphs to the natural environment. To take them in reverse order, in *Political Liberalism* he presents 'our relations to animals and the order of nature' together with the problems of duties to future generations, international relations, and the principles of health care, as 'problems of extension'.[4] The question is whether the principles of justice he has worked out for the case of co-operating adult citizens can be extended to deal with these other issues. In the case of animals and the natural world he seems to imply that no simple extension is possible,[5] but that we can none the less find common political grounds for adopting environmentally friendly policies by appealing to the welfare of present and future human beings. He then considers the view that such an anthropocentric approach fails to assign the proper kind of value to nature, but his response is to conclude that 'the status of the natural world and our proper relation to it is not a constitutional essential or a basic question of justice as these questions have been specified. It is a matter in regard to which citizens can vote their nonpolitical values and try to convince other citizens accordingly.'[6] As I understand it, this implies that more far-reaching environmental policies than an anthropocentric approach would justify might be adopted by a majority vote of citizens, but justice would not rule one way or the other on the question. Rawls here completely fails to address the issue of the effect of environmental policy on the distribution of primary goods, which for him of course *is* centrally the subject-matter of justice. What if a majority vote to preserve an endangered species meant that fewer material resources were provided for the worst-off group in society?

If we turn back to *A Theory of Justice* we find only the briefest mention of the environment in the course of a general discussion of the issue of public goods, treated standardly by Rawls as goods which are indivisible and which can therefore only be provided for everyone or no one.[7] Rawls makes the familiar point that because of free-rider problems such goods cannot be supplied through economic markets, and must therefore be provided directly by the state. In his discussion of the branches of government he charges the 'allocation branch' with correcting for externalities by the use of suitable taxes and subsidies, and among the cases he has in mind here is that of an industry which imposes costs on others by polluting emissions. So we can say that in certain well-defined cases Rawlsian justice would include environmental measures to ensure that individuals did not disturb the fair balance of benefits and burdens by imposing costs like pollution on others or by free-riding on public goods. But Rawls asks finally whether it might not be legitimate for citizens to make further public expenditures beyond those required by justice as so far defined, which would presumably embrace such things as preserving and/or increasing access to areas of natural beauty, safeguarding endangered species, and so forth.[8] His answer is that such expenditures must be unanimously agreed upon by the citizens, which means that the costs must be so distributed that everyone gains on balance from the expenditure.[9] It follows that if I care nothing about the erosion of the Lake District or the fate of the Large Blue, I cannot be made to contribute to the costs of salvaging them. Rawls makes this quite explicit: 'There is no more justification for using the state apparatus to compel some citizens to pay for unwanted benefits that others desire than there is to force them to reimburse others for their private expenses.'[10] The picture presented here, then, is that distributive justice comes first, but if people are willing to contribute some part of their rightfully held resources for environmental or other such public goods, this is a permissible, but not mandatory, development. Environmental values are treated as preferences which may be pursued only within the limits set by the primary scheme of distribution that justice requires.

If we turn now to Ronald Dworkin, we again find that a theory of justice whose subject matter is conceived as being the proper assignment of resources to individuals—in Dworkin's case, equality of resources—has difficulty in finding any place for environmental goods. I know of only three places in his many essays where Dworkin approaches this issue. One occurs in the course of a complex discussion of the 'baseline' from which the resource auction that defines equality is to take place.[11] The problem is roughly this: if we say that people have equal resources when no one envies the bundle of resources that another has obtained through competitive bidding at an auction in which each has equal purchasing power, we must also consider both how the lots at the auction are constituted, and what rights and restrictions are attached to the ownership of any particular lot. Generally Dworkin favours liberty-maximizing solutions that disaggregate lots into their component parts and that give people maximum freedom to do what they wish with the items they bid for success-fully. But then he contemplates the possibility that some people will use their resources in a way that other people value negat-ively, such that, if these others had known in advance what the use would be, they would have altered their pattern of bids. The example Dworkin gives is of someone who decides to erect a glass box on a plot of land that forms part of what would otherwise become a harmonious Georgian square: had the other owners known of this possibility, they might have combined to outbid the audacious modernist. Such informational failures may, Dworkin thinks, justify measures such as zoning regulations and pollution controls as part of the baseline.

So we find Dworkin making room in his theory of justice for environmental measures that serve to control the negative extern-alities that one individual may impose on others, much as did Rawls. In his essay 'Liberalism', however, we find a rather differ-ent argument which, if successful, would justify a general policy of conservation of natural resources.[12] Here Dworkin points out that without such conservation 'a way of life that has been desired and found satisfying in the past' will become unavailable to future generations, so that on grounds of neutrality there is a case for conservation. He does not say explicitly what that endangered way of life consists in, but we may suppose that he has in mind something like Thoreau sitting down by Walden Pond, which would no longer be a live possibility if commercial development engulfed all of the inhabitable terrain.

It is difficult to see this briefly stated argument as having much force, when one reflects that there are countless ways of life that meet the condition laid down in the last paragraph, and which would therefore qualify for special protection under Dworkin's expanded version of liberalism. Dworkin's avowed neutralism about the value of different ways of life prohibits him from saying that there is anything of special value about a life lived in harmony with nature that sets it apart from the life of the idle fop or the religious recluse, either of which may become difficult to sustain in an egalitarian and commercial society.[13] In each case there has presumably to be some judgement made about how many additional resources it is reasonable to expend in order to keep open the possibility of a particular way of life, and no strong argument for environmental conservation could possibly be built on such a flimsy footing.

Finally Dworkin comes down rather firmly on the other side of the fence when he discusses the case of an individual with environmental commitments. This is the case of Charles, who 'hopes that no distinctive species will ever become extinct, not because he enjoys looking at a variety of plants and animals, or even because he thinks others do, but just because he believes that the world goes worse when any such species is lost. He would overwhelmingly prefer that a very useful dam not be built at the cost of losing the snail darter.'[14] Dworkin makes it clear that Charles's ambitions must be treated simply as preferences which give rise to no particular claims of justice. His voice should be counted equally with those of others when the decision about the dam is made, but no special weight should be given to his beliefs.

Taking Rawls and Dworkin together as representatives of the liberal theory of justice, we can sum up by saying that environmental goods may enter the theory at three points. First, those features of the environment that are really essential to a sustainable human existence—like breathable air—have first claim on resources in the same way as, say, national defence. If principles of justice are there to guide us in distributing the fruits of social co-operation, then anything that counts as a necessary precondition of any co-operation at all should be seen as lexically prior to more specific distributive principles.[15] But this only applies to a few very basic environmental goods. Second, the creation of environmental goods and bads may disturb the fair assignment of resources or other primary goods, as when the pollution you generate lowers the value of my land, and here justice supports environmental policies as the most effective way of controlling such external effects. Again this is limited to those features of the environment that have a tangible impact on the distribution of primary goods to individuals. Finally people may simply value environmental goods even though these neither count as essentials of human existence nor affect their share of primary goods—for instance, they may value the continued existence of the snail darter. Such valuations are regarded by the liberal theory as preferences which should count equally (but no more than equally) when political decisions are taken. But within what limits may such decisions be made? At this point the liberal theory becomes ambiguous. In some places both Rawls and Dworkin appear to envisage majorities voting to devote resources to environmental, along with other aims, (or in a variant of this Dworkin envisages public officials conducting a cost-benefit analysis which weighs Charles' devotion to the snail-darter against others' preferences for the dam being built in a 'Benthamite calculation'[16]). But this collides with the claim that 'justice is the first virtue of social institutions' or 'the right is prior to the good', which entails that individuals cannot have their just shares of resources reduced by a majority vote or a utilitarian calculation, and leads to Rawls's much more restrictive view that environmental goods in this third category may only be provided with the unanimous agreement of citizens. Only if a particular good can be created or protected using resources which each of their previous holders is willing to give up for this purpose is it legitimate for the state to act.

It seems, therefore, that much that is of concern to environmentalists—preserving landscapes and ecosystems, safeguarding endangered species of animals and so forth—gets fairly short shrift in the liberal theory of justice. But, without begging the question, why should this be seen as a shortcoming of the theory? Its defect is that it trades in the currency of a restricted list of primary goods without showing convincingly that these should indeed take priority over other sources of value. Primary goods are supposed to be goods that everyone wants as much of as possible whatever his or her specific plan of life. But what if many people would be prepared to give up income and other benefits in order to enjoy a richer environment, at least once they have secured a minimum bundle of Dworkinian resources or Rawlsian primary goods? May people not have plans of life which are better advanced through environmental provision than through further dollops of commodities or income?

This suggests amending the theory of justice so that environmental goods can be counted as primary goods alongside the remainder of the list. The basic structure should be seen as providing people not only with liberties, opportunities, and wealth, but with an environment whose features they value positively. Although the environmental goods are not (normally) assigned to particular individuals, nevertheless in reckoning each individual's share of social resources we should include the environmental goods to which he or she attaches value.

But this immediately raises the question of how the value of environmental goods is to be computed. How should we decide what sacrifices (either of disposable income or of public goods of other kinds) it is fair to require people to make in order to preserve the habitat of the Dartford Warbler or the Large Blue? The most obvious answer is to attempt a cost-benefit analysis of the environmental goods in question for each person. That is to say, we should use a technique such as contingent valuation (where people are asked how much they would be prepared to pay to safeguard or restore some environmental feature) to establish a monetary equivalent for each environmental good. The use of such techniques has been widely and critically discussed in the environmental literature—much of the criticism focusing on the wide variation in the answers received to 'willingness-to-pay' questions, depending on the form of the question and the context in which it is asked—but I do not want to enter the debate at this level.[17] Instead I shall address the wider issue of whether this is the right way to introduce environmental goods into the theory of justice.

From my reading of the literature, most environmentalists are very sniffy about cost-benefit analysis, even in cases where they think that it is likely to yield the 'right' answer, as they see it, to some environmental issue. Why might one reject cost-benefit analysis as a way of establishing the value of environmental goods? One reason would be that if we try to discover how much income people are prepared to give up to have an environmental good— either by asking them or observing their behaviour when they have to make a choice—we will end up valuing the environmental good on too narrow a basis, that is in terms of the use value people derive from its existence. This charge is quite convincingly rebutted by writers like David Pearce, who point out that environmental value ought to be seen as a composite of actual use value; option value (the value people attach to the possibility of using or enjoying some environmental resource like unspoiled countryside even though they are not now doing so); and existence value (the value people attach to the continued existence of a species or a habitat, for example, even though they have no intention of observing or visiting it).[18] Whatever method is used to measure costs and benefits ought to be designed to capture all three sources of value.

A second claim is that environmental goods are incommensurable with goods like money—it is simply impossible to say how much money would compensate you for the loss of an environmental feature. This claim is sometimes backed up by the observation that many people refuse to respond to questions about their willingness to pay for environmental preservation.[19] However I am not convinced that such refusals necessarily demonstrate incommensurability. People are notoriously unwilling to make hard choices: if asked whether they would be prepared to give up A in order to have B, both highly valued, there is a very understandable tendency to try to find a way of having your cake and eating it, and therefore to avoid answering the question directly. Furthermore, refusing to say how much you would be willing to pay to have a lake kept free from chemical pollution may be a way of indicating that you don't think that the cost of keeping the lake clean should fall on you. In other words you regard this as an externality for which someone else—a factory owner, for instance—should be held responsible).[20] In general, the incommensurability argument is hard to sustain. Presumably people are prepared to set priorities *between* environmental goods: they are prepared to say that preserving an area of virgin forest is more valuable than rebuilding so many miles of dry stone walling. The next question is whether similar judgements can be made when prices are attached—if it costs £1m to preserve the wood, and £250,000 to rebuild ten miles of wall, which would you rather have done? To resist this question is to leave yourself open to the charge that you have no consistent way of choosing between different packages of goods. Would you rather preserve the wood or restore *fifty* miles of wall? A hundred miles of wall? Unless someone thinks that there is never any need to make choices between environmental goods, or just refuses to say which good she prefers when presented with such a choice—neither of which strike me as intellectually defensible attitudes—money equivalents are going to be inferable from the choices that are made.[21]

A further, and more powerful, argument against cost-benefit analysis is that people's valuations of environmental goods are better regarded as judgements than as preferences, in particular because they are likely to depend on a good deal of information about the exact nature of the good they are being asked to value. John O'Neill gives the example of a drab-looking area of marsh whose ecological value cannot be properly grasped without absorbing a good deal of information about what makes that particular habitat special.[22] A trained observer looking at the marsh sees something different from the ordinary person. So to value the marsh properly we would need to consult people's informed preferences rather than the ones they happen to have now.

This certainly constitutes a strong practical challenge to the use of cost-benefit analysis for many environmental goods. However, I want to insist that even when all the evidence is made available, the question still remains how much value people attach to a particular environmental good—a question that we should normally expect different people to answer differently. So even if we want to say that questions about the value of the environment are questions of judgement, the judgement involved is going to be one that combines matters of fact with an irreducible element of valuation. Even when we know everything there is to know about the marsh, some of us may still find little or no value in it.

Here I am resisting the view that we should value environmental goods, not by some more-or-less sophisticated form of cost-benefit analysis, but according to an objective account of the value they have for human lives. Such views appear to be popular among environmental philosophers. O'Neill develops a neo-Aristotelian argument to the effect that a good human life must involve the development of capacities which include the capacity to understand and appreciate nature, so someone who (subjectively) places no value on environmental features reveals himself to be leading a less-than-fully adequate life. Bob Goodin argues that concern for the natural environment stems from the considerations that:

(1) People want to see some sense and pattern to their lives. (2) That requires, in turn, that their lives be set in some larger context. (3) The products of natural processes, untouched as they are by human hands, provide precisely that desired context.[23]

Though Goodin does not say so explicitly, the implication of this must surely be that someone who professes herself indifferent as to whether an untouched natural feature—a piece of wilderness, say—survives or not is making a mistake; she is yielding up part of what gives 'sense and pattern' to her life. So it could not be in her interest for the wilderness to be used up to provide her with a higher income or more goods of other kinds. To put this back into Rawlsian terms, untouched natural products are to be seen as primary goods for persons regardless of their particular, subjectively held, conceptions of the good.

These views seem to me overstated. Even if it is true of many people that their conception of a meaningful life involves reference to natural processes outside themselves, it is surely very far from a universal truth.[24] Goodin's first and second premises are far more plausible than his third, if the third is taken to mean that *only* untouched natural products can provide the 'larger context' that people need to make sense of their lives (think of a religious tradition as an alternative). But if the claim is merely that untouched nature is valuable to *some* people for this reason, then we are right back to the central problem that we are wrestling with, namely how to set your interest in preserving certain natural features free from human interference against my interest in having land available to build a bigger and better football stadium for my team to play in, and so on, with the interests of everybody else.

Another way to put this point is to remind readers that we are trying to work out how environmental goods should figure in a theory of social justice whose task is to adjudicate between individuals' competing claims on resources of various kinds. You may believe that everyone would enjoy a richer life if they could be persuaded to take up the kind of attitude to nature that both O'Neill and Goodin in slightly different ways are describing, in which case it would certainly be reasonable to try to convince them of its value. But it is not reasonable to establish a regime of distributive justice which by privileging environmental goods assumes that people already value nature in that way when empirically we know that they don't.

So far I have been defending the view that environmental goods should be valued, for purposes of social justice, by finding out as accurately as possible what quantity of other goods different people would be prepared to sacrifice to have them. But now I come to a difficulty which I take to be crucial for the standard cost-benefit approach. The problem is that when people make judgements about the value of environmental goods, (for instance in response to willingness-to-pay or willingness-to-accept questions), they are likely already to incorporate into their answers a social perspective. That is to say, when asked what they would be willing to give up to preserve Sequoia National Park or the snail darter, the value they record may not just be a personal estimate of how much worse off they would be without the park or the bird, but an estimate of how much worse off their society, (or even perhaps humanity), would be. (This corresponds to Mark Sagoff's claim that when people make judgements about the environment, they are behaving as citizens rather than as consumers.[25]), And this makes it quite inappropriate to use the values obtained in this way to work out a theory of justice between persons (i.e. in deciding how to count environmental goods against goods of other kinds in calculating each person's index of goods). What the cost-benefit analysis is giving us, in many cases at least, is not a figure for how much people benefit personally from environmental goods, but some amalgam of that and their estimate of how much *other* people will benefit; the judgement recorded is partly an impersonal or other-regarding one.[26]

But although we have uncovered a serious weakness in the

cost-benefit approach, we are no nearer finding a solution to the problem we are addressing. There is no reason to think that the judgements people make about the value of the environment in answer to survey questions will converge, nor is there any reason to think that, in so far as they are based on estimates of how much value others attach to environmental goods, they are at all reliable. To say 'I would be prepared to give up such-and-such an amount of resources to protect Sequoia National Park from commercial development, and this is because of the value *to everyone* of preserving areas of wilderness' is to say little of any substance if, (as seems very likely), I have no way of knowing how much other people care about wilderness. So there are likely to be large differences in the values recorded for natural features, even among well-intentioned people, and we seem to be no further ahead.

The response of writers such as Sagoff at this point is to say that the question becomes political, and it is to be resolved by political dialogue between citizens. Each puts forward his or her environmental proposals, together with the reasons behind them, there is debate in which conflicting opinions can be presented, and finally a common decision is reached. In somewhat similar spirit, Barry suggests that the requirements of justice in such cases become procedural: each person puts forward her own ecological (or non-ecological) viewpoint and tries to convince others of its validity, then finally some procedure such as a majority referendum is used to make a decision about whether, say, the dam is to be built or the snail darter saved. So long as the procedure is endorsed by principles of justice, Brian Barry claims, the outcome will also be endorsed, indirectly, as just.[27]

I am generally sympathetic to the idea that political deliberation is the appropriate way to resolve issues in cases like this.[28] But before turning our backs on the question of social justice and the environment by saying, in effect, 'let's just hand over environmental issues to democratic procedures', we need to open up the black box a little to see what might be going on when environmental proposals are being debated. Let me sketch a couple of possibilities. One is that people are educating one another about the real value of environmental features. Earlier I borrowed the example of a dull-looking but environmentally rich piece of marshland. In such cases, I may be unperceptive or ignorant, and you may be able to persuade me that the marsh has value on grounds that I already accept, in which case our final judgements will converge. A second possibility is that the participants may be invoking communitarian grounds. That is, they may link proposals about the environment to a wish to preserve the general character of the community in which the political debate is taking place, and this argument may weigh with others who attach no direct value to the environment itself. For instance, I may be an urban American who hates the countryside. But I may also value living in a country with a distinct national culture, and I may see, or may come to see, that for Americans the presence of untamed nature is an important element of national identity.[29] So I may support proposals to preserve wilderness areas even though for me the wilderness has neither use nor option nor (direct) existence value.

In either of these cases—a spontaneous convergence of judgements about environmental value, or a shared recognition of the importance to the community of some environmental feature— the outcome of political debate would be legitimate in more than just a procedural sense. By the same token, it would give grounds for setting aside other demands of social justice. If, knowing the facts we all (or nearly all) agree that a particular piece of heathland or forest should be preserved, then this may justifiably trump other demands on our resources, for instance increased spending on social services. We would have made, democratically, a judgement about priorities which in this case came out in the environment's favour.

I suspect, however, that such cases will be quite exceptional if we consider the full range of environmental issues. Where it is a matter of preserving a species, for instance, it is very unlikely that there will either be convergence in judgements, or the possibility of convincing appeals to communal values (the exceptions might be species with symbolic significance, such as the bald eagle). We are back to cases where people can be expected to attach quite different weights to environmental goods even under conditions of full information. So what is going on inside the black box when political deliberation occurs? Presumably people are trying to

convince one another that they really do care about the continued
existence of the snail darter (or not as the case may be) and trying
to show how much they care about it, in the sense of how high it
stands in their list of priorities. What goes into the final judgement, say a majority vote on the dam versus the snail darter? In
the best case, public-spirited citizens will be expressing a judgement on what they regard as a fair resolution of the conflict. They
will weigh the arguments of those who support the snail darter
against those who point to the value of the energy and the water
resources the dam will create, stand back from their own preferences and try to decide which proposal has justice on its side.[30]

But in that case we (and they) need substantive principles of
justice to guide us in weighing the claims of those who value the
preservation of the snail darter against the claims of those who
value, say, cheaper energy. The deliberative procedure simply *qua*
procedure cannot deliver justice, because at a crucial point in the
process a substantive judgement has to be made. If the wrong
principles are applied by those making the decision, then the
decision may be unfair even though in every other respect the
correct procedure has been followed. So we are driven back once
more to the question of how, substantively, environmental goods
should figure in our theory of justice.

I suggested earlier that we should regard environmental goods
as primary goods, to be counted alongside other goods when
computing what proportion of social resources has been devoted
to each person. For present purposes I am leaving it open what
the principle of distribution should be—candidates might include
equality, or a patterned principle such as desert, or the Rawlsian
difference principle. The suggestion is that, if we begin from a
situation in which no environmental goods are provided but
resources of other kinds are allocated as justice requires, then
we should try to promote environmental values in such a way that
the distributive pattern remains unchanged when environmental
goods are incorporated into the index. Thus, if the principle is
equality of resources, we should aim for an outcome in which
each person enjoys an equal share of resources overall, where the
share is calculated by combining the goods that she holds privately
with the environmental goods that she enjoys along with others.

The problem, as we have already seen, is how to compute the value of environmental goods when this index is constructed.

At this point I want to return to the argument about cost-benefit analysis. The problem with this, as we saw, is that when people are asked to put a money value on some environmental feature, they are liable to switch to the citizen perspective and endeavour to make a public judgement about the social value of the feature in question—often saying, as a result, 'this piece of nature should be preserved regardless of cost'.[31] What we want, first of all, is for people to say how much natural objects matter to them personally. When this primary information is available, for everyone or for a sufficiently large cross-section of the community, we can then as citizens make a second-order judgement about what justice requires.

The rationale for this two stage procedure can be brought out if we take a more prosaic case, say the decision to build a public swimming-pool (which, let's suppose, will be available to everyone without charge when it is built). Before we can decide whether to build the pool, we need to know what value different people attach to having the opportunity to swim, which we could find out by asking, say, what annual fee they would be prepared to pay to have access to the pool. Armed with that information we could then see whether the resources needed to build the pool could be found in such a way as to preserve fairness. It would, for instance clearly be unfair to levy a poll tax for this purpose if it turned out that those less well off placed a lower value on the pool than the better off. Without the primary information it would be impossible to decide, except by pure hunch, whether the pool should be built at all, or how it should be funded. So our citizens need to address two questions: how much value they personally attach to having a swimming pool, and then, in the light of that information, what decision to reach about building it.

The same procedure, I am suggesting, should be used in the case of most environmental goods. Unless it is possible to achieve a high level of consensus about the importance of such a good, the right approach is to try to discover people's private valuations first, and then to enter these as evidence in public deliberation about environmental justice.[32] So, although I am not proposing that cost-benefit analysis should be used mechanically to resolve environmental disputes, I am claiming that without something like cost-benefit analysis as a first step, a just resolution of such disputes will turn out to be impossible.

It may of course prove to be impossible in practice to obtain reliable private evaluations through cost benefit analysis because those questioned insist on taking up the role as citizen and answering from a social perspective. In current circumstances this is understandable, because such analysis as is now conducted only gives ordinary people one chance to influence public policy. They are not asked (first round) 'How much would you be willing to pay to preserve the Dartford Warbler?' and then (second round) 'Here are some options for preserving the Dartford Warbler, and here also are the figures we got in answer to our willingness-to-pay question. What, in your judgement, should the government now do?' With only one bite at the cherry, they may reasonably use the willingness-to-pay question as an opportunity to record their judgement that bird-habitats are sufficiently important to enough people to make preserving them a priority. So we have to envisage a more consistently democratic procedure for making environmental decisions, and place cost-benefit analysis within that framework.

Environmentalists may still resist the analogy between the swimming-pool case and the Dartford Warbler case, arguing that in the first instance all that is at stake is the amount of personal enjoyment or benefit someone gets from having the pool available for use, while in the second case concern for the fate of the Warbler represents a value judgement about the importance of protecting birds and other forms of wildlife. Although the two cases are indeed significantly different in some respects, my argument has been that, from the perspective of social justice, they must be treated alike. People may reasonably disagree about the value of many, perhaps most, environmental goods, just as they may reasonably disagree about the value of works of art or different styles of music. These differences reflect differences in personal experience, taste, and belief, and although we can try to persuade others to revise their valuations, in general there is no reason to expect a consensus to be reached (the exceptions are the cases I identified on pp. 166–67 above). So long as disagreement about the value of various environmental goods remains, the public provision of such goods has to be regarded, from the perspective of justice, as a benefit provided to some but not to others.

It may be illuminating here to consider a parallel case: suppose people ask for public funds to build churches of different denominations, each group believing sincerely that theirs is the right way to worship God. The basis of each claim is not the amenity that members will enjoy personally from having the church built, but the fact that without the church God cannot be worshipped in the way that matters to Him most. How, from the perspective of social justice, should we treat such a claim? If public funds are indeed provided to build one such church, we must surely record the provision of the funds as a benefit going to the congregation in question, despite the fact that their claim is based not on a self-regarding desire but on a sincere belief about what is impersonally valuable. How is this case different from that of a group who demand the preservation of a piece of virgin forest on the ground that this constitutes an intrinsically valuable ecosystem?[33]

I have suggested in this chapter that if we want to include environmental goods in the theory of justice, we should see them as falling into three broad categories. First, there are goods which can be attached directly to other primary goods, including the basic conditions of a healthy human existence, and the absence of environmental harms such as pollution which would reduce the value of other primary goods. These fit naturally into standard liberal accounts of justice such as those of Rawls and Dworkin. Second, there are goods about which we may hope to generate sufficient agreement, through public discussion, that their provision would not pose substantive issues of justice: a democratic procedure, leading to consensus, would be sufficient. Third, there are many other goods which are valued differently by different people, and which, therefore, have to be counted as primary goods when calculating the index of those who value them. Here, I have argued, there is no alternative to cost-benefit analysis as a means of finding the trade-offs people wish to make between environmental goods and resources of other kinds.

What would follow from all of this in practice? It is clear that the state must be centrally involved in the provision of goods in the first two categories, with public policy and legislation aiming to secure basic standards of environmental safety and protection, and environmental aims that are genuinely shared emerging through the democratic process. With goods in the third category, however, the state's role is more open to question. I have already taken note of the practical limitations of cost-benefit analysis as presently conducted. If costs and benefits cannot be identified with reasonable accuracy, it may be better for environmental goods in this category to be provided primarily by voluntary organizations, with members showing their level of commitment through the time and money that they are willing to devote to each organization. Against this it may be argued that there is potentially a free-rider problem here: people may value the preservation of bird-nesting sites, but hope that enough others will join the Royal Society for the Protection of Birds to make their own contribution unnecessary. If this proves to be so (and the membership levels of the various environmental organizations suggest there are ways round the problem) there may be a case for the state re-entering the ring through a system of earmarked taxation: when filling in their tax forms, people would have the opportunity to indicate how they would prefer some part of the money to be spent. Under this system you cannot (legally) avoid paying your fair share of tax overall, but you can indicate that you want it used for purchasing works of art for the national gallery rather than saving the Dartford Warbler, if you value the first above the second.

Environmental philosophers will probably find this too weak a response to the host of environmental problems that we presently confront. There is an understandable tendency to present these problems in apocalyptic terms, and to treat all environmental goods as though they fell into the same fundamental category. In contrast to this, I share the liberal belief that in many areas, including this one, people's personal values or 'conceptions of the good' may diverge radically, and that a defensible theory of justice must accommodate such divergence. As I have tried to show, environmental goods *can* be incorporated into the principles of social justice, but only if we are willing to draw some distinctions, and renounce apocalyptic fundamentalism.

7

An Extension of the Rawlsian Savings Principle to Liberal Theories of Justice in General

M. L. J. WISSENBURG

1. Introduction

The idea that we have obligations to future generations has always been a forceful argument in support of environmental policies. The nature of obligations to future generations is also a topic of intense debate in mainstream liberal political thought, yet liberalism has traditionally shown little interest in questions of an environmental nature. In this text, I discuss the role of these obligations in liberal thought and give them a green twist.

One of John Rawls's most original and fundamental contributions to the theory of social justice has been the savings principle.[1] In just four sentences and a footnote somewhere at two-thirds into his latest book, *Political Liberalism,* Rawls replies to his numerous critics of the preceding twenty years with an elegant new defence

This research was sponsored by the Foundation for Law and Public Policy (REOB), which is a part of the Netherlands Organization for Scientific Research (NWO). Parts of an earlier version of this chapter were published in M. Wissenburg, *Green Liberalism: The Free and the Green Society* (London: UCL Press, 1998). I am deeply indebted to Andrew Dobson, Bob Goodin, and Sasja Tempelman for their extensive comments on an earlier version of this text; to my colleagues in the Department of Politics, University of Nijmegen, particularly Grahame Lock, for their sincere scepticism, their interest, suggestions, and support; and last but not least to André Mahieu for tolerating the excessive use I made of his café and coasters to sit back, reflect, and write.

of this principle.[2] It is my object to show that the new defence is not only better than the old one, although still not unproblematic, but that it also has relevance for theorists who do not want to work within a Rawlsian framework of original position and contract theory. I shall argue that it in fact offers a very satisfactory basis for any liberal principle of justice between generations— given a small number of side-constraints. Finally, I hope to demonstrate that this new argument in favour of a savings principle *as such* may not help us much further in determining the precise *contents* of that principle, but that it does support a strong minimum condition for justice between generations.

In the remainder of this section, I shall summarize Rawls's new defence of the savings principle and discuss the differences between the old and the new Rawls. Section 2 lists the main conditions under which the savings principle is justified in the context of Rawls's theory of justice, and argues that each of these conditions can be made less demanding. Thus, Rawls's argument for a savings principle can be generalized to apply in the context of nearly every liberal theory of justice. In section 3, I discuss the form of a savings principle ensuring justice between generations and reject four comprehensive formulations of the savings principle, some of which have gained a certain popularity among green political theorists. I then introduce an alternative, more formal reading and defend this as a logical implication of the generalized argument for a savings principle: the restraint principle, according to which justice between generations demands maximum restraint in the use of natural and artificial capital. In the concluding section 4, I discuss some striking consequences of accepting a savings principle and of interpreting it as a restraint principle.

When he first introduced the idea of a savings principle, John Rawls rejected the notion that individuals in the original position have obligations to their immediate descendants simply because they do.[3] A move like that might make persons in the original position far too distinctly individual and would certainly contradict the basic assumption that people in the original position are mutually disinterested. He did, however, assume that (abstract) next generations have valid claims on (abstract) present generations. This assumption justified the introduction of a further motivational assumption: people in the original position were to be imagined as representatives of bloodlines, 'as being so to speak deputies for a kind of everlasting moral agent or institution'.[4] On the other hand, these representatives, to whom Rawls refers on other occasions as heads of families, are biased in a way: they are expected to represent the interests of at least the next two generations but not their bloodline's 'entire life span in perpetuity'.[5] As a rather straightforward implication of these assumptions, persons in the original position will agree that a savings principle should be included in the list of principles of justice. Yet Rawls finds it impossible to specify this principle beyond the point of saying that it depends on a society's level and rate of development.[6]

Despite the small number of pages Rawls devoted to the issue of justice between generations, his account of it has drawn an impressive amount of criticism. For one, it has been pointed out that Rawls, when describing his representatives, seems to have had fathers in mind rather than mothers—to be specific, fathers of traditional Western nuclear families. He also seems to assume that having and caring for children is in some way natural, a universal practice and a universal possibility.[7] Oddly enough, the people in the original position are not expected to represent children or their special interests, one of which probably is, incidentally, a healthy environment.[8] Finally, Rawls received criticism on the way he deduced the need for a savings principle from the assumptions he made: the logic of the argument would be inconclusive.[9]

Rawls has indirectly replied to these comments by answering yet another critique. It has been noted that there is a contradiction within the set of assumptions that make up the original position. Apart from the fact that people in the original position are not supposed to know how old they are or to which generation they belong, Rawls assumes both (a) that everyone in the original position is mutually disinterested and that (b) everyone cares for his or her descendants' fate. Condition (a) implies that the contracting parties will not be interested in any kind of savings principle at all: condition (b) implies that they will be. This appears to be a contradiction, and Rawls has admitted as much.[10]

In *Political Liberalism*, Rawls's answer consists, essentially, in two

very simple moves: he drops condition (b) and redraws the outlines of the original position in such a way that the contracting
parties will 'agree to a savings principle subject to the further
condition that they must want all previous generations to have
followed it'.[11] I shall refer to this new condition as condition (c).

In this new version of the original position, condition (b) has
become redundant: whether or not people care about descendants
is no longer relevant. Rawls still believes that it is a reasonable
condition, and to that degree he refuses to give in to well-founded
criticisms, but at least in so far as justice between generations is
concerned, Rawls's private convictions now no longer affect the
argument.[12]

Instead, condition (a) turns out to do nearly all the work.
People in the original position may be disinterested in the fate
of others, but they care a lot about themselves. It is precisely to
this feeling that the new original position is expected to appeal: it
makes the savings principle mutually beneficial. Let me give a first
and deliberately imperfect illustration of this: if your grandparent
offered you 5,000 on the condition that you promise to give your
grandchild 5,000 at say the same age, and the alternative is to start
in life with nothing but the clothes in which you were born, it
would be irrational not to accept your grandfather's offer.

Of course, handing down Rawls's interpretation of pounds,
primary goods, from generation to generation rather than money
from parents to children is far more ingenious: it implies promising to hand down goods to a next generation, *regardless* of whether
one has or wants or likes children. It is, moreover, not just a fair-
weather principle: Rawls demands that the savings principle be
formulated in such a way that it would be accepted by all
generations, even if economic times are rough. The savings principle will have to be flexible enough to guarantee that no generation will be worse off *relative* to any previous generation, that is,
relative to the circumstances in which each generation lives. The
new defence is furthermore foolproof against breaking promises
made to dead people because promises are made to generations
rather than individuals. Then again, it is not foolproof against a
generation that decides to take the money and run, unless we
assume that these people have a sense of justice or obligation.

Fortunately, Rawls already assumed the existence of 'a sense of justice' in his old original position.[13]

At this point, two questions naturally arise: 'What's to stop, precisely, the generation in question from taking the money and running?';[14] and '. . . on what sort of psychology is that generation-skipping concern systematically more plausible than the original story about caring about our immediate descendants in Rawls I?'[15] The answer to both is simple: rationality.

It may look as if the presence of a sense of justice is essential to the argument, and it is, to some extent. However, this cannot be held against Rawls himself. One of the reasons why the new original position cannot perform too badly in comparison to other available solutions *in re* obligations to future generations is that they all rely on something like trust. In fact, all these solutions must necessarily rely on trust: that is what obligations are all about. It is therefore not unreasonable for Rawls to assume the presence of a sense of justice; he can do no other. Nor can anyone else. There seem to be no physical or legal means or incentive to really ensure 100 per cent compliance with these moral obligations—simply because anything you give to others is lost for you. Apparently, the only alternative to a sense of justice on earth is to argue that one gets one's reward in heaven, which is a totally different view on obligations to future generations than the one persons in the original position would be sensitive to.

Now Rawls makes one important improvement on the orthodox understanding of justice between generations[16]—visible, for instance, in condition (c): generations exist next to each other, not one after the other: 'society is a system of cooperation between generations over time'[17]—it definitely does not say 'a system of transfers from one generation to the next'. Yet is seems that this more realistic conception of generations does not change the substantial role of trust.

Imagine the following situation: a first generation, let us call them the Lost Generation, has made great sacrifices on behalf of the next generation, the Babyboomers, and let us say that the Lost Generation has made them promise to save something for the next, third generation, Generation X. A demand that the

Babyboomers do not do worse for Generation X than the Lost Generation did for them might be construed as a kind of moral blackmail: one does not choose to grow up in the circumstances of ever increasing prosperity created by the Lost Generation any more than one chooses to be born Spanish. So let us assume that the Lost Generation is reasonable: it demands that the Babyboomers do not do worse for Generation X provided they actually can. The important thing is this: Generation X may find out that the Babyboomers made and broke a promise to the first generation—because the Lost Generation is still around in old peoples' homes complaining about the unreliability of their children, or because they read *Political Liberalism* page 274, or for any other reason. As far as Generation X is concerned, any agreement it might have had with its fellow citizen Babyboomers then breaks down; Generation X will stick strictly to the mutual disinterest condition and can, if it feels that way, make the rest of the Babyboomers' days hell. In fact, defection by some Babyboomers is already enough to prove to contemporaries of *any* generation that the defectors cannot be trusted with generations that do not yet exist, nor with *existing* people of any generation.

It is true then that trust plays a crucial role in the new Rawls's justice between generations, but there is no altruism in it, no other-regarding attitude—just self-interest and mutual disinterest. Note that in the example given other-regarding motives do not come into play at all. Since generations exist as contemporaries, defecting generations impose a cost upon society of which they will have to pay a part: defection destroys the basis of trust on which society was built. The other generations can perhaps go on as before in their co-operative venture but they will have learned that no one can be trusted—a lesson that cannot be too healthy for the survival of society.

To put the point more systematically, Rawls assumes in condition (c) that new generations enter an already ongoing system of social co-operation. On entry, they have a choice between accepting the existing rules (the principles of justice chosen behind the veil of ignorance) or rejecting them. Rejection would mean losing the social bond and with it the advantages of social co-operation. Since it would be irrational to reject a system of rules that does not make one worse off and might actually improve one's situation, the new generation will accept the existing rules, including the savings principle. Once included in the system of co-operation, any generation can choose at any time between keeping its promise or breaking it. They will only do the latter if they stand to gain from defection. Being mutually disinterested *individuals,* they will set off the losses incurred by leaving society against the gains of either individual exclusion and solitude or a life in the company of other untrustworthy defectors. Under the standard assumption that the primary social goods are rights and liberties, opportunities and powers, income, wealth and self-respect,[18] it would be irrational for any individual to step out of society and lose these goods. Moreover, being reasonable persons in the original position, they would devise a system in which they would not want to risk losing out if others—or even a whole generation—were to step out of the contract. Hence, the contract rests upon general mutual consent and not upon one-sided promises. In all these considerations, the elementary factors are rationality, mutual disinterest, and trust in the other's rationality. Altruism has no role in it.

Note that the possible existence of as yet non-existent future generations is irrelevant to the Rawlsian argument. There is no way to protect them directly against 'thieves'—stealing from them is easier than stealing candy from a baby. Instead, they are protected indirectly at any given moment by a principle that means to protect the interests of existing generations. Incidentally, this saves Rawls from having to discuss the objection[19] that we have obligations to the next generation we create because we put them on the spot, but not to any third generation our descendants create because that is *their* responsibility.

There is one serious problem, though. We cannot assume that a well-ordered society already exists or that people in the original position design principles for a society that already meets the right principles. With his condition (c), Rawls explicitly assumes that the system of co-operation is already in existence: the savings principle will not be accepted unless one can want previous generations to have accepted it. However, it seems that a first generation would only lose by accepting the savings principle, hence would not be motivated to accept the arrangement. The original position of course has no first generation. The veil of ignorance precludes knowledge of the generation to which one belongs, so that given Rawls's standard assumptions about the original position, people in it will none the less accept a savings principle. Yet there are first generations in real life. Every change in the structure of a society, every move towards a more just society, is made by a first generation that will (ideally) judge its own performance in relation to what people in the original position would decide. If the latter cannot represent a situation which the former experience on a regular basis, a choice situation that will influence their well-being—then there may well be something wrong with the reflective equilibrium between our considered convictions and the conditions of the original position.[20]

The only answer that avoids an appeal to altruism would run as follows: since all next generations will 'want' the previous generation to have agreed to the savings principle, their mutual basis of trust would fail to come about if one generation defected—in which case all generations, including the first one, would lose out. And given Rawls's list of primary social goods, it seems reasonable to assume that the costs of defection will far outweigh the benefits, even for a first generation. To put it bluntly, it is in granddad's interest to invest in his grandchild; he thereby gains the trust and support of two generations.

Rawls has this time given us an internally perfectly consistent justification for the choice of incorporating a savings principle in the just society.[21] The sheer mutual advantage of such a principle ensures that mutually disinterested persons behind a veil of ignorance will choose it; the combination of rationality and mutual advantage ensures that it will be stable principle.[22] But Rawls has done far more. First, given the assumptions on which the original position is built, he has implicitly shown that a savings principle, hence a form of justice between generations, is a necessary condition of the just society. Since the savings principle operates to the advantage of every next generation, it would be irrational not to choose it. Conversely, its absence from a society would make that society unjust, i.e. biased in favour of previous generations. Such a society would lack a basis for trust and hence for its stability and survival. Second, by representing generations as contemporaries, persons in the original position know that for most of their lives, their well-being will depend on generations that are not even around yet. Thus, by ensuring justice between existing generations, Rawls has implicitly also ensured justice towards non-existent future generations. Perhaps this goes two steps further than Rawls himself wished to go, but it is an obvious and unavoidable consequence of his train of thought.

2. Extending the Validity of Rawls's New Argument

Next to the general assumptions made in *A Theory of Justice* concerning the guarantees needed for an impartial construction of principles of social justice, Rawls needed only one additional assumption, condition (b) and later (c), to explain the emergence of a savings principle. Even condition (c) itself is redundant, to a degree: if persons in the original position want more rather than fewer primary goods, it is rational for them to want previous generations to have followed an appropriate savings principle since that always benefits next generations. What condition (c) actually adds to the original version of the original position is the existence of different generations as partial contemporaries.

In this section I want to show that Rawls's argument for a savings principle can be adapted to fit a far wider range of liberal theories of justice. Justice between generations, in the form of a savings principle, will turn out to be an essential trait of nearly every liberal theory of social justice. I shall do this by first weakening the conditions of Rawls's original position, thus extending the argument to liberal contract theories in general. As the idea of a contract is a vehicle for moral arguments rather than an argument in its own right, the conclusions reached can subsequently be shown to be valid for all liberal theories of justice with only one exception.

First then, we will have to revise all the conditions Rawls needs in order to support a savings principle—that is, conditions (a) and (c) as well as others:

(1) Mutually disinterested individuals who,

(2) in order to fulfill their reasonable plans of life

(3) prefer more rather than fewer primary social goods, which are

(4) relatively scarce, and

(5) can be made available on a wider scale through social co-operation.

These individuals are endowed with:

(6) the knowledge that there are (simultaneously) similarly conditioned previous and next generations,

(7) a sense of justice,

(8) a veil of ignorance that covers their identities,

(9) general scientific knowledge about the structure and nature of societies,

(10) a preference for the maximin principle,

(11) the legitimate authority to establish, (re)distribute and limit property rights.

Provided these conditions apply, individuals will want a savings principle to be established and they will want it to take such a form that 'they must want all *previous* generations to have followed it'.[23] (Note that (1) to (6) imply Rawls's condition (c).)

Most of these conditions can be rephrased without any difficulty in terms that fit other liberal theories of justice. Condition (2), for instance, is innocent enough to fit any conception of liberalism since they all understand the individuals' plans of life, in some form or other, as the core value of liberalism. We can simply leave it up to individual theorists to define 'reasonable'. This first change in the structure of the original position being made, the logic of Rawls's argument still stands: what matters is not the content of plans of life or whether they are admissible in the original position, but the fact that there is something relevant at stake for persons choosing principles of justice.

Conditions (3) to (5) can be adapted in a similar way. All we need is a common expression for the means required to fulfill plans of life, a concept of which 'primary social goods' is one conception among many. For this purpose I shall use the term 'rights'. Let us assume that social justice is about the distribution of unspecified things (the specification depends upon the theory and theorist) that can be distributed in the form of rights. In other words, we distribute goods and represent them as rights, but we could have chosen another term—say, claim, good, benefit and burden, vehicle of utility, etc. We shall also assume that rights are distributed to individuals only. The idea that individuals are the primary recipients of justice fits in best with liberalism, since liberals usually only and at most care for collectives as preconditions of the individual's freedom to pursue her plan of life.[24]

Since individuals are assumed to care for their plans of life, they obviously also care about having the rights necessary to that purpose, and about having more rather than less of them. Furthermore, the assumption of relative scarcity (where 'relative' can be further specified within a particular theory) is standard—there is little practical use in talking about distributive justice under conditions of abundance or extreme scarcity.[25] Assumption (5) is also standard within liberal theories of justice and needs no further revision. Again, these changes do not influence the basic structure of the argument in favour of a savings principle.

We can move beyond the requirement of general scientific knowledge (9) by demanding that persons in revised original positions have access to all the relevant information available and use it in a rational way—again leaving it up to the specific theory to determine whether 'rational use' means 'complete and comprehensive use' or whether there is a limit to the amount of information that contracting parties can cope with. Again, this new assumption is incorporated in some form or other in all liberal theories of justice and does not change the structure of Rawls's argument.

It seems that we cannot change the requirement of a veil of ignorance (8) without also adapting condition (1), mutual disinterest. The more parts of the veil are dropped, the more mutually disinterested individuals become rational individuals, goal-maximizers. They thus lose their impartiality and start to design principles to their own immediate advantage, and that does not obviously include an interest in the fate of future generations. However, condition (6) warrants that persons in an original position will know that a stable system of social co-operation safeguarding their liberties and opportunities can only succeed if, at the same time, it satisfies enough other parties who may be members of other generations. The latter may not be a common assumption in liberal theories of justice (they often do not even discuss the topic of intergenerational justice) but it is both intrinsically reasonable (because realistic) and in no way incompatible with liberal views of justice. Hence, even without (all elements of) the veil of ignorance, it will be reasonable to accept *a* savings principle: everyone (except the first generation) stands to gain from it. Note, though, that the way in which the contracting parties are characterized in specific theories will certainly influence the *form* of the savings principle. In a society of perfect altruists, for instance, the appropriate savings principle might well require perpetual starvation of every generation for the sake of every next generation. In a society of perfect egoists, on the other hand, next generations would receive nothing more than their bargaining power allows them to extract from their predecessors.

Note that the extension of conditions (1) and (8) to rational individuals with or without elements of a veil of ignorance has one disturbing consequence: it allows for coalitions and majoritarian decision making on principles of justice. Societies can, after all, usually survive the disappearance (or in this case, non-inclusion) of one or more of its members. None the less, even a society of minimal size contains (by assumption) more than one generation. Hence, the structure of the argument still remains intact.

As for the sense of justice (7) which gives Rawls his basis for trust, we do not have to demand more than that the contracting parties will not break agreements without good reason; being rational, the defector knows that defection brings less gain and more costs.

The penultimate condition that can be extended concerns the contracting parties' preference for the maximin principle (8). We shall adapt it by dropping it. In fact, the maximin principle is redundant in Rawls's argument for the *idea* of a savings principle but it deserved mentioning because it affects the precise *form* it can take. It has been argued, for instance, that the Rawlsian version of a savings principle would copy the difference principle (in the defence of which the maximin rule plays a crucial role): persons in the original position would, or should if Rawls had done a better job, distribute goods over generations to the benefit of the least advantaged, i.e. the powerless non-existing next generations.[26] This is not the place to discuss this idea—let us just note that the defence of the idea of a savings principle does not depend on a specific attitude towards risks, but on the pure rationality of gaining anyway, relative to a society without a savings principle.

The last condition to be adapted is (11), which requires that contracting parties have a legitimate authority to establish, (re)distribute and limit property rights. It is only here that we may meet real difficulties. Not all liberals, especially not libertarians, if liberalism is understood in a broad sense, will accept that anyone other than the possessing individual has the right to use or abuse her property.

The claim I shall make here is that condition (11) is reasonable, at least within a liberal frame of thought, and that it should not be weakened or strengthened. Hence, the type of libertarian theory in which property rights[27] are assumed to be absolute do not fit into the picture; they cannot contain a savings principle except one based on the voluntary compliance of individuals. Then again, I shall also argue that such theories are untenable.

The short version of the argument runs as follows: not all rights can be absolute (valid everywhere and anytime) and inalienable (non-transferable). In practice, a world of merely absolute and inalienable rights is impossible to live in, as it leads to instances of *fiat justitia pereat mundi:* anyone or any set of individuals who can save lives but refuses to would legitimately make life hell. It is also incompatible with liberal democracy. Hence, there are limits to private property rights.

In the long version, one crucial assumption must be made in advance—an assumption, since it can only be defended partially. Any distribution of rights, I would argue, is conditional on the absence of better arguments in favour of another (principle of) distribution.

The theorist who would argue that some principle or other is 'objectively' true, regardless of human opinions, arguments, theories, and debates, defends what is known in ethics as an absolutist position. Even if they can be proven, objective principles cannot be defended, indeed need not be defended, since they are valid without consent. If consent is missing and the true view is shared only by a select group, as is bound to happen in pluralistic societies, objective principles offer no practical help whatsoever in shaping society. The liberal theory of justice excludes appeals to a higher moral truth accessible only to the chosen few, as indeed do most theories of justice and morality. The truth may be in heaven, but, to paraphrase Michael Walzer, the law is made on earth.[28]

Liberal theorists also reject the alternative 'relativist' position according to which principles need not, indeed cannot, be defended since there is no shared yardstick by which to measure them. Even if they could live with the idea that all morality, all social institutions and views of the good are ultimately accidental, they do not believe in the impossibility of an advancement towards some form of consensus or *modus vivendi* on the basis of a shared minimal conception of reason.

To quote a famous investigator: if we exclude the impossible, whatever else remains, however improbable, must be the truth. In this case, having excluded relativism and absolutism, what remains is an optimistic faith in the persuasive force of logic, of arguments. Hence, no claim to the validity of any moral principle can be accepted without argument.

Our axiom says that rights must be distributed on the basis of good arguments. It does not say that we, or contracting parties in an original position, are free to hand out ownership and user rights to *every* possible thing in the world. Rawls's theory is ambiguous at this point. He assumes on the one hand that no-one deserves the capacities with which one is born, so that these natural endowments can be seen as resources for society—and society then decides on the development and use of its citizens' endowments, plus whatever they gain through their use. Michael Sandel has correctly pointed out that this is a *non sequitur:* just because I do not deserve my Nobel prize qualities as a writer does not mean that society does.[29] We need a further argument to allow society, or in fact anyone, to take possession of faculties and goods, use them and distribute them. But on this topic, Rawls is silent. He seems implicitly to accept John Locke's view that mixing one's labour with nature can make a product one's own—where in this case 'one' is society rather than an individual, since society ultimately 'owns' the means by which nature is transformed into goods. However, he gives us no reason to believe that mixing one's labour is a sufficient condition for the creation of ownership rights.

What we need here is an argument to justify original acquisition—looting nature—*as such,* regardless of whether society or the individual performs the act of acquisition. In classical liberalism and in some libertarian circles,[30] the solution to this problem is to think of original acquisition as a natural right. Once we reject the natural rights assumption, as arbitrarily as Nozick accepts it,[31] we are left without any justification of original acquisition, of any subsequent transfer of goods and of the use we make of them. Since I see no way of solving it, I shall ignore this problem here and join the *communis opinio* among liberals in simply assuming that there can be such a thing as legitimate property.

It is slightly easier to defend the idea that *individuals* can have property and that, therefore, persons in an original position should recognize private property rights. To paraphrase William Galston: even though neither the individual nor society deserved an individual's natural endowments, the way a person directs the development of her talents should be considered a private achievement.[32] Society or my social environment influence me but they do not make me; they merely create the favourable circumstances in which, or the duress under which, I develop and employ my talents. Hence, and other things being equal, society or my causers in society cannot claim credit for the use I make of my talents—only I can.

We may then assume that there can be individual ownership rights. We have as yet no reason to believe that there can be ownership rights to everything, but there is reason to believe that *some* things can be owned. Finally, we have as yet no reason to believe that an ownership right to *x* implies that one can do everything one likes with *x,* i.e. that ownership is an unconditional right, one with which no one may interfere. There is a case for believing that at times an ownership right will be a right to use rather than (absolutely) possess a thing, and to use it only in particular ways, places, periods, or circumstances only.

What makes many rights conditional is the fact that no matter how scarce or abundant they may be, claims to them can be compared, evaluated, and ordered—and even in absence of competing claims a claim need not become a right. The fact that only one person applies for, say, a subsidy is not enough reason to give it; we also need a positive reason to recognize her claim as valid. Hence the strength of arguments determines whether we should agree to a particular distribution of conditional rights or to a principle of distribution. Because we have no yardstick for the ultimate truth or validity of principles, we have to accept, first, that any conditional right that can physically be withdrawn can also be withdrawn morally should a stronger argument come along, and secondly, that a right to x is not a right to x-plus—a right to pluck apples is not a right to cut down trees.

Thus, condition (11) can remain unchanged provided two further assumptions are made: we have to assume that arguments for the just distribution of specific rights may not be final, an assumption that should be built into distributive principles; and we must assume that the set of distributable conditional rights is non-empty. We then end up with the following list of conditions:

(1) Rational individuals (i.e. goal-maximizers) who,

(2) given a plan of life that satisfies some condition of admissibility (reasonableness),

(3) prefer more rather than fewer of those rights that are defined as relevant by their plan of life; rights to goods that are

(4) relatively scarce and

(5) become available through social co-operation.

These individuals are endowed with:

(6) the knowledge that they are contemporaries of similarly situated next and future generations,

(7) a common basis of trust: the willingness to justify at least a possible defection from the scheme of social co-operation,

(8) either some, or all, or none of the elements of the veil of ignorance,

(9) all available relevant information, which they use in a rational way,

(10) the legitimate authority to establish, (re)distribute and limit property rights, assuming
    (a) that there are distributable conditional rights, and
    (b) that arguments for the just distribution of specific rights may be overruled by better arguments.

We have moved from Rawls's own contract theory to Rawls's theoretical clones, first and second cousins and beyond, and each time we extended the conditions of Rawls's original position, we saw that the validity of the argument for a savings principle remained unaffected. By now, the argument has been shown to work for virtually every liberal theory that can be represented as a contract theory—the exception being libertarian theories in which ownership is a natural right, and we have rejected the latter as unsound. It is now possible to drop the contractarian façade and explain why *any* liberal theory of justice, contractarian or not, should contain a savings principle. What the ten conditions above describe is a typically liberal view of society: goal-maximizers with a plan of life, for the realization of which they need private property rights, rational individuals who stand to gain from social co-operation. In the presence of persons from different generations, it is simply rational for goal-maximizing individuals to seek the mutual benefit of a savings principle.

It is important not to lose sight of the limitations of this account. We had to assume that nature may legitimately be exploited and that exploitation can give rise to legitimate ownership rights. We still know nothing about the precise contents of the savings principle. More importantly, we cannot extend the validity of the argument beyond liberalism. If, for instance, individuals and their plans of life were products of society or incarnations of a culture (as they are in communitarian theories), the appeal to mutual advantage, self-interest, and individual liberties, and opportunities loses its force.

The implications of these few sentences on page 274 of *Political*

Liberalism are nevertheless quite interesting. We now have reason to believe that Rawls can defend his savings principle, that liberals in general need to include a savings principle in their respective theories of justice—and that (some form of) obligations to future generations is a *conditio sine qua non* of any liberal theory of justice. The obvious question then is: what form will this obligation take?

3. The Restraint Principle

The Rawlsian defence of the savings principle results in a side-constraint for, rather than a principle of, justice between generations: it has to be a principle to which we want ourselves to adhere as much as we want previous generations to have adhered to it. We had little to report on the precise contents of the savings principle. In this section, I hope to move one step beyond the purely formal observation that a liberal theory of justice must contain a savings principle. I shall first discuss four possible interpretations of the politically popular demand for sustainability, that is, the demand that we ' . . . meet the needs of the present without compromising the ability of future generations to meet their own needs'.[33] In all of these, the aim is to ensure that humans ought to pass their planet on to future generations 'in at least no worse shape than they found it in'.[34] I shall refer to this condition as 'no worse off' (NWO). So as not to complicate matters too much, I shall ignore the so-called identity problem: different policies will create future generations made up of different people whose well-being can only be compared to non-existence.[35] I shall furthermore assume that we are only saving material goods for future generations, although the argument can be extended to cover immaterial goods—institutions—as well. Unfortunately, all this is not enough to make these principles viable. I therefore introduce an open-ended principle instead: the restraint principle, which demands (roughly) that rights, within the limits of necessity, should be distributed in such a way that they remain available for redistribution.

Let us start with the uncomplicated idea that the savings principle would be satisfied if present generations leave the world no worse off than when they entered it. As it turns out, NWO might well be acceptable for people in a Rawlsian original position but not under most other circumstances. It is a fair-weather principle, assuming the possibility of continuous growth of welfare or at the very least of a steady state economy. In deviating cases, and regardless of what other arguments can be offered in its support, NWO is not an optimal answer—not to our question, and not to the demands of green political theorists for a principle that ensures sustainability. Imagine the following oversimplified situation: we have at t_1 a generation g_1 with a welfare of w_1. Instead of welfare, one can of course read freedom, primary goods, sets of rights, options, and so forth. Our g_1 that has the opportunity of investing in the future in such a way that it:

(a) may improve but will not lower its own welfare: $w_1 \geqq w_1'$
(b) leaves the subsequent generation g_2 worse off than it would have been without investments, i.e. $w_2 < w_2'$, and
(c) leaves next generations $g_3 \ldots g_n$ better off than they would have been: $w_3 > w_3'$, $w_4 > w_4'$, $\ldots w_n > w_n'$[36]

As an illustration, imagine that the first generation cuts down all its man-made forests, sells the wood and leaves the land in a derelict state. The next generation will have to live with wasteland, the generations after that will have access to both economically useful wood and aesthetically attractive wilderness. (Contrary to Brian Barry's opinion then[37] we can make our remote successors better off by making our immediate successors worse off.) From the point of view of a green theorist this situation is to be preferred to the one in which NWO had been applied. The same happens to be true for the goal-maximizing individuals described in the previous section. As a rule, they cannot lose but stand to gain from violating the principle. NWO makes them worse off any time an investment disadvantages one single future generation or perhaps even one single future individual. Thus, they would never choose this as their savings principle. Even Rawlsian risk-avoiders would have to reject NWO: putting themselves in the position of g_2, they would have to accept NWO since it leaves them better off, but NWO would lead to subsequent generations being worse off than they could be, so they would have to reject it as well. Rawls's minimax condition and NWO are logically incompatible. Note, finally, that NWO takes no account of the population size. Imagine that g_2 comes into the world finding the same amount of resources its predecessors found, only the population size has doubled. It will have to live in misery if it is to hand over exactly as much as it found to the third generation.

Let us now adapt NWO and turn it into a Pareto-optimal principle: generations should only invest in future generations if that leaves no one worse off and at least one person at least as well off as would otherwise be the case. The first thing to note is that this principle demands, at least, that persons in an original position are mutually disinterested as regards each other's fate. Egoists have no reason to accept Pareto-NWO. Secondly, nothing substantial changes as regards our example: Pareto-NWO will leave generations g_3 and following worse off.

The way forward seems to be to accept that generations can legitimately be made worse off, under certain conditions. Consider, thirdly, this Pareto-minimum rule: no generation should leave the subsequent generation in a position in which it cannot lead a life that is better than sheer misery. The implication of this rule is that each generation should see to it that no next generation falls below a certain basic level of welfare and that, apart from this, anything goes. Consequently, every generation is free to rob its successors of endless other opportunities they could have had—which will be unacceptable to anyone who risks ending up in a later generation.

Finally, consider a combination of these three rules: generations should not be made worse off than preceding generations, unless the overall gains outweigh the overall losses, and provided no generation falls below a minimum standard. Apart from the principle's insensitivity to population size, and apart from the obvious problem that we might have to work with an infinite number of future generations to establish whether there is an overall profit at all, this rule will certainly not be acceptable to risk-avoiders. Moreover and generally speaking, it allows one to sacrifice the well-being of one generation to a perhaps minute gain for others in cases where all generations could perhaps be very well off.

There is a way, though, to formulate a savings principle that will appeal to persons in original positions in general and without exception. The principle in question is the restraint principle, which demands that:

> no goods shall be destroyed unless unavoidable and unless they are replaced by perfectly identical goods; if that is physically impossible, they should be replaced by equivalent goods resembling the original as closely as possible; and if that is also impossible, a proper compensation should be provided.

The restraint principle can only be overruled by the quest for survival, i.e. if there is no other way to preserve a present life worth living other than by harming a future life. (I shall return to the question of necessity and inevitability below.) As a consequence, the restraint principle does the exact same work as we intended NWO to do—it leaves no one worse off than physically possible—without the disadvantages attached to NWO.

Now how can this principle be defended? First, of course, by pointing out that it does what NWO was supposed to do—but that will not convince liberals. In their case, an appeal to the logic of rights seems more appropriate. We assumed above that rights are conditional, i.e. dependent on the better argument. Now think of rights as sets, as complexes of permissions (duties, freedoms, etc.) to use one specific object to one specific purpose in one specific way at one moment in time and one place in the universe. The rights involved in owning, say, a forest then consist of a long range of 'molecular' permissions describing what one may and may not, should and should not do, at any time with each of the elements of which the forest is made up. As in real life, the owner is, for instance, free to hunt rabbits in it but not foxes, free to let it grow naturally or cut the dead wood, free to sell it but not to fell it. In short, she can use it but not in every way she might want to.

If conditional rights are seen as complexes of permissions, it becomes possible that, under certain circumstances, some rights simply cannot legitimately be attributed. Arguments in favour of a specific set of complex rights can only bring one so far and no further. A valid argument for picking fruit from trees here and now legitimizes only those acts that are necessary to the purpose. It is not necessary to cut down the tree to get hold of the fruit, therefore, a right to possess or take possession of the fruit does not entitle one to cut down the tree.

More to the point, there is a particular type of permission that can but should not be given: the permission to destroy objects of conditional rights. No argument except pure necessity can legitimize that we destroy anything that could be used by anyone else for a better reason. Consequently, we are 'custodians rather than owners of the planet'.[38]

In support, we do not have to appeal to the intrinsic value of nature, nor to the interests of distant future generations. The presence around us of six or more generations of actually existing individuals suffices. Conditional ownership depends on arguments, the soundness of which may change over time or depending on the information we have. Today, my word processor is of almost vital importance to me, but tomorrow I may no longer need it and it may become indispensable for my neighbour at the university. At this moment, my government may decide to build a new national airport in an ecologically relatively unimportant corner of the country. Within weeks, it may learn that it is the only piece of nature that can be saved from a sudden catastrophic outburst of acid rain, thus forcing it to withdraw its earlier decision—as long, of course, as it has not actually been effectuated.

Others may turn out to have better claims on goods than I have—they merely have not yet made those claims, have not been able to do so, or have not been heard. They may even be unaware of their own good reasons, as it takes time to grow up and develop or discover one's plan of life. In this context then, a first-come or finders-keepers principle is not a warrant for justice—my claim may be prior in time without being prior in terms of urgency or need. Whenever there is a choice between destroying a good, thus depriving others of present or future options to realize legitimate plans, or merely using it without limiting other people's options, we have a duty to chose the latter.

Hence, there are things we just should not destroy unless using them is unavoidable and there is no other way to use them except by destroying them. Even then, we ought to try to replace it by the best possible substitute, so as to leave as much room as possible to protect the interests of other claimants—whose claims, after all, may be better. In other words, we may demand that an object should not be destroyed unless unavoidable, that if it must be destroyed it should be replaced by an identical object, that if this is impossible an equivalent object should be made available, and that if the last is also impossible, a proper compensation should be provided.

Thus far, the restraint principle seems to be a logical implication of the argument for a savings principle: it is consistent with individual self-interest, even to the degree that it minimizes risks for risk-avoiders, and it ensures that future generations inherit as much as they can without present generations losing anything essential. Yet the demand that nothing be destroyed 'unless necessary' might form a weak spot in the restraint principle. In point of fact, it depends on the contents of the specific liberal theory of justice where exactly the border lies between necessity and indulgence. As far as the restraint principle is concerned, the problem is not where this border lies but whether it makes sense to draw a border like this at all.

In everyday life, we actually do make a distinction between what I would like to call (basic) needs and (further) wants. Extreme situations excluded, we would say that 'mere survival' is a pure need and 'the fiftieth Rolls Royce' a pure want. What justifies this distinction—both in everyday life and in theory—is, for one part, the fact that some but not all goods, acts, rights, etc. are necessary conditions for a tolerable life and necessary but not sufficient preconditions for a morally good or rewarding or full life.[39] What the latter consists of is, again, up to the individual theorist to decide. Secondly, we have a moral duty to care about the availability of these necessary preconditions more than we have for the presence of less important goods. Only if these basic conditions have been met can humans be free to take responsibility for their own behaviour and actions—only then can they be moral agents.

Assuming then that the difficulty of defining a precise criterion of 'need' or 'necessity' cannot count against the in itself sensible idea of a distinction between basic needs and further wants, the restraint principle can be as valid and sensible as the principle of which it is an interpretation: the savings principle for justice between generations.

4. *Conclusions*

As we saw in the first two sections, the new version of Rawls's argument for a savings principle to promote justice between generations is valid both under the conditions of Rawls's own original position and in the context of liberal theories of justice in general, provided they meet some quite innocent criteria. To rephrase this part of the argument in a very compressed form: all rational individuals who stand to gain from social co-operation and who live together as members of different generations will also find a savings principle to be to their advantage, provided it is formulated so that they will want previous generations to have followed it as well. Being mutually beneficial, rejection of such a principle would be irrational. This makes justice between generations, and the savings principle in particular, a necessary condition for the stability and (therefore) survival of a liberal society.

In the previous section, we discovered that there is at least one way in which this abstract idea of 'a' savings principle can be given more body. Since the distribution of rights depends on the strength of arguments, since arguments for an act x can only justify x and any acts necessary to x, and since such arguments are only valid at the time of, or for the duration of, x, any argument like that necessarily lacks support for an act that is *not* necessary to x. We reformulated this conclusion in the form of the restraint principle, which demands that conditional rights are user rights and that they cannot include a right to destroy the object of a right unless destruction is unavoidable, in which case the good in question should be replaced or restored, or a proper compensation should be provided—in declining order of preference.

Because a savings principle for justice between generations is a necessary condition for the survival of liberal democracy, viz. a reasonable scheme of co-operation between co-existing subsequent generations, and because the restraint principle is a justifiable interpretation of the idea of a savings principle, the restraint principle itself becomes a necessary condition of liberal democracy.

It is worthwhile considering some of the implications of this conclusion for a moment. A first implication should not be too surprising: if there are rights that can only be distributed on a conditional basis, then property rights can no longer be considered sacrosanct. We already know that they are not absolute in real life and positive law, we now also have confirmation that they need not be absolute from a moral point of view, that is, that they cannot only be distributed but also redistributed.

Secondly, the restraint principle quite elegantly solves part of the problem of justice between existing, and therefore, morally relevant generations and non-existing, and therefore, not necessarily relevant generations. It protects the interests of future generations by protecting those of present generations: its effect will be that we leave the world no worse than we found it on entry, in so far as that is humanly possible, but its acceptance does not imply that we also accept the NWO or any other fair-weather principle.

The restraint principle also extends existing connections between the mainstream debate on social justice and the more marginal debate on justice between generations by what comes down to one simple move: recognizing that abstract 'generations' are not distinct entities that appear on, and disappear from, the stage one after the other, but exist as contemporaries of different ages involved in the same co-operative venture. This same move makes it possible to ignore the delicate question of the moral status of non-existent persons and generations without denying that obligations may exist.

Moreover, the restraint principle creates a link between these two debates and the debate in green political theory on the preconditions for a sustainable society. Note, for example, that the restraint principle protects more than humans only: it also incorporates non-human nature. The restraint principle demands that, unless there is no way to avoid it, no rock, animal or plant should be destroyed, no species made extinct. It also demands that if this is impossible, the most similar possible alternative should be made available: nature should be replaced by nature, not by concrete. It puts the onus of proof for the legitimacy of environmentally harmful acts on the bad guys.

Fifthly and finally, the restraint principle, as a moral principle, points to some serious shortcomings in real life with regard to the preconditions present society creates for future generations. The fact that the restraint principle allows one to criticize practice from an 'internal' liberal-democratic point of view rather than from an external, 'green' perspective is, in this context, perhaps less important than the discovery that these stains on the reputation of liberalism are for real.

8

Sustainable Development and the Accumulation of Capital: Reconciling the Irreconcilable?

TED BENTON

1. Introduction

In economic, environmental, and development policy communities, in the planning departments of Local Authorities, in the public statements of Non Government Organizations (NGOs), government departments, big firms, and international agencies, and even in the thinking of radical 'green' social movement organizations, the concept of 'sustainable development' has near-sacred status. But the apparent consensus disappears as one investigates the diversity of meanings attached to the term in its deployments by these very different interests and organizations.[1] In this chapter I want to explore a small part of this diversity in uses of the idea, focusing on a central tension between the radical normative aspirations of the concept in its paradigmatic exposition, on the one hand, and the obstacles to the realization of those aspirations posed by key features of the current distribution

I have benefited greatly from participation in the discussions of the Red-Green Study Group, and the wider Green Left. I have learned much and gained inspiration from successive groups of graduate and undergraduate students at Essex University. I was also privileged to participate in the ESRC-sponsored discussions on Sustainability and Social Justice held at Keele University, and to receive the patient and generous editorial help of Andrew Dobson. Finally, I would like to acknowledge the ESRC's award of a senior research fellowship (H52427505494).

of economic, military, and political power, on the other. This exploration will pay attention to the institutional context under which the 'discourse' of sustainable development emerged and subsequently came to hegemonize policy-formation and legitimation in the areas of environmental protection and economic development. The chapter concludes with a brief analysis of the prospects and limitations of a strategic use of the normative dimension of the notion of sustainable development in struggles against an unjust and destructive world-order.

As W. M. Adams shows, the idea of sustainable development is a synthesis of several quite heterogeneous patterns of thought and normative concerns.[2] Among these is, first, a primarily Western tradition of nature preservation, linked initially to hunting interests as well as scientific ecology, which fed into international pressure on Third World (here and elsewhere I use admittedly inadequate terms such as 'Third World', 'North/South', 'developed/underdeveloped' and so on merely to indicate radical unevenness and inequality in the world economy) countries to maintain nature reserves in the post-colonial period. A quite distinct source was the explosion of concern at the end of the 1960s about global growth-dynamics in a finite world. Though the global models which predicted 'overshoot and collapse' unless decisive action was taken were widely criticized, the moral panic they generated did succeed in getting ecological destruction onto an emerging global political agenda.

However, there was more than one strand to this new field of concern. One dimension was properly described as 'neo-Malthusian' in its alarm about population growth.[3] Since the rates of growth were highest in the Third World, the policy implication was that to avoid global disaster, Third World leaders had to be persuaded to take action on population limitation. Where, as in the more widely discussed *Limits to Growth* report,[4] the analysis was broadened to include the resource and pollution implications of industrial growth, there were still requirements to be made of Third World countries: if their aspirations to 'development' were to be realized, this would take us well beyond the carrying capacity of the earth. The panic, then, concerned not just Third World population growth, but also the ecological implications of global generalization of existing Western levels of industrialization and material living standards.

The synthesis which eventually gave rise to the idea of sustainable development emerged in the preparatory discussions for the United Nations Conference on The Human Environment held in Stockholm in 1972. In essence, concern about environmental protection was perceived by many Third World political leaders as a priority for the richer, industrialized nations which, having degraded their own environments, wished to prevent necessary development in poor countries. There was also understandable suspicion on the part of previously colonized countries that environmentalism was a cover for a new form of imperialism. In order to ensure the necessary involvement of a substantial number of Third World governments it proved necessary to demonstrate positive linkages between development and environmental protection: the simple opposition between growth and finite limits had somehow to be softened.

The conference led to the establishment of the United Nations Environment Programme and provided the stimulus for the subsequent *World Conservation Strategy.*[5] In Adams' view this document remains residually neo-Malthusian, with the primary emphasis on conservation, but now justified in terms of the benefits for humans of sustainable management or protection of ecosystems, as well as wild and cultivated genetic diversity. Between 1980 and the publication of the Brundtland report, *Our Common Future,*[6] the emergent discourse of sustainable development became more fully integrated into deep concerns about world poverty, and the glaring inequalities perpetuated by prevailing patterns of global trade and capital flow. The work of the Brundtland Commission coincided with famine in Africa, which claimed an estimated one million lives, the pesticide leak at Bhopal, which killed two thousand people and blinded or otherwise injured some two hundred thousand, and the catastrophic Chernobyl nuclear accident. The notion that we were witnessing a crisis of global dimensions, in which socio-economic and ecological aspects were inseparably intertwined was manifest.

Our Common Future argued for synergy between growth (as necessary to the development aspirations of the South) and environmental protection. The case was made that poverty is an important cause of environmental degradation, so that growth aimed at the alleviation of poverty can serve the twin aims of social justice and environmental protection. It was further claimed that ecologically irresponsible growth policies can hinder further industrial development through undermining necessary environmental conditions of production itself. The kind of development pursued in the already industrialized world had raised living standards at too high a cost in terms of resource use and pollution. A qualitatively different 'development path' would be required to meet the aspirations of the world's poor in an environmentally sustainable way. The key point here is that the report questions the (neo-Malthusian) assumption that economic growth is directly correlated with environmental degradation, and so limited by fixed environmental parameters ('carrying capacity'). Technological innovation and improved social organization can be looked to as ways of getting the benefits of global economic growth without risking environmental disaster. A central feature of this vision is enhanced management of environmental resources in the interests of 'sustainable development'. The oft-quoted Brundtland definition of this concept, (development which 'meets the needs of the present without compromising the ability of future generations to meet their needs'[7]), ingeniously rivets together the major concerns of inter- and intragenerational justice with the demand for environmental protection.

The project envisaged in the report is to revitalize the global economy, in 'a new era of economic growth'. But for growth to meet the criteria of sustainable development it must be targetted at alleviating the conditions of the world's poor, and 'based on policies that sustain and expand the environmental resource base.'[8] The view of the social justice dimension of sustainable development offered by Brundtland gives priority to the 'basic needs' of the poor, but it also speaks of giving opportunities for all to 'fulfil their aspirations for a better life,'[9] and of the poor getting their 'fair share' of the resources necessary for growth. The aim of equity will be furthered by greater 'citizen participation in decision making', and greater democracy in international affairs.

2. Some Normative Issues

This normative vision and the analysis which underpins it is very persuasive, but serious doubts can be raised about it, both as a source of normative criteria, and as a practical project. First, there is some equivocation in the way the report conceptualizes intragenerational justice. Securing the 'basic' needs of everyone as a priority[10] conforms to most 'lay' notions of justice, as well as to the core moral intuition of Rawls's influential 'difference principle'. However, given the extreme inequalities now evident both within each society and across the globe, the scale of redistribution required to meet the basic needs of the poor might be relatively slight compared with a more ambitious aim of a 'fair' or 'equitable' distribution of the world's wealth. Moreover, the proposal that opportunities to fulfil ambitions for a better life should be extended to everyone suggests that the vision is of a development path which benefits even the currently affluent. The implication is an expectation of growth in the world economy which will meet the needs of the poor without demanding politically risky costs to living standards in the industrialized countries.

A second set of problems has to do with the concept of need itself. Given the global character of the project defined by 'sustainable development', a cross-culturally valid concept of need would be required. The reference to 'basic needs' suggests a hierarchy of needs, in which some requirements get priority over others. This might mean, for example, treating requirements of organic survival—physical security, food, water, clothing—as 'basic' compared with more culturally specific requirements such as rights of religious observance, or preservation of culturally meaningful traditional ties to particular places. Alternatively, it might mean giving priority to certain requirements over others which might still be held to be universally applicable—such as emotional security, civil liberties, freedom of conscience and 'self-actualization', (as in Maslow's immensely influential theory of need[11]).

Either way there are difficulties. For many people, attachment to culturally specific requirements is more important even than the meeting of basic physical need. Not only are there many instances of willingness to sacrifice life in the defence of abstract values such as 'freedom', ethnic identity, and the 'fatherland', but there is also the experience of profound demoralization and self-destructiveness which commonly results from the displacement of indigenous peoples by 'development' projects. Similarly with Maslovian hierarchies of need. There is a tendency to confuse questions of causal with moral priorities: certainly we must eat if we are to think, but it does not follow that eating gets moral priority over thinking.

The very distinction between basic and non-basic needs is problematic for (at least!) two reasons. One is that the force of the concept of need itself is compromised. The difference between a need and a mere want, or preference, has to do with the necessity of the former, and it is this connotation of necessity which gives the attribution of needs its moral power. Either something is necessary, or it is not. One way to deal with this problem is to distinguish between orders of need in terms of their necessity for the meeting of various purposes. So, for example, we might distinguish mere survival from flourishing, thriving, or living well. Basic needs might be the set of requirements for survival, whilst higher order needs might be required for flourishing. But, (and this is the second difficulty), to accept basic needs in this sense as defining priorities is to aquiesce in a grossly reductive view of human nature. The kind of operation mounted by aid agencies in the face of refugee or famine emergencies, where large populations are gathered in camps, and provided with basic necessities of food, water, shelter, and (hopefully) physical security comes close to this. Clearly these operations are necessary as responses to immediate emergencies. However, they presuppose a view of 'basic needs' as survival requirements which is appropriate to (again, hopefully) short-term interventions, but could not be acceptable as a normative criterion for long-run 'sustainable development'.

To anticipate somewhat, my claim is that for humans there is an irreducibly normative, and, more broadly, cultural dimension to the social practices through which needs are met. To meet needs in a way which is proper, or appropriate to humanity is to meet them in ways which satisfy normative, cultural requirements. So, for humans to meet their need for food is not solely a matter of consuming a certain necessary minimum bundle of nutrients, but it is a matter of collecting, preparing, and socially consuming what are culturally recognized as foods according to the customs and standards of the people involved. So, through participating in one and the same social practice, people affirm and reproduce their cultural identities and meet their nutritional requirements, but this may also be a medium through which emotional bonds are established and social solidarities maintained. From this example we can see that what in some societies may become hived off as institutionally separate opportunities to satisfy 'higher' needs (theatre, music, art) may also be understood as implicated as 'moments', or aspects of social practices which also satisfy 'basic' needs. The suggestion here is that instead of a formal hierarchy of needs determining priorities in the allocation of goods, we should think, rather, in terms of modes of life, comprising patterns of social practices, whose integrity allows for a multi-dimensional meeting of the needs of participants.[12]

We can take this line of argument a little further. To recognize multi dimensionality in human need, and to think of needs as integrally involved with one another in the practices through which they are satisfied is to cast doubt on the coherence of some of the most widely used formulations and practised instruments for reconciling considerations of justice with the requirements of 'development'. Where indigenous people are displaced, there is generally a commitment to 'compensation', or to relocation. In the case of biodiversity conservation, the Convention on Biological Diversity acknowledges the obligation on the part of the developed countries to share the 'benefits' of biotechnologies developed through their access to Third World resources and to financially support poorer countries in meeting their obligations under the Convention. In both cases there is a presumption of substitutability, and of equivalence in exchange, between various possible 'satisfiers' of needs.

However, in the case of people who are physically displaced by development projects, developers and governments commonly promise 'compensation'. There are numerous case-studies of the catastrophic consequences of failure to deliver on these promises—to the point where such failures can be seen as inherent structural features of this type of 'development' project. A recent example is the displacement of indigenous people by the construction of the Chixoy dam in Guatemala. A leaked World Bank document reflected on the 'mismanagement' of the resettlement of 2,500 Mayan indians displaced by the dam. This involved '369 Mayan Indians—mainly women and children—being tortured, shot, stabbed, garrotted, and bludgeoned to death by the Guatemalan military in punishment for their community demanding they be properly compensated for the loss of their homes to the dam'.[13] Worldwide some 60 million people have been forcibly displaced to make way for big dam projects since 1950, with consequent homelessness, unemployment, disease, hunger, and loss of cultural identity.[14] But even in the event of 'compensation' promises being kept, with the relatively successful targeting of 'basic needs' for shelter, food, clothing, and so on, the integrity of a mode of life which connects people with one another both in the present and across the generations, and also links them with the physical contexts and media of their social lives, has been destroyed.[15]

In cases where 'compensation' takes financial form, or a promise of technology transfer, other problems arise. Financial compensation is only of use to people to the extent that they already do, or are able to be tempted into meeting their needs through capitalist market relations. The same is true of technology transfer. Technologies should not be thought of as disembedded units of 'tackle' which can be made to serve human purposes, more-or-less independently of their physical and socio-cultural context. To accept genetically modified crops, or high-yield varieties of staple foods as developed by the R and D departments of the big agribusiness companies is to be committed to a whole-scale transformation of local agro-ecosystems and of rural class relations, bringing with it a growing integration with, and dependence upon, international flows of capital and goods.[16]

So, what is presented in the text as a fair exchange of benefits turns out in the real world of differential power relations between North and South, and globalizing capitalist relations, to be a powerful force for extending the reach of market relations into localized and often largely subsistence-based agricultural and indigenous communities. There is, of course, room for debate about whether it is in the interests of such local communities to be integrated within the sphere of international markets and capital accumulation. It can be argued, for example, that patriarchal relations in some such 'traditional' communities are such that giving women opportunities for wage labour, even at very low rates of pay and under poor working conditions, can still be in relative terms empowering for them.[17] Also, as this implies, it may be that some groups will benefit while others lose. At this point there arise fundamental questions about the diversity of sources of inequality and social division within 'communities'. Not only would any adequate understanding of the moral issues involved have to take into account the interconnections of ethnicity, race, gender, class, caste, and lineage-based divisions, but also the connections of all of these with differential access and control over environmental resources and conditions. However, the very existence of this debate is an index of the untenability of the *assumption* that those values which are lost when development deals are struck can be calculated in a common unit of exchange with the benefits 'development' is supposed to bring.

So, the 'development deals' on offer within the post-Rio framework of sustainable development are not redistributive in any straightforward sense, to be compared with, say, cash benefits to the poor in an already industrialized market society. They are interventions which transform peoples' relationships both to one another and to their physical and biological conditions of life. As they do so, they not only meet existing needs, (if, indeed, they do even this), but also generate new patterns of need and dependency.

Questions of justice are clearly appropriate to situations such as these, but it is hard to see how either liberal or communitarian approaches to distributive justice are adequate to the moral challenge they pose. The Rawlsian difference principle supposes a common unit according to which we can judge who is better, who is worse off. The abstract individualism of the difference principle also renders it insensitive to the importance of the quality of meaningful relations between participants in a form of social life as constitutive of their well-being. The difference, for example, between co-operative and 'mutualist' divisions of labour, governed by shared normative understandings, and divisions based on the cash nexus, is such that participants may judge themselves to be better or worse off, quite independently of any resource transfers to individuals. The shift in many UK educational institutions from centralized accounting to devolved budgets and internal markets is a good example of this. Of course, this could be dealt with by excluding such considerations from the sphere of distributive justice, whilst still recognizing their wider moral significance. However, to do so would be to drastically narrow the range of goods (and bads) whose distribution could be evaluated in terms of considerations of justice. Implicitly, therefore, such a narrow conception of justice would beg the question in favour of those patterns of institutions, mainly liberal democratic capitalist ones, which come closest to its social ontology and implicit view of human nature (competitive-individualist, material-welfare maximizing, achievement-oriented, and so on).

For rather different reasons, 'development' as conventionally understood poses serious challenges to a communitarian view of justice. For one thing, the proposed 'development deals' span 'communities' which are not just spatially but also morally and culturally far apart. Making development aid contingent on improvements in human rights, the empowerment of women, or grass-roots participation in decision-making, for example, often does not conform to the values of would-be recipient states. Moreover, the normative frame brought to bear by such states themselves may express the interests or cultural values of social elites which have access to state power, as against the norms and values of local communities whose lives are to be directly affected by big development projects. Which community and whose values take precedence? Finally, since the transformation and/or fragmentation of local communities is an invariable consequence (intended or not) of development strategies, there is a paradox in the acknowledgement of 'community' as the grounding for norms of justice, and support for forms of intervention which set in motion the undermining of community integrity. If this is right, then consistent communitarians must oppose such forms of development deal, no matter how unjust, (by outside standards), such traditional local communities might appear to be.

3. Practicalities: Sustainability and Contemporary Capitalism

So far I have suggested that the most persuasive version of the concept of sustainable development, Brundtland, still leaves some important questions unanswered in its linkage of justice with the concept of need. The moral and political significance of these unanswered questions can be illuminated by considering what the 'development deal' signalled in the discourse of sustainable development, and in the international conventions which spell it out in more detail, implies in terms of practical implementation in the current world-order. A very understandable response from an advocate of the concept would be to acknowledge that the empirical cases which are the grounds for my expressions of disquiet are examples of 'development' conducted under the old rules—they are exactly the kinds of disastrous intervention which the project of sustainable development is designed to displace. It is quite true that 'Agenda 21', which seeks to give substantive policy content to the new vision of development, does emphasize the importance of decentralizing decision-making to local communities, facilitating of grass-roots participation, empowering of disadvantaged and marginalized sections of communities, using appropriate technologies, and so on. The Convention on Biological Diversity, also, clearly enjoins the contracting parties to 'respect, preserve and maintain knowledge, innovations and practices of indigenous and local communities embodying traditional lifestyles relevant for the conservation and sustainable use of biological diversity and promote their wider application.'[18]

This is an important objection to my line of argument so far. It is certainly true that big international players such as the World Bank and some transnational companies have responded to NGO and social movement pressure. The withdrawal of the World Bank from the Narmada Dam project in India, and Shell's promise of 'openness, transparency and consultations' in its Amazonian operations following global condemnation of its activities in Nigeria[19] are well publicized examples. However, there are many respects in which the legal and institutional proposals issuing from the Rio process, and promulgated through the discourse of sustainable development serve to confirm and regulate the most objectionable features of 'traditional' development. So, to return to the Convention on Biological Diversity: co-existing in its provisions with the lofty sentiments expressed in Article 8, is a clear commitment to the commercial interests of the pharmaceutical and agro-business complexes. The crucial and much contested Article 16(2) states:

In the case of technology subject to patents and other property rights, such access and transfer shall be provided on terms which recognise and are consistent with the adequate and effective protection of intellectual property rights.[20]

Through this provision, the Biodiversity Convention is integrated with the requirements of international patent law which, under powerful pressure from the biotechnology industries, is increasingly friendly to the patenting of living organisms, varieties, and genetic materials. As R. McNally and P. Wheale argue:

But whereas the patenting system, as internationalised under GATT, ensures that advanced industrial countries reap the benefits of the transfer of their comparative advantage—gene technology—there is no equivalent international system whereby less developed countries can ensure they gain the benefits of their comparative advantage, biodiversity. . . . Although biodiversity is unique and the result of the stewardship of indigenous peoples who have recognised, protected, developed and utilized its potential over many years, it cannot be left alone and patented in situ. The patent system rewards extraction, not conservation and stewardship.[21]

In other words, not only is this 'development deal' undermined in its redistributive aims but also in its preservationist aspirations, as expressed in Article 8, by the current international trading regime.

There is also now a growing body of case-study evidence of ways in which some Western-based conservation organizations are prepared to ignore, or even collaborate with extreme state-sponsored violence against indigenous peoples in the interests of wild-life conservation. It is alleged, for example, that tens of thousands of the Karen people of Burma have been forced to work unpaid on infrastructural development, whilst some 30,000 more have fled into the jungle or across the border into Thailand. This is because they live in an area being developed by the Burmese government into one of the largest nature reserves in the world. According to recent first-hand accounts '. . . the Burmese army is clearing the Karen area, razing entire villages, killing, raping, enslaving.'[22] The project is expected to attract millions of eco-tourists, and also includes the laying of a gas-pipeline by Total and Unocal. The Burmese government claims the support of the respected World Conservation Society and the Smithsonian Institution. A spokesperson for the former is quoted as saying: 'We do not sanction forced relocation, torture or killings. But we have no control over the government. We are in Burma because it is one of the highest biodiversity countries in Asia.'

Nevertheless, the normative commitments to long-run protection of cultural and biological diversity, and to distributive justice remain integral to the most widely advocated visions of sustainable development. Even if specific conventions and treaties equivocate, compromise, and retreat, and even if what remains is undermined by the institutional and power relations under which such documents are 'implemented', there may still be something worthwhile in the mere statement of the aspiration. The concept of sustainable development and the various authoritative texts which put it into the arena of public debate can provide a legitimate basis for social movements to criticize particular projects and institutions in terms of their own declared aims. I will return to an evaluation of this more critical use of the discourse of sustainable development it a later stage of the argument.

For the moment, there are some other features of 'sustainable development' which demand exploration. Thus far we have considered, rather too briefly, the concept of sustainable development primarily from the standpoint of intragenerational justice, the concern with meeting 'the needs of the present'. The introduction into the concept of concern for the needs of future

generations is what distinguishes the idea of 'sustainable' development from other 'alternative' and radical approaches to
development. The critical literature surrounding the concept is,
of course, full of questions about this idea. How many future
generations are we to be concerned with—or does the concept
require sustainability into the indefinite future? How do we know
what the needs of future generations will be? How can we weigh
the demands for justice of those who live today against the
hypothetical demands of people who do not yet exist? Given
current advances in genetic knowledge and engineering, how do
we know what future generations will be like? Given the profound
cultural changes which have occurred in most societies even
within the last generation, how do we know what future generations will want? In terms of available natural resources, how can
we know whether it will matter to future generations that we use
up finite supplies. It may be that future technologies may make
future generations independent of resources which are currently
indispensable, or that we destroy things which have no utility for
us. (Future technologies may render essential features of the
natural world which to us seem quite useless.)

These are all important questions, but here I want to focus on
the status of the norm of sustainability itself. I take it that the term
refers to a property which a practice, or maybe a complex of
practices making up a social formation may or may not have—i.e.
the property of being able to be maintained through (more or less
extensive) spans of time. This, in turn, can be analysed in terms of
the longevity of the elements, relations, and external conditions
set in motion by the practice(s), and the availability of the means
of replacing them as they die, wear out, get used up, degraded,
and so on. Sustainability, in other words, concerns what historical
materialists call 'social reproduction'. When requirements for
social reproduction are not met, or when their availability
becomes problematic, the result may be a 'crisis' of the social
system. It is important to bear in mind that social reproduction
can be rendered problematic in a variety of different ways.
Habermas, for example, wrote of 'legitimation crises' deriving
from the *ad hoc* character of state interventions into the economic
system under late capitalism, and 'motivation crises' deriving from

dislocations between system-requirements and the life-worlds of individuals. For Habermas these forms of crisis were displacements of the crisis tendencies endemic in earlier phases of capitalist development, which manifested themselves as directly economic: recurrent periods of business failure and mass unemployment alternating with periods of economic expansion.[23]

The various traditions of twentieth-century Marxism and Critical Theory have tended to focus their accounts of crisis tendencies and endemic instabilities on social relational contradictions and dislocations internal to the social system. However, more recent work, associated with the American writer Jim O'Connor[24] and others associated with the journal *Capitalism, Nature, Socialism*[25] have begun to theorize the forms of social crisis which derive from the characteristic relationship between specifically capitalist economic relations and their external conditions. In O'Connor's view there is an inherent tendency for capitalist economic growth (expanded reproduction of capital) to degrade or destroy the very conditions for its own continuation. This contradiction between the forces, (and relations), of production and the conditions of production is referred to as a 'second contradiction of capitalism'. (The first being that between capital and labour.) In O'Connor's account the conditions of production include infrastructures of various kinds, agricultural land, and workers themselves, as well as naturally 'given' conditions such as pollution-sinks, material and energy resources, and other broadly ecological conditions. The systemic crises resulting from this contradiction cannot be resolved by firms at the economic level, and they generate pressure for state intervention to repair and restore degraded or destroyed conditions to enable further capital accumulation. This is the broad framework of analysis for an understanding of environmental politics in capitalist societies.

Without engaging in a detailed discussion of O'Connor's argument we can, I think, use its broad outlines as a way of posing some questions about 'sustainability' in an increasingly globalized capitalist economy.[26] First, why should we think there is a tendency for capitalist production to undermine its own conditions? A seemingly obvious answer might be that the logic of capitalist competition generates a long-run growth tendency in the system, inevitably producing more pollution and making more demands on natural resources. But this would be to fall back into the questionable neo-Malthusian assumption that growth as such and environmental protection are incompatible. Are there any reasons for expecting *specifically capitalist* economic growth to be inherently environmentally damaging? One reason for thinking so begins with the same recognition as neoclassical environmental economics. This is that many environmental 'goods' are free-access or common-property goods which are in limited supply, contribute to wealth creation, but are unpriced. Neoclassical assumptions lead us to expect such goods to be over-used and so degraded or destroyed. Thus, for example, D. Pearce *et al.* argue:

The elementary theory of supply and demand tells us that if something is provided at a zero price, more of it will be demanded than if there was a positive price . . . For example, by treating the ozone layer as a resource with a zero price there never was any incentive to protect it. Its value to human populations and to the global environment in general did not show up anywhere in a balance sheet of profit or loss, or of costs and benefits.[27]

The policy implications on the same assumptions are that environmental goods would be protected if they could be turned into capitalist private property and traded at their true market value, or, if that proved impractical, treated 'as if' they had a market price, and their use introduced into economic calculations on that assumption.

For the moment, let us distinguish the diagnosis from the treatment. The neoclassical diagnosis is an acknowledgement that environmental degradation is endemic to capitalist markets, so long as environmental 'goods' and services are not fully integrated into the market system—that is to say, so long as they are not produced, reproduced, bought, and sold as other commodities are. Now, most environmental economists acknowledge that it is impractical to fully commodify all environmental goods. Some necessary infrastructural investment will not be made by private capital because it is too risky, or has no prospect of sufficient return on capital. Some naturally given conditions, such as fresh air, have a physical character which, so far, prevents exclusive private appropriation, whilst others have characteristics of temporal duration such that there are inherent limits to rates of return on capital invested. In still other cases there are restraints deriving from the political and cultural systems—the obstacles to fully capitalist production of children in relation to labour markets derive from both sources. For anyone thinking of starting a family now it would be difficult to predict the state of the labour market at the point when the contemplated offspring would be old enough to enter it, and even if such predictions were available there might hopefully be some resistance to the idea that the prospect of selling the labour power of one's offspring for a profit should be the prime motivation for parenthood.

This being generally accepted, it follows that reproduction of the conditions of production in general, and environmental protection in particular cannot be left to the market. The idea generally favoured by environmental economists is that we should rig markets in such a way that economic agents have to behave *as if* environmental goods had prices. As Michael Jacobs has pointed out, the common assumption that there is a radical difference between market instruments and old fashioned 'command and control' in environmental policy is mistaken.[28] Direct government control over environmentally relevant behaviour and such devices as tradable permits and green taxes are both forms of intervention in markets, and both of them require significant extensions in the exercise of state power.

We have, then, an interesting consensus between neo-Marxist and neoclassical economists to the effect that left to themselves, capitalist market forces degrade their own environmental conditions. Capitalist growth is not sustainable without effective extraeconomic policy interventions to constrain environmentally damaging patterns of economic calculation. This poses three related questions. Are there reasons for thinking that current forms of institutionalization of capitalist economic organization are especially likely to generate environmental problems? If so, what are the prospects, given current institutions and power relations, for resolving those problems? What relationship do rival interpretations of the idea of sustainable development have to the moral and political issues posed by our answers to the first two questions? The discourse of sustainable development broke from the prior assumption that growth and sustainability were incompatible, but it retained the assumption that capitalist economic growth was both compatible with, and necessary to, the meeting of need and the fairer distribution of the world's resources. This may be a further assumption which we need to break from.

First, then, is contemporary capitalism inherently ecologically destructive? There can be no doubt that capitalism is a broad framework for organizing economic life which has shown the most extraordinary flexibility in adapting itself to the most unlikely contexts and innovating to meet recurrent challenges and obstacles. Its success has been so overwhelming that few now contemplate the feasibility of a post-capitalist future. However, serious obstacles are looming, some of them consequences of its very success. In considering some of these, it will be helpful to distinguish between the mechanisms which generate crises in the relation between capital accumulation and its external conditions, on the one hand, and the potential obstacles to successful extra-economic strategies for crisis resolution, on the other.

Among the reasons why there is a general tendency for capitalist economies to degrade their environmental conditions is that they institutionalize two 'logics', or modes of calculation which have no necessary mutual correspondence. They embody a commercial logic, which works on the assumption that all costs and benefits can be aggregated into magnitudes of a single, monetary unit, and so are on that basis mutually exchangeable, and seeks to minimize costs for the sake of maximal returns on investment. This is also a logic which sets a higher value on present than on future benefits (discounting). However, this purpose can only be met on condition that capitalist firms also embody another 'logic', according to which differently skilled and qualified workers are employed to carry out different tasks in an overall division of labour, and hierarchy of command, using energy resources, tools and machinery, raw materials, physical space, etc. in appropriate proportions for the production of marketable goods or services. Although scientific and technical innovation may render these elements in the 'labour process' mutually substitutable on a one-by-one basis, for any more-or-less delimited period, the *qualitative* differences between the different conditions, media, materials, agents, and products of the enterprise and the appropriate mix between them all, set definite boundary conditions to the operation of the enterprise, and so are absolutely central to its sustainable management.

Now, given that the selective pressures which determine survival of the unit of capital are those of success or failure in market competition, it is the commercial logic which predominates over and sets the demands which the labour process logic is required to meet. It is thus the 'logic' of abstract monetary calculation and the drive for maximum short-term gains which predominates over the forms of calculation appropriate to the labour process—understood as a practice which combines together qualitatively incommensurable skills, materials, and techniques under definite external conditions in the production of 'concrete' use-values. This is the core dynamic which drives the tendency of production under capitalist market relations to stretch and override its boundary conditions, and so to over-exploit both its labour force and its ecological and infrastructural supports. Whilst neoclassical economics acknowledges that non-marketed goods are liable to be over-exploited, the above analysis suggests that there is a *dynamic tendency* in market systems for this to happen. Moreover, it suggests that this is a consequence not of market 'failure', but of the very forms of calculation (maximization of abstract value, as distinct from production of qualitatively differentiated use-values) which constitute markets.

But there are reasons to think that this general tendency of capitalist markets is likely to operate with increased intensity under contemporary forms of institutionalization of capitalist relations. There are five broad features which are significant here. Four of them are included within the currently fashionable topic of 'globalization'. The first is the increasing ratio of internationally traded to domestically traded goods, and the increasing mobility of capital across national boundaries. The second related tendency is the continued rise in dominance of financial over industrial and commercial capital. The third is the increasing significance in the world economy of transnational corporations.

The fourth is the international trading regime operated by the World Trade Organization (WTO). These developments are, of course, facilitated by new communications technologies and more rapid modes of transportation. These changes in the international organization of capitalist production and distribution all intensify what Anthony Giddens has called the 'disembedding' of economic activity.[29] That is to say, economic wealth creation is increasingly detached from dependence upon, and constraints entailed by, local conditions of action. Transnational logging companies can and do make short-term profits by unsustainable exploitation of local forests and then shift operations to other countries. Large-scale investors in financial markets are able to shift capital from one branch of industry to another in pursuit of short-term gain without bearing any responsibility for the consequences for local jobs or environments. The international trading regime outlaws as 'protectionist' attempts by national governments to use environmental considerations to regulate its foreign trading relations ('As feared, in every case brought before it to date, the WTO has ruled in favour of corporate interest, striking down national and subnational legislation protecting the environment and public health at every turn'[30]).

The fifth environmentally problematic feature of the current phase of capitalist development is the large-scale incorporation of scientific and technical innovation into the product development and marketing operations of large-scale industry. Not only has there been a big shift of research into the private sector in all of the OECD countries, but public sector research is increasingly funded according to criteria which highlight potential for commercial exploitation. Some commentators, most notably Anthony Giddens and Ulrich Beck, draw attention to the 'high consequence' risks associated with at least some of the new large-scale technologies, such as nuclear power generation, chemical plant, and genetic engineering.[31] These risks are held to be ineliminable (but rather rendered 'improbable'), and potentially catastrophic. We might add to these another category of risks—such as BSE/CJD—which derive not from new technologies but rather from the new forms of intensive food production and industrial processing combined with neo-liberal pressure for deregulation.[32]

4. Reform Environmentalism and its Limits (Deregulation as an 'Own Goal')

However, the very recognition that these features of the current world economy are generating both socio-economic and ecological damage on an unprecedented scale is one source of the discourse of sustainable development. Whilst the 'disembedding' of economic action from the forms of control exercised by nation states, (often in response to labour and environmental movement pressure), boosted economic growth on a global scale, the finite character of that global arena soon became apparent, though not quite in the way the *Limits* team had expected. The emergence of a new order of global ecological issues such as climate change, ozone depletion, the loss of wild and cultivated biodiversity, was the outcome both of the threat to future capital accumulation posed by the social and ecological consequences of previous decades of unregulated growth and of the recognition by technocratic and business elites that this was the case.

But any serious political economy of the growing Northern demand for environmental protection has to recognize that not all industrial sectors operating internationally favour such regulation. Petrochemical and other mineral extraction and connected industrial interests generally do not, and as is well known, have formed effective 'anti-greenhouse' coalitions. Also, those sectors which do demand regulation have interests in very different kinds of regulation. So, for example, tropical biodiversity is increasingly seen as an important arena for research and product development by the mainly Northern-based pharmaceutical industry. International agreements are required to ensure *in situ* protection of this biodiversity, but such agreements are of no use unless they also confer rights of access to the companies, and property rights in the resulting products. Bilateral deals between transnational companies and nation states can often secure these conditions more effectively than can international conventions. One example of this is the deal between US-based Merck Pharmaceuticals and the Costa Rican National Biodiversity Institute. The deal gives Merck the right to screen, develop, and patent products from the Costa Rican rain forest. R. McNally and P. Wheale comment:

If the Costa Rican example became a model for countries elsewhere, the world's stock of biodiversity would become the monopolistic property of the handful of companies rich enough to purchase exclusive rights to it. Given that Costa Rica is estimated to hold five per cent of the world's biodiversity, the entire global stock could be sold for just US$20 million.[33]

Uncertainty about the implications for the interests of US-based biotechnology firms was an important source of hesitation on the part of the US government in signing the Convention on Biological Diversity at Rio. By contrast, cultivated biodiversity, which is increasingly important for the agribusiness sector, can often be preserved *ex situ* in gene banks, and does not necessarily require the preservation of 'traditional' farming systems.

So, a significant part (to say the least) of the global environmental agenda is driven by the perceived requirements of large-scale transnational business sectors to secure necessary legal, socio-political and ecological conditions for continued capital accumulation. This is, for them, the core meaning of 'sustainable development'. The hegemony of this interpretation of the concept has been made possible by its translation into the concepts of neoclassical economics.[34] So, even in the work of David Pearce *et al.*, and notwithstanding their undoubted commitment to the environmental cause, there is a detectable transition from the attempt to 'investigate some of the economic underpinnings of the idea of sustainable development'[35] to an outright incorporation of it into the language of economics:

An 'economic function' in this context is any service that contributes to human well-being, to the 'standard of living', or 'development'.[36]

So nature, in so far as it contributes to human well-being is an economic category—'natural capital'. Pearce *et al.* provide arguments for a notion of sustainable development which treats a relatively large part of 'natural capital' as non-substitutable by human-made capital, and therefore deserving of preservation as part of the heritage of future generations. Alan Holland's critical treatment of this idea elsewhere in this volume is exemplary. Suffice it only to add that the environmentalist intentions of Pearce *et al.* are entirely subverted by their incorporation of nature's contribution to human well-being under the concept of 'natural capital'. To assign nature's 'services' a market price which expresses its 'true value',[37] is precisely to include it among the world of commodities, to be exchanged with other commodities of equivalent value: substitutability, in the sense of equivalence to a common standard of measure, is entailed in their endorsement of the commodification of nature.

However, as we have seen, there are strong reasons for thinking that 'the second contradiction of capitalism' cannot be addressed at the level of economic action, but requires extra-economic intervention. But the very shifts in the international organization of capital accumulation that are responsible for the emergence of global socio-ecological obstacles to further capitalist growth also undermine the conditions of possibility for the effective regulation that capital requires. In periods of relative economic closure and immobility of capital, nation states have been quite effective in imposing forms of regulation on firms with respect to health and safety, local environmental externalities, wage rates, working hours, and wider labour-force welfare provision. This has been especially true in industrialized liberal democracies with powerful and unified labour movements. However, the neo-liberal strategy of removal of trade barriers and enhanced international mobility of capital has involved the deliberate abandonment on the part of national governments of large areas of regulatory power, and rendered national economies increasingly dependent on unaccountable international economic conditions and collective actors.

This is sometimes equated with a loss of power on the part of national governments, but in so far as governments are aligned with the interests of increasingly internationalized economic elites the new economic (dis)order empowers them *vis-à-vis* internal labour and other oppositional social movements. The resulting conditions are very favourable for short-term capital accumulation, since they reduce labour costs, enhance the power of managements over working conditions and practices, and the power of firms over local planning authorities and labour market conditions. They also favour the off-loading of infrastructural and environmental costs. However, what may be advantageous to individual firms and some sectors of the economy in the short term may not be favourable to the long-term sustainability of the economy itself, nor to the continuing legitimacy of the prevailing economic and political system. It is the growth of 'elite' recognition of this that has fuelled a certain turning away from the bleak economism of neo-liberalism towards a more centrist weak communitarianism on the part of many intellectuals and politicians of the right. The same recognitions are at work in business and technocratic elite support for strategies of 'sustainable development'.

However, the forms of reinstitutionalization of international political economy listed above have entailed an abandonment on the part of national governments of key areas of economic sovereignty. This means that even where a 'long-termist', enlightened view becomes influential in industrial pressure groups, policy communities, and political parties, the social and political resources to implement the appropriate strategies are simply absent. Public-sector research expertise has been dissipated or privatized, regulatory powers have been either severely weakened or discredited, or both, and taxation has been successfully represented as a social evil. Powerful arguments for 'green taxation' largely fall on deaf ears, partly because governments fear public resistance to further taxation (a resistance fuelled by their own rhetorics), and partly because green taxes, along with high levels of environmental regulation and welfare provision, are strong disincentives to inward capital investment.

Moreover, the ideological sources of social integration which sustained high levels of environmental regulation, social welfare, and security in the post-war period throughout much of Europe have also been undermined by the disintegrative consequences of neo-liberalism wherever it has been hegemonic.

If nation states lack the means to impose the sorts of restraints required to make growth in their 'national' economies sustainable, then the focus for concerted action has to be international and ultimately global diplomacy. The European Union has had some significant success in imposing environmental standards across the

Union, but it is arguable that intensifying international pressures for 'competitiveness' are likely to undermine such environmental and welfare standards that have so far been achieved. At the global level, the work of UNEP and the processes set in motion by the Earth Summit at Rio in 1992, have been the focus of hopes for an international regime of sustainable development. Though Rio was undoubtedly very significant in raising global public awareness of the seriousness of the issues it addressed, the practical outcomes have been very limited. The agreements reached contained few legally binding targets, and vast divisions of interest between different nation states and regions led to a reduction of much of the text to the status of pious rhetoric. Key divisions, especially between the already-industrialized 'North' and the so-called 'developing' countries of the Third World had their roots in the structure of the international economic order. Nothing agreed at Rio significantly affected this, whilst international negotiations on the framework for international trade, and the role of the International Monetary Fund (IMF) which could well have done so, were carried on without reference to the Rio process. As Michael Grubb *et al.* point out:

The interminable references to the special circumstances of the developing countries are nothing to do with restructuring international economic relationships, and little to do with enhanced aid; they are simply protective clauses which assert that developing countries are not committed to anything unless additional money is made available. Since it is clear that money is not remotely available on a scale which is comparable to the estimated needs, this can be seen as casting an immense shadow over the whole UNCED exercise.[38]

There are, then, reasons to fear that current forms of institutionalization in the world economy simultaneously intensify global environmental degradation *and* undermine the conditions of possibility of effective legal and political intervention to resolve the problems posed by it. So, even if we take a narrow view of 'sustainability' as maintaining the conditions for continued (capitalist) economic growth, the prospects for achieving it seem slight, short of very profound changes in global economic relations which go far beyond anything proposed in the Rio agreements.

In the absence of such changes, the prospect is a rather bleak one. There are already signs of increasing use of coercive measures both by powerful nation states and by transnational corporations to ensure access to, and commercial exploitation of key resources. These vary from outright military action, through sponsorship of 'wild' capitalist exploitation of mineral reserves, as in parts of the former Soviet Union, to symbiotic bilateral deals between corporations and repressive Third World regimes.[39]

5. Sustainable Development as Critique?

Taken together, these dynamic tendencies in the current world (dis)order cry out for both social justice and ecological protection, but exhibit few signs of the emergence of means to deliver either. So, if the flawed reform strategy of 'sustainable development' is all that stands between us and this very bleak prospect, there clearly is a case for sceptics to sink their differences, join the 'broad church' of support for environmental reformism, and learn to sing the hymn of sustainable development. This case looks stronger if we remind ourselves of the normative demands of the Brundtland formulation, and some of the formulations of Agenda 21 and other Rio documents. As we saw, there is a shared commitment to prioritizing the basic needs of the poorest communities now, protecting the environmental conditions for the need-meeting of future generations, preserving traditional and indigenous knowledges and ways of life, encouraging participation on the part of marginal and disadvantaged sectors of the population, and extending grass-roots democratic involvement. The above arguments have been an attempt to expose the deep tensions between these normative aspirations, on the one hand, and key features and tendencies in the global political economy, on the other. Given the current institutional forms, power relations and economic norms which govern patterns of growth in the world system, the proposal to 'target' growth at meeting the needs of the poorest whilst preserving the environmental needs of future generations is simply not a feasible option. The prevailing institutional forms are such as to favour the subsumption of residual normative commitments to justice and environmental protection into an economistic reading of 'sustainability' as a project aimed at preserving the resource base for future capital accumulation on a global scale.

But this exploration of the tensions in the idea of sustainable development, given current institutions, suggests the possibility of a critical deployment of the idea which moves, so to speak, in the opposite direction to the dominant reading. This would be to adhere to and strengthen the normative aspirations at the core of the Brundtland approach, whilst using these as a platform from which to argue the case for radical changes in economic organization and ideology: for building institutional means to impose restraints on the mobility of capital and resources, for strengthening local self-sufficiency, and for 're-embedding' economic activity and technical innovation within revitalized democratic civil societies and legal-political orders wherever this is possible. Much of this is implicit if not always explicit in the texts of the Rio process, but there is still too little recognition of how fundamentally this normative project flies in the face of existing institutional frameworks and concentrations of military, economic and political power. If it is to gain ground, any alternative vision of sustainable development must combine its normative commitment to social justice and ecological protection with a critical political economy which can take root in the practice of grass-roots social and political movements.[40] Such movements as the coalitions against big dam construction in India and elsewhere, the international co-ordination of campaigns against rain-forest destruction, involving indigenous peoples, NGOs and media personalities, the increasingly significant 'environmental justice' movement in North America,[41] the 'greening' of the Trade Unions and Labour movement, the emergence of Local Exchange and Trading Schemes, whole-society transitions to green development strategies, such as are currently under way in Cuba,[42] and local projects funded by some of the more radical voluntary aid charities are just so many indications that there remain effective challenges to the hegemony of globalizing capital. Whether these can coalesce around viable long-term alternatives to unsustainable capitalist globalization remains to be seen. My claim is simply that if there is hope, it is in the strengthening of coalitions around such movements and activities, rather than in reliance on the 'green-wash' of the big corporations, and the merely rhetorical adherence to sustainability on the part of many powerful nation states.

But there are three broad respects in which even the normative dimensions of the Brundtland version of sustainable development also stand in need of criticism and correction. The first is the criterion of sustainability itself. The centrality of this concept in the evaluation of economic growth strategies has had the effect of displacing other normative issues relevant to the conduct of economic life. So, for example, an approach to forestry which involves the replacement of old-growth forest by plantation mono-cultures may be defended as sustainable, in that cropping and replanting may be in balance, and many of the ecosystem-functions performed by old-growth forest may be performed equally effectively by the plantation which comes to replace it. For example, Professor J. Lawton of the UK NERC has been quoted as saying:

I think the answer to the question of species redundancy will not please the conservationists. I think that is regrettable. It could turn out that the planet could be an awful lot simpler and still work perfectly well.[43]

However, the loss of biodiversity may be held to be significant both in its own right, and in virtue of the loss of the woodland as a source for subsistence food-gathering, ancillary forest products, and aesthetic meanings for local human populations. Exclusive concern with sustainability implies insensitivity to the multi-dimensional role played by many natural and semi-natural environments in peoples' lives, and the ways these can be jeopardized and undermined by forms of development which may still satisfy the criterion of 'sustainability'.

As we saw above, the Brundtland concept of sustainable development and the 'development deals' constituted in the Rio agreements also countenance technology transfers and financial compensation in exchange for access to traditional and indigenous knowledges and (for example) biological resources. These forms of compensation presuppose the profound social and cultural transformations involved in the penetration into rural communities of monetary exchange and growing dependency on wider economic forces. Again, normative issues are posed by such changes which are not directly addressed in the texts of the Rio agreements. Finally, the criterion of 'sustainability' bypasses a whole agenda of normative issues which arise directly 'at the point of production': issues of trade union rights, ethnic and gender discrimination, working conditions, rates of pay, health and safety, employment security, and economic democracy. In large measure the take-up of the discourse of sustainable development by powerful international actors such as the World Bank and IMF has enabled a narrowly defined environmental ethic to displace this wider agenda of economic welfare and democracy.

At least some of these limitations could be met in the terms of an elaborated concept of sustainable development by way of a more inclusive conceptualization of needs. As we have seen, both Brundtland and the Rio agreements tend to work with a notion of 'basic' needs, and with the assumption that needs will be met largely through market transactions in a money economy. If issues left out of account by the narrowness of the concept of 'sustainability' as the prime criterion for evaluating economic organization are to be addressed through the elaboration of the concept of need, then a much broader conception of needs will be required. In particular, the needs for satisfying and fulfilling work, for convivial working relationships, and for democratic participation in decisions about how both human working capacities and material resources will be allocated to different sectors of production and distribution would be included in any concept of need adequate to a fully rounded concept of human individual and social flourishing. To this we might add the further cultural and political-institutional requirements for dialogic resolution of differences of view on all of these questions, and the necessary economic autonomy of communities, within whatever geographical boundaries are meaningful, to order their need-meeting interaction with nature according to their own values and priorities.

Finally, Brundtland pays some passing attention to non-utilitarian, 'moral, ethical, cultural, aesthetic, and purely scientific reasons for conserving wild beings.'[44] But—not surprisingly, given the urgency and scale of the human suffering which the report places at the centre of its concerns—the predominant reference to the importance of non-human nature is in its role as a 'resource-base' for the meeting of human needs. The moral orientation of the report, and, indeed, of the concept of sustainable development in more-or-less all of its applications, is thus, in the jargon of environmental ethics 'anthropocentric'. With some qualifications, nature is valued for its capacity to sustain human need-meeting. Sustainability enjoins us to exploit the resource-base more rationally, with long-term aims in view. But here the equivocation between 'basic' needs as survival conditions, and 'needs' as requirements for a fuller vision of human flourishing becomes significant. If we take seriously the report's brief acknowledgement of 'moral, ethical, cultural' and other reasons for restraint in our dealings with non-human nature this already takes us beyond a mere resource-conservationist view of the desirable relation between human societies and non-human nature. Robyn Eckersley's valuable typology of environmentalisms includes what she calls 'human welfare ecology' as an approach which acknowledges the multi-dimensional character of human need in relation to non-human nature: needs for aesthetic, spiritual, and cultural engagement.[45] To take these dimensions of human need in relation to nature seriously would add further reasons for a strategy of 're-embedding' economic activity within the normative order of democratically constituted civil societies and legal-political institutions—for, in other words, radical shifts in the direction of economic democracy. Even this, however, stops short of the 'ecocentric' perspective advocated by Eckersley. For her, even human welfare ecology remains anthropocentric, and does not address the case for acknowledgement of the inherent value of non-human beings and relations, independently of their relationship to the meeting of any specifically human needs.

But it does not seem to me that the distinction between human welfare ecology and ecocentrism is quite so easily made. If we consider the content and significance of those cultural orientations to nature and the forms of fulfilment associated with them which are referred to by such terms as 'spiritual', 'ethical', 'aesthetic', then it is clear that an indispensable moment in them all is an attitude of respect, even of awe, towards the non-human. These are not forms of instrumental action. We do not 'use' nature as a 'means' to the gratification of our desire for beauty or inspiration, but simply open ourselves to the power of nature to inspire. So, to preserve, and to hand on to future generations the conditions of possibility of such valued experiences entails restraining, and eventually defeating those social and economic forces which destroy both the non-human world itself, and our personal and cultural resources for finding it valuable.

PART III

9

Must the Poor Pay More?
Sustainable Development, Social
Justice, and Environmental Taxation

STEPHEN TINDALE AND CHRIS HEWETT

1. Introduction

Sustainable development is an extremely political concept. To many it is simply another phrase for environmental protection. To others, particularly the governments of the Third World, it means allowing the poorest in society to catch up with the rich countries of the North. By focusing on the objective of meeting human needs, it masks the tensions between short-term social and environmental goals which have often divided campaigners, both on the global and national stage. If these tensions are ignored then the concept becomes meaningless and ultimately undeliverable.[1]

Of course it is often the case that ecological and developmental imperatives pull in the same direction—poverty *is* a great cause of degradation of the natural world. There is much evidence to suggest that it is the poorest in society who suffer most from the consequences of pollution. Sustainable development has also introduced a new form of equity to be concerned about: the concept of intergenerational equity. Policies which can address both social and environmental issues are clearly desirable but may not have the instant effects which circumstances, and electorates, demand. Most social issues are immediate to people's lives and require urgent action. Many environmental issues, however, whilst having a bearing on individuals' circumstances, are problems of the future and therefore appear to be a lower priority.

The result of this conflict of priorities can result in bad policy decisions. It is undeniably the case that some policies which are desirable for environmental reasons will exacerbate inequalities and social injustice. Similarly, some measures to improve short-term social conditions can simply increase environmental risks for future generations.

It is the role of the policy-maker to juggle with these priorities, and the decisions made are ultimately political judgements. The most important point to stress is that, as with most policy decisions, the problem is not treated in isolation. All environmental policies should be examined for their impact on social justice and vice versa. The introduction of VAT on domestic fuel in the UK in 1994 brought the conflicts of social and environmental objectives into sharp focus. Work since then has shown that a more sensible approach is possible and certainly desirable.

This chapter concentrates on environmental taxation, since this raises the issues in their most acute form. But the notion that environmental regulation avoids the problem is mistaken. It is impossible to say in the abstract whether taxation or regulation is the more regressive: it all depends on the issue. Minimum efficiency standards might increase the price of consumer durables, which would hurt the poor more than the rich. Higher standards of drinking-water have undoubtedly caused suffering among low-income households, since the cost of meeting them is passed on to customers via water bills. In a market economy, the burden of both taxation and regulation tends to fall on the customer. And this, from an environmental perspective, is as it should be. It is the consumers who create the demand for a product who are the true polluters, not the manufacturers who meet that demand. It is the consumers who should pay.

In any case, most commentators accept that taxation and regulation have to be used in harness. Consider the case of transport. Let us assume that we want to tackle pollution and urban congestion. The options available are taxes or road-pricing, minimum fuel efficiency standards, mandatory pollution controls on vehicles, and traffic bans. The impact of transport taxation on low-income households is considered in detail below; for now it is sufficient to note that higher taxes will be progressive across the population as a whole, (since the poor cannot afford cars), but regressive among car-drivers. Banning cars in urban areas would in a sense be more equitable—though if taxis were allowed it could be said to discriminate against those unable to afford taxi fares. Efficiency standards and pollution controls could also be said to be even-handed in their impact (although if, as the car manufacturers claim, they will make vehicles more expensive there will be a regressive impact at the point of purchase). So should one reject taxation and opt instead for these regulations? The answer is that one should not—one should go for *both* taxation and regulation, because they are not really equivalent at all. Traffic-free city centres are greatly to be desired, but much of the traffic will then be displaced into the suburbs. Greater fuel efficiency and stricter emissions standards are similarly to be welcomed, but without policies which manage demand for transport their impact will be overwhelmed by increases in vehicle numbers—as is predicted to happen with catalytic converters. To say that environmental regulation is less regressive than taxation is like saying that the government health warning on cigarette packets is less regressive than tobacco taxes: it may be true, but it is not very relevant, since the one will not be effective without the other.

2. Are Green Taxes Unfair?

The most widely heard argument against environmental taxes is that they hurt the poor. Public support for the concept of 'fair taxation' remains strong, as the Conservatives discovered when they introduced a poll tax—an approach which had offended medieval conceptions of social justice, and was therefore unlikely to appeal in the marginally more enlightened twentieth century.

Conceptions of fairness were also instrumental in defeating the government's attempt to implement the second tranche of VAT on domestic fuel. The concept of progressive taxation is supported by substantial majorities in all EU countries—for example 87 per cent in Germany, 85 per cent in the UK, 84 per cent in Italy.[2]

An exception to this general support for progressive taxation appears to be made for 'sin taxes' on tobacco and alcohol. Public acceptance of these is so strong that it overrides concerns about distributive justice which in other contexts are regarded as paramount. When the government was defeated on the second tranche of VAT on domestic fuel, the Chancellor introduced instead a package including higher taxes on alcohol and tobacco which were more regressive in their impact than the original measure. But because fuel is essential, whereas tobacco and alcohol are thought not to be, there was little protest.

The UK tax system has become more regressive in recent years. In 1979, the top fifth of the population (in terms of income) paid 38 per cent of their income in tax, while the bottom fifth paid only 31 per cent. By 1992, the figure was 34 per cent for the top fifth and 39 per cent for the bottom fifth. Broadly regressive changes have included a steady shift from direct to indirect taxes, reductions in top rates of income tax, and the freezing of the lower-rate threshold in 1993 and 1994.

There are, however, different ways of looking at progressivity and regressivity. One way, the theoretical approach, is to look simply at the incidence of taxation. An income tax is more progressive than a sales tax. A second, more practical way is to look at what the government proposes to do with the revenues. A package in which the government levies income tax and uses the revenue to subsidize opera tickets is *less* progressive than a package in which the government levies a sales tax and uses the revenue to pay welfare benefits to the poor. (The most regressive approach is to tax poor people and use the receipts to subsidize the opera—this is called the National Lottery.)

Of course, the most progressive package would be one in which the government levied an income tax and used it to pay welfare benefits. This has been the traditional approach of the Left, the heart of social democracy. It should certainly not be abandoned.

Indeed, at a time of widening inequality there is a need for more rather than less redistribution of income and wealth. However, the political constraints need to be recognized. Not all the expenditure a progressive government would like to take can be funded through direct taxation. In this situation, one has to weigh up the social cost of inaction as well as the impact of a tax increase. For example, the lack of books in state schools is highly regressive in its impact—richer parents buy their children either the books or a place in a private school. Unreliable and expensive public transport is primarily of concern to the one-third of households who do not own cars, which are predominantly, though not exclusively, those in lower-income groups. Would it be progressive or regressive to impose an indirect tax in order to increase spending on education or public transport? This is again a question which cannot be answered in the abstract.[3]

Environmental taxes have been criticized by some on the Left as 'rationing by price'. This is a strange statement. In a market economy, that is how most goods and services are apportioned. There are some things, like health and education, which should be outside the market—free at the point of use. But none of the candidates for environmental taxation, except perhaps domestic energy taxation, come into this category. Road use is currently free, but food is 'rationed by price'. Which is the more essential? Genuine rationing—rationing by coupon—would be more equitable. It would also be politically impossible, and in any case not ideal. If the coupons were tradable, the rich would end up with them anyway, though the poor would have more money from the sale of their coupons. A non-tradable system would simply drive trading underground.

Current environmental patterns are highly inequitable, with poor households suffering more from pollution, local environmental degradation, and so on. One has to ask, therefore, whether environmental taxation is more regressive than inaction. The answer, of course, is that sometimes it is, sometimes it is not. It all depends on the nature of the problem and the nature of the tax. The blanket assertion that environmental taxation is regressive therefore oversimplifies the picture. Cuts in government expenditure or a failure to act to protect the environment may be even more regressive. The distributional impact of green taxes should be assessed on a case-by-case basis.

Some environmental taxes will fall on business—taxes on toxic emissions, for example—so the regressive impact will be limited. An increase in business costs is likely to be mildly regressive if it feeds through into higher prices to the consumer, but a tax reform which redistributes rather than increases business taxes is likely to have a broadly neutral impact on prices. Other environmental taxes will fall indirectly on individuals, but can be collected through a progressive mechanism. An example is a landfill tax, which will increase the cost to local authorities of disposing of municipal waste (although most of the impact will be on the industrial sector). The local authority will be able to recoup its costs through local taxation, be it property- or income-based. Unfortunately, in the UK local taxation is itself not very progressive, but this need not be the case. Alternatively, if the tax is levied centrally, central government could choose to use some of the revenue to increase its support revenues to local authorities. Nevertheless, there are legitimate concerns about the impact of some green taxes.

Domestic Energy Taxes

The main areas of concern are the taxation of domestic energy, and transport taxes. Environmentalists and opposition politicians may have argued, correctly, that the British government's decision to impose VAT on domestic fuel was motivated by financial rather than environmental considerations. But the fact remains that other proposals for energy taxation, such as the European Commission's carbon/energy tax proposal would have had a broadly similar impact on domestic energy prices, albeit phased in over a longer period.

The government argued, correctly, that most other European countries have a tax on domestic fuel. But it ignored a crucial difference. Other Northern European countries with climates similar to or colder than Britain's have far stricter regulations governing the insulation standards of their housing stock. They simply do not have the draughty, damp, and impossible-to-heat properties which are so common in the UK. Energy use is therefore much more closely correlated to income—those who use more energy do so because they own more appliances or indulge in more luxuries. Until Britain reaches similar levels of energy efficiency with our housing stock, comparisons with domestic energy taxation in other Northern European countries will be entirely bogus. Moreover, even the Nordic countries are now hearing complaints from social-policy groups that further taxation of domestic energy would be regressive.

The social impact of higher fuel bills in the UK is illustrated by a study carried out at the University of York's Social Policy Research Unit.[4] The survey found that those households with incomes in the top 20 per cent spend 4.2 per cent of their budget on fuel, while those in the lowest 20 per cent spend 12.1 per cent. The burden is therefore nearly three times greater for low-income households than for more affluent households. Only 46 per cent of those in the lowest quintile have gas central-heating (the most energy-efficient form of space heating); the figure for the highest quintile is 75 per cent.

There are also different impacts for different types of household. Families with children spend over £13 a week on fuel, while pensioners and single householders spend £8–£10 a week. Single pensioners spend 16 per cent of their budget on fuel, as do lone parents with children under five. Those living in private rented accommodation, (the most energy inefficient form of tenure), also have proportionately high fuel bills and less incentive to invest in efficiency measures, since they may not stay in the property long enough to reap the benefits. These figures illustrate the difficulty of designing a targeted compensation package.

Low-income households are less able to cut back on fuel use by changing equipment or installing energy-efficiency measures, which can have a high capital cost. Indeed, energy use in the domestic sector overall is far less responsive to price than in the industrial and commercial sectors.[5]

An Eco-bonus

The low elasticity, together with the regressive impact of higher domestic fuel costs, suggest that the price mechanism should not be used to encourage efficiency in the domestic sector. However, domestic energy taxation could be made acceptable if the revenue was used to give a lump sum payment to each individual, or possibly to each household. This is generally referred to as an 'eco-bonus', and has been the subject of extensive discussion in a number of countries. It is possible to see the eco-bonus as a forerunner to, or component of, a broader Basic Income, a proposal which has found support among a number of economists. (James Meade argued that Basic Income should be funded, in part, through environmental taxation.)[6]

An example of how an eco-bonus might work in practice is given by Stephen Smith (although he does not use the term) of the Institute for Fiscal Studies (IFS). Smith calculates that the average cost to British households of the EU carbon/energy tax would be £2.11 per week, if all the revenue collected from households was returned to them in a lump sum payments of £2.11 to each household. This would be substantially more than the extra tax paid by poor households, but much less than the extra tax paid by rich households. Thus the package overall becomes progressive. However, this does not necessarily mean that all poorer households will be better off; there may be some low-income homes with high fuel use. Pensioners, the unemployed, or the ill who are at home all day clearly need more fuel than those who go to work. So, an element of targeting would probably need to be built in, increasing the administrative complexity and running the risk of missing some of those most in need.[7]

A Tax-free Fuel Allowance

An alternative would be to give each household a tax-free fuel allowance. This would mean that only excessive use of energy would be taxed. The Dutch energy tax applies only for use above 800 cubic metres of gas and 800kWh of electricity. The notion of charging for excessive use is an approach which merits serious consideration—it could be applied for example to water use as well as energy. It is not in itself a guarantee against regressive impact—those groups who for the reasons mentioned have especially high fuel use may well go above the threshold. Special cases could be compensated through the benefits system—although this is subject to the concerns expressed above.

Insulation Programmes

A third alternative would be to spend money insulating the homes of the poor. This should certainly be done: it would pay dividends in terms of public health and social justice as well as environmental improvement. It is the appalling state of the British housing stock which makes taxing domestic energy so regressive: these concerns simply do not exist in most other countries. Universally available improvement grants have been withdrawn in recent years, and although there are some good schemes still in existence, such as the Home Energy Efficiency Scheme, they do not match the scale of the problem. A tax neutral package would not of course produce any extra revenue to increase spending on insulation programmes. But even assuming a government was prepared to go in for a 'tax-and-spend' package of increasing domestic energy prices and using the revenue to upgrade the housing stock, there is an important constraint. The work should be done *before* any tax increase. Otherwise many poor people will be left in the cold while they wait for the extra insulation.

However, it is possible to envisage a situation in which the private sector, (either energy utilities or, perhaps, building societies or others involved in property), put up the funds to carry out a programme in advance of the tax being imposed, and were recompensed from the proceeds of the tax. A scheme such as this could sensibly be administered through the Energy Savings Trust.

The Liberal Democrats have recently recommended an ingenious approach in their energy policy paper *Conserving Tomorrow*. A carbon tax would be introduced, but vouchers covering a proportion of the fuel costs would be given to those on low incomes living in badly insulated homes. These could be used either to pay a proportion of the bill, or else to pay for energy efficiency investments.

The Conservatives' imposition of VAT on domestic fuel, a blatant breach of faith with the electorate undertaken without any prior thought about compensation or measures to improve the housing stock, was rightly condemned as pernicious. Sadly, it has made sensible discussion of a non-regressive package of measures including higher domestic energy prices very difficult. It would not be impossible to design such a package, and at some stage it should be attempted. In the meantime, the case for environmental reform of the tax system needs to be decoupled from the debate about VAT on fuel. It would be straightforward to exempt the domestic sector from any further energy taxation, and this is probably the way forward. Those economists and environmentalists who argue that this means ducking the issue should remember that domestic energy taxation *has* increased by 8 per cent. Commercial energy taxes have increased not at all.

3. The Social Impact of Transport Taxes

Increasing the cost of motoring is less problematic than increasing domestic energy prices. This will be a broadly progressive measure over the population as a whole, since most poor people cannot afford cars. However, it will be regressive within the car-owning community. And the fact that poor people cannot afford cars today does not mean that they do not want to be able to afford them in the future.

The impact of transport taxes is considered in detail in a paper from the IFS entitled *The Distributional Consequences of Environmental Taxes*.[8] The report notes that 'there is a close relationship between affluence and car-ownership. The richest decile are, on average, over eleven times more likely to have the use of a car than households in the poorest decile, in which less than one household in ten has the use of a car. Moreover, households in the richer deciles are much more likely to have access to more than one car.' (See Table 9.1 and Fig. 9.1.)

The IFS authors found that increasing the price of petrol by 55 pence per gallon (taking it to the highest real level it has attained over recent decades) would mean that the lowest income decile would pay an extra 0.22 per cent in tax (measured as a percentage of total spending), while the highest income decile would pay an

TABLE 9.1. *Car-ownership, by decile of gross income*

Decile of gross income	Average no. of cars	Percentage having use of cars
1	0.09	8.5
2	0.21	19.3
3	0.42	40.1
4	0.57	51.6
5	0.75	66.1
6	0.93	76.7
7	1.05	83.2
8	1.19	89.4
9	1.45	93.9
10	1.80	96.2
AVERAGE	0.84	62.5

Source: adapted from P. Johnson, S. McKay, and S. Smith, *The Distributional Consequences of Environmental Taxes*, IFS Commentary 23 (London: Institute for Fiscal Studies, 1990).

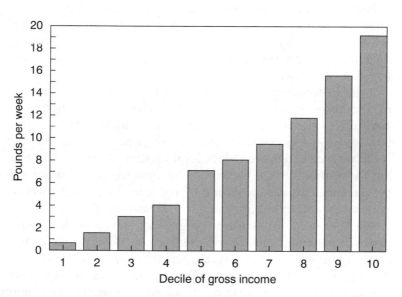

FIG. 9.1. *Petrol spending, all households*
Source: *see Table 9.1.*

extra 1.04 per cent However, this happy picture is altered if one considers not all households but only those which own cars. Within this group, the lowest decile pay 1.19 per cent more in tax while the highest decile pay 1.07 per cent more. There will also be groups of people particularly hard hit, and they would need to be compensated. The disabled, for example, may not be in a position to benefit from better public transport. Some of the revenue from higher petrol taxes could be used to increase the disability allowance.

Those who live in rural areas inadequately served by public transport would also be adversely affected, although phasing the taxes in gradually will give these people the chance to invest in smaller, more fuel-efficient vehicles. One way around this specific problem would be to invest in providing public transport alternatives in these areas, although this would depart from the principle of fiscal neutrality, and there are parts of the country which will never be adequately served by public transport. A second would be to levy lower rates of tax in rural areas, although this carries the danger of so-called 'tank tourism', in which urban drivers travel into the country to fill up—often quite irrationally, since they spend more on the petrol used getting there than they save from the lower cost.

A third alternative would be for central government to use some of the revenue to increase support payments to rural local authorities—possibly related to needs assessment. This need not be a departure from overall fiscal neutrality, since the local authority could then be obliged to reduce local taxation. This idea has been put forward in the past by the Liberal Democrats, and appears to be the most promising means of compensating rural dwellers without compromising the need to increase fuel prices.

We also need to consider the general argument that higher petrol taxation is only progressive because poor people cannot afford to drive—not because they do not want to. It may not damage their weekly income, but it may well damage their aspirations. Making something to which they aspire even more unattainable is hardly good social policy.

Behind this argument is the assumption that in an ideal world everyone would own or have access to a car. This is partly to do with status, but primarily because it is increasingly difficult to exist in a modern motorized society without one. Amenities are spread out over a wide area, public transport is run down, cyclists are too often run down too.

It does not need to be like this. Only 2 per cent of all journeys in the UK are made by bike, compared to 10 per cent in Germany and 28 per cent in the Netherlands. Contrary to popular belief, the Dutch have not always cycled: the high levels of cycling are a result of public-policy decisions made in the 1970s. Cycling rates in Germany rose by 50 per cent between 1981 and 1991. Cities such as Copenhagen, Freiburg, and Groningen have shown, through extensive provision of trams, buses, and cycle lanes, pedestrianization, and sensible planning policies, that it is possible to arrange matters differently, to avoid or even reverse car dependency. In Freiburg, 60 per cent of journeys in 1976 were made by car; by 1992 this had fallen to 46 per cent. Walking and cycling had increased from 18 per cent to 28 per cent.

There has been a recent increase in the number of bicycles bought in the UK. The British now own fifteen million bikes. However, many of these are not regarded as a means of transport but as a leisure accessory. People drive into the country with their bikes on the back of the car rather than cycling them around the town. Better, safer cycling facilities could well reveal a latent enthusiasm for cycling among Britons.

However good the cycle-tracks or public transport provision, there will still be some purposes for which a car is highly desirable. It is easier to do the weekly or monthly shop by car, however good the public transport system, although it would not necessarily be so if supermarkets reintroduced home deliveries. People with small children may find it difficult to enjoy a holiday without a car. Access to affordable car use for such purposes—through low-cost rental services, for example—is desirable. It should be remembered that most people do not have access to a car most of the time—only around two-thirds of households have a car, and within this group there are very many families where one person drives to work and parks the car in the office car park all day, leaving the other partner to shop, etc. on foot. As so often, arguments about the equity of change hides the inequity of the *status quo*.

What are the alternatives to higher petrol taxes, and would they be less regressive? One is to allow things to continue as they are, to control car use through congestion. This is highly inefficient economically, socially, and environmentally since cars sitting in traffic jams emit a high level of pollution. As we saw earlier, it is poor communities that tend to suffer most from the resulting pollution, although British business suffers to the tune of £15–20 billion a year, the figure the Confederation of British Industry (CBI) puts on the cost of congestion.[9] Although road building appears to be out of favour with the public at present, failure to act on managing demand for traffic will inevitably lead to calls for an increase in the supply of road space. New roads will be built through the hearts of communities, and these communities will not be the haunts of the well-heeled.

The easy political response is to say that congestion will be tackled through better public transport. Leaving aside the question of whether this would be enough to manage demand adequately in the absence of higher petrol prices, where in the current political climate is the money going to be found to invest in and subsidize a modern, efficient, and safe public transport system? In an ideal world one might wish to increase income tax in order to fund a better transport system—as well as better education, better healthcare, better policing, better prisons, higher welfare benefits, higher overseas aid, and so on. In the real world, sadly, this is not possible. Education has been identified by both Labour and the Liberal Democrats as the top priority, and (though this would come as a surprise to some members of these parties) it is possible to have only one top priority at a time. If governments do not increase their revenues, they will not have the money significantly to increase spending on public transport. Since increases in income tax and VAT do not appear to be on the agenda, to reject higher transport taxes is to accept the *status quo,* complete with congestion, pollution, and road rage. Poor people might want to drive tomorrow. What they want and need today is a decent public transport system. Failing to provide one is the really regressive policy.

5. Unemployment and Poverty

The greatest cause of poverty in Britain today is unemployment. Any package of measures which increases employment is therefore likely to be progressive. Environmental taxes might be mildly regressive if introduced in isolation. But if they make it possible to reduce unemployment, the net impact would be positive. Green taxes would stimulate environmental industries, which in itself would create employment and improve the UK's long-term industrial prospects. And they would produce revenue, which could be used to create employment, though wage subsidies, higher public spending on labour-intensive sectors like health and education, or reductions in taxes on labour.

The Institute for Public Policy Research (IPPR) has recently published a report proposing a package of new or increased environmental taxes—including a commercial and industrial energy tax, higher road fuel duties, an office parking tax, an end to company-car tax perks, a higher landfill tax, and a quarrying tax—and corresponding reductions in Employers' National Insurance Contributions.[10] According to modelling carried out for the IPPR by Cambridge Econometrics, this would result in 252,000 extra jobs in 2000, and 717,000 in 2005. There would also be substantial reductions in carbon dioxide and nitrogen dioxide emissions and wastes arising.

What about the impact on low-income households who do not see their income rise due to increased employment? They will benefit from the environmental improvement; often disproportionately so. But will they be better or worse off in financial terms? The only tax change which bears directly on households is higher petrol duty, and low-income households could relatively easily be compensated for this. The other tax changes might feed through to consumer in the form of higher prices, though reductions in labour taxes will leave many producers unaffected or better off. The overall impact on the Retail Price Index (RPI), as we have seen, is negligible. But do the poor buy more of the energy-intensive goods which might increase in price? The main items in low-income household budgets are housing, food, fuel, clothing, and household goods.[11] Of these, housing costs and fuel would be unaffected; food, clothing, and household goods would be made cheaper.

It is possible, then, to design a package of reforms which leave both the poor and the environment better off. But it should never be assumed that this happy result is inevitable. As Michael Jacobs has pointed out, unless environmental taxes are specifically designed to be progressive, they probably won't be.[12]

10

Ecological Degradation:
A Cause for Conflict,
a Concern for Survival
KOOS NEEFJES

1. Introduction

In this chapter I would like to bring a perspective to the debate on environmental sustainability and social justice which differs from that of other contributions. It is rooted in situations of turmoil rather than stability, of relative lawlessness, an absence of effective environmental policies, and/or substantial and open political discourse. These situations are extreme, but not exceptional, since wars and other forms of conflict and the breakdown of nation states are very much things of our times, in most continents.

In other contributions to this volume arguments regarding weak and strong sustainability and about how to achieve social justice within a particular policy approach are put forward. The majority of texts seem to assume a relatively well organized democratic state in which individuals can inform themselves and policy choices can actually be made regarding economic growth

This chapter has benefited from discussions after the presentation of a draft version during the seminar series 'Social Justice and Sustainability', organized by Andrew Dobson of the Department of Politics at the University of Keele. Much appreciated suggestions and comments were also given by some of my (former) colleagues, including Chris Roche, Robin Palmer, Ros David, and Suzanne Williams. The contents obviously remain entirely my own responsibility.

and the use of natural resources. But this is not always and everywhere the case, as is explained here in section 2.

Historically, and in particular since about the time of the invention of agriculture a very large majority of the world's people have suffered relentlessly from a lack of food and comfort in generally degrading ecological environments, increasing population, ever-changing production technologies, and increasing social inequalities. This process is now accelerating rapidly: at a global scale increasing numbers of people enjoy material well-being but inequality is becoming more extreme than ever and ecological degradation is no longer solely of a local nature, nor could the natural environment in all cases be restored, even if we wanted to do so (see section 3).

Section 4 gives an overview of more recent analyses of the cause and nature of conflicts around the world, and in particular the importance of the role of resource degradation. There are analysts who portray a very gloomy situation of collapsing states as a result of population increase, environmental degradation, and so on. Others focus on the internal logic of 'predatory political economies' and try to formulate ways of dealing with them instead of suggesting that they are inevitable for some neo-Malthusian reason.

In section 5 ecological change in relation to conflicts is illustrated with concrete cases, with ecological degradation as a cause for further social disintegration, ecological degradation as a resource for survival as well as war, and the idea that ecological change and social justice can be pursued in a democratic way whilst conflict is ongoing or threatening.

The conclusions in section 6 are that:

- peace is an important precondition for social justice and ecological sustainability;
- strong sustainability cannot be pursued in a situation of poverty, rapid population growth, economic decline, and weak systems of governance;
- economic growth is actually a precondition for peace in many conflict situations;
- central to any policy should be participation of local people in governance and project management and the development

of democratic structures, even in a situation of conflict or threatening conflict, in order to achieve some level of social justice and ecological sustainability through the strengthening of civil society;

• the international redistribution of claims on use of natural and economic resources must be considered in various ways, in order to deal fairly with the problem of population increase.

2. Sustainability and Social Justice in Conflicts?

Bryan Norton[1] elaborates on 'strong sustainability' and its (potential) measurability. He defines strong sustainability as a situation in which 'prior generations act so as to maintain, in addition to general, social capital, the 'natural capital' necessary for people in future generations to face an acceptable range of opportunities'. The 'natural capital' is that part of the resource base which cannot be substituted through technological innovation or otherwise. Choices that are made at present should not close off choices (for resource use) in the future, and thus the key criteria that he develops is something like the optimization of future opportunities. This means, in particular, that the (physical) irreversibility of ecological change should be avoided, which should be 'in principle specifiable in physically describable and measurable terms'. Measurement of strong sustainability, i.e. of the state and change of natural capital, can only happen within a highly local context, and 'must include a sense of past and of the future . . . and the people who have co-evolved with the place'. He argues that local communities must be involved in processes of value-articulation in order to achieve that, which requires that they 'articulate a core sense of values'. He also introduces a concept of resilience, meaning that certain thresholds should not be exceeded, thereby preventing (ecological) systems from flipping into new system states. If this resilience were measurable we would have an indicator for the maximization of future options of resource use. He concludes by proposing the development of an options/constraints index in which measurable physical aspects are combined with the 'desirable choice options for the citizens who occupy the region' (see Norton ch. 5, in this volume).

Strong sustainability obviously cannot be reached, and measurement will be pointless, in a situation where extreme exploitation of natural resources is taking place in order to fuel a war or to survive in a crisis. Interestingly, Norton also writes 'provided that a community can articulate a core set of values that unite them . . . it may be possible to identify some "indicator" . . . [for] options within that environment,' in other words, a society needs to be stable enough and coherent in order to define conditions for strong sustainability. And 'The creation of a sustainable society, I believe, is much like creating and implementing a constitution.' It may be true that ecological systems can irreversibly flip into other system states as a result of strong impacts on natural resources, and highly exploitative situations just before, during, or immediately resulting from violent conflicts may create just that.

Andrew Dobson[2] gives us a typology of sustainabilities, a kind of elaboration of a scale from weak to strong sustainability. The most important distinction between concepts of sustainability seems to be the different answers to the question of substitutability of capital for natural resources: can we discount the future values of resources to a present monetary value *and* expect ecological sustainability to be achieved? Those who affirm this are at the weak side of the spectrum. He also shows that there are different approaches to the question of 'what to sustain?' (for strong sustainability, see e.g. Norton: irreversible natural capital), and, furthermore, his typology depends on questions related to the relative importance of future needs and wants. At the stronger side of the typology the interpretations of sustainability tend to find reasons for ecological preservation 'for nature's sake', without referring exclusively to human needs and wants, and the debate about substitutability becomes largely irrelevant.

Whatever the level of substitution of natural resources for capital, substitution itself will only occur in a situation of some kind of economic development as a result of, or side effect of, resource use. Otherwise resources are only *exploited,* and this may be the case where resource competition reaches the level of armed conflict, or where survival has become the only paradigm.

David Miller[3] distinguishes three groups of environmental goods, the first two of which should be under some form of state control and could be valuated; they include externalities such as air pollution. He comes close to the conclusion that cost-benefit calculations of environmental goods in the third category (such as protecting a rare animal species) are ultimately impossible to agree on because they are always based on subjective judgements of individuals, and the idea of social justice is therefore hard to square with such environmental goods. Only a democratic political process can lead to just distribution of environmental resources, but he adds that a cost-benefit analysis based on judgements of individuals should be a first stage in such a decision-making process.

Wissenburg[4] explores the idea of population policies as a means of achieving sustainability within a liberal democratic political system. He concludes that there is, given liberal democratic principles, actually very little scope to equitably limit individuals' procreative liberties, and that 'control of the population size . . . is acceptable only in the most extreme circumstances, where the survival of mankind is stake'.

But when does that occur, and who is to judge and/or implement such draconian measures? It seems unlikely that 'mankind' will perish as a result of some kind of environmental apocalypse, but rather, that there will be 'pockets' of disaster as a result of increasing competition over resources, affecting some and not others. There are, and will be, winners and losers, and in order to understand that better we have to focus the analysis on justice between groups and states, and not only on justice between individuals.

It seems that all these theses share the assumption of a well organized, at least more or less functioning political system, with relative peace and the resources to implement policies. Under those circumstances social justice and sustainability can be discussed and pursued by individuals and groups or movements, and some success will be achieved. But what about situations where political stability is not particularly obvious?

What about situations where resource competition 'gets out of hand', situations where conflict is mediated through the use or exploitation of environmental resources, and situations where conflicts are fuelled by and result in environmental exploitation? Let us first look at some history of environmental change and suffering.

3. A History without Sustainability and Social Justice

Ponting has written eloquently about the history of environmental change caused by human beings[5]. He elaborates on the fact that for more than 99 per cent of the 2 million years since *homo erectus* invented the first tools people have been dependent on hunting and gathering. This life-style was relatively easy in the sense that there was no constant threat of starvation, diets were diverse, and people had plenty of leisure time (although unfortunately chess had not yet been invented). The ecological impact of human beings was very limited and primarily of a local nature. There are even examples of the conservation of some natural resources by hunter-gatherers, but there is also proof of over-hunting to the point of extinction of some animal species. Certain methods of population control employed in those days seem rather harsh today, such as infanticide and abandonment of elderly people. There is no doubt that people influenced their environments in many subtle ways, even before the development of agriculture from about 10,000 BC.

Ponting explains the development of agriculture as a result of increasing population pressure, i.e. technology had to be developed in order to cope with local shortages that resulted from an ever-increasing demand; this happened independently in South-west Asia, China, and Mesoamerica. In a gradual process that took thousands of years, livestock and crops were domesticated, villages and later towns emerged, different tools and irrigation were invented, and, importantly, social differentiation appeared, with the development of religious, political, and military elites. He writes that 'at the root of these social changes was a new attitude to the ownership of food'.[6] For example, records from Mesopotamia of about 3,000 BC and later show the centralized control of the elite over the urban population, food, and production systems. They also show a decline in wheat production, which is explained by gradual salinization of soils as a result of irrigation. This kind of environmental degradation combined with increasing pressures from the elite for agricultural intensification and population growth was an important cause for the demise of several city-states and civilizations. A contributing factor to the downfall of the Roman empire, Ponting writes, was declining food production following environmental degradation in several provinces.

An important point that he makes is the suffering, the permanent situation of near starvation, in which the peasantry live and have lived throughout the world and centuries even *with* agriculture. A majority of say 95 per cent of the population of all parts of the world were producing for their own consumption and for the maintenance of a small and oppressive elite, employing levels of technology that resulted in yields that were just about sufficient in most (i.e. 'normal') years. Freak weather or other sudden shocks like plagues would uncover their vulnerability and outright famine would result. Furthermore, problems with production combined with demand must have been exacerbated by often extremely high taxes of warring elites. He mentions many examples of famines in Asia, Europe, and Africa throughout (recent) history that easily match the scale of famines in Africa in e.g. the 1980s. Even under normal circumstances the peasantry depended largely on vegetarian and rather monotonous diets. This situation persisted everywhere around the globe until the second half of the nineteenth century when some countries, particularly in Europe, managed to import large quantities of food and other products from their colonies, and after which fertilizer and mechanization could start increasing agricultural yields dramatically (these latter observations are supported by Slicher van Bath (1960)[7]). But a central part of Ponting's thesis is that throughout most of the past thousands of years human population sizes were virtually continuously too large for the level of available technology and environmental potential, and thus food supply was continuously insufficient whilst occasional yet regular departures from the 'normal' led to disease, starvation, famine, and migration, which were effectively population checks.

Amartya Sen explains some twentieth-century famines primarily through a failure of 'exchange entitlement mapping', i.e. the alternative commodities (especially food) that a person can acquire in exchange for what they can offer, i.e. their 'endowments', which can include their labour, savings, and possessions and produced goods.[8] He speaks of 'direct entitlement failure' when for example a peasant produces less food for herself which may be due to environmental reasons; 'trade entitlement failure' happens when for example a labourer's wage is stable whilst food prices rise. Sen argues that his model enables the analysis of social, economic, and environmental effects on different groups in a society and overcomes the limitations of analytical approaches that focus on overall food production in explaining famine. For example, the Great Bengal Famine of 1943 has generally been explained by a lack of total rice supply, whilst Sen shows that overall shortages were not at all extreme. The famine hit rural labourers and craftsmen hard, but not as hard as peasants and sharecroppers, whilst some government and army personnel were almost unaffected. All this is partly explained by sharp food-price rises whilst rural salaries stayed roughly the same, or in Sen's language, there were sharp movements in exchange entitlements. These movements are explained by, for example, inflationary pressures in the war economy (printing banknotes), speculation, and panic hoarding, 'a moderate short-fall in production', and expanding income, subsidies, and distribution arrangements for urban-based groups that were associated with the war effort (in particular the army and industry).

Sen's model is fundamentally about differential economic rights to resources, goods, and means of production. Environmental rights appear to be implicit in the 'endowment vector' as is technology and technological knowledge. His model does help understand how command over such endowments impacts differentially on people in times of a particular crisis, but it does not explain how these factors themselves evolve over longer periods of time.

The importance of population growth for technology development and thus production potential is a central aspect for

Harrison.[9] This writer reviews, amongst other things, approaches to population control throughout history, mentioning for example the ideas of infanticide, and of migration, and colonization in ancient Greece and Rome in order to stabilize population numbers. He then goes on to discuss different positions in debates about modern population policies: Malthus, who proposed (as a kind of natural law) that agricultural production increased arithmetically, whilst population increases geometrically and thus much more rapidly, allowing the conclusion that famines could be seen as a natural process of population control; Marx and George who saw poverty primarily as an outcome of inequality; and Boserup, who argued that high population densities were the main driving force for agricultural/technological change.[10]

Harrison then proposes to bring these different positions together and elaborates on a model in which he tries to assess *environmental impact* as a result of changes in *population, consumption, and technology*.[11] These three factors relate to each other, and factors like poverty, market freedom, inequality, and property rights influence environmental change indirectly. Consumption is in his view extremely difficult to curb and must be minimized through 'change in values and culture'. He explains that population is very difficult to influence in a direct way, and he argues in favour of guaranteeing women's rights, provision of good health care and family-planning facilities, poverty alleviation, more equal distribution of assets, and economic growth. Population growth is a driving force for technological development particularly in times of (environmental) crisis, and this would then potentially lead to a more sustainable situation. Environmental impact can thus be minimized *in particular* through technological developments that reduce the environmental stress that huge numbers of high consumers cause, and that is coming about under stress and crisis. He calls this the Third Revolution, after the agricultural and industrial revolutions.

Paul Ekins' analysis, however, makes it clear that it is highly unlikely that technological development alone could solve the current and future environmental problems of pollution and resource consumption if the majority of the world's population reach resource consumption levels anywhere close to the affluent populations of this era.[12] Over-consumption and issues of re-distribution of resources and entitlements to pollution have to be addressed if future crises are to be averted. Very high densities of affluent people in Europe for example have access to resources from elsewhere, which is expressed particularly well through the notion of 'ecological footprints' of consumers.[13]

It is in fact only very recently that we have become aware of the global dimension of environmental change, often expressed in terms of 'global commons': the sink function of rain forest is important because of global warming and climate change result-ing from greenhouse-gas pollution, the hole in the ozone layer potentially affects the whole world, acid rain affects countries far away from where the problem is caused. These global problems have so far not caused large numbers of people to migrate or to die, but we can see some huge disasters looming. Meyer-Abich shows that impacts of climatic change are expected to be largely negative ecologically and socially, and they will be felt primarily by lower-income groups, people in dry-lands, city slum dwellers, and residents of islands and lowlands.[14] We can expect more floods in Bangladesh and Egypt, more protracted droughts in Africa, and widespread skin cancer in Australia, i.e. mostly (potential) disasters that affect others than those high-consumers who actually cause the problem.

Throughout history the demise of one empire or state has been accompanied by the rise to (local) power of another, and the degradation of environmental and production potential has led to migrations of people. The peasantry may not have noticed much difference between one or another elite that controlled their surpluses. Migrations were certainly not always without violence, particularly not when it concerned larger groups of people, but the idea of migration has changed with the arrival of the nation state as we know it from the nineteenth and twentieth centuries. It now seems normal to expect that most refugees, whether they flee war, famine or less dramatic economic decline, will ultimately go back to their country of origin, even though they may have migrated to a place with much more space and potential for agricultural production or other livelihoods. The elimination of this option for long-term survival prompts the question about which options are left, and more radically, a question about rights and obligations of people from one nation state towards natural resources elsewhere.

Ekins explains that current high levels of resource consumption by the world's elite consumers can never be attained by all; he doubts whether technological change can cater for a sufficient improvement in resource efficiency.[15] But even if we do not work with the assumption that all of the world's people aspire for that level of consumption, if we just look at the question of survival of the more vulnerable groups of people then it seems that economic growth and technological change still have a very important role to play, in particular if local and global environmental degradation is not halted and reversed. There appear to be increasing numbers of local conflicts around the world, and increasing migration and starvation, possibly fuelled by environmental crisis and resource competition. The next section explores how can we analyse that in a useful way.

4. Resource Competition and the Breakdown of Societies

The term 'environmental refugees' is explained by Norman Myers as 'people who can no longer gain a secure livelihood on their homelands because of long-term environmental problems such as soil erosion, deforestation, desertification, and record droughts.'[16] He claims that there are currently about 25 million such refugees in the world, compared to 23 million who have fled political, ethnic, and religious problems. And, for example, through global warming and sea-level rise we can expect many more millions of environmental refugees in future. It is obviously very difficult to distinguish these groups of displaced people, and indeed he acknowledges that the problem of environmental refugees 'is equally a crisis of social, political and economic sorts'. It seems that labels are not all that important, but that we require some clarity regarding the origins of crises through looking at the connections between all these factors, and not to separate one, (environmental degradation), from the rest.

According to the Oxfam Poverty Report[17] the number of refugees in the world has increased from roughly 16 million in 1988 to 23 million in 1993, whilst there were then about 26 million 'internally displaced' (the official definition of refugee implies that one has to have crossed an international border). The report also says that 'of the 82 major armed conflicts which took place between 1989 and 1992 all but three occurred *within* states'. The nature of these conflicts has changed compared to earlier wars in the sense that civilians have increasingly become targets as well as participants. The causes of these conflicts are, according to the report, diverse, and include 'ethnic tension, denial of political rights, poverty and competition over scarce resources', while it argues that the effects of such conflicts (and in particular migration) can no longer be ignored by other countries.

In an influential yet much criticized paper Kaplan paints a picture of a world future in which chaotic anarchy can almost not be avoided, and the forerunners are in Africa, Asia, and Latin America where nation states are collapsing and in inner cities in the industrialized world where crime rates are rising alarmingly.[18] This would all be caused by a mixture of reasons, including population growth and environmental degradation. But are the places with violence, famine, and migration indeed completely anarchic, and impossible to really understand?

New theories are being developed in order to understand crises like war and/or drought-related famine and population movement better, to look at the driving forces and internal rationale, and to be able to respond better in such situations. The names through which this process is being understood are 'slow onset emergencies', 'permanent emergencies' and 'complex emergencies'. The central idea is that economic and environmental decline and increased competition for resources such as land, and other factors slowly erode the resilience of large groups of people. A relatively minor drought, ethnic or political confrontation, or other reason may then spark off violent conflict, displacement, and/or famine. Often 'humanitarian crises are intentionally created, and powerful political and economic pressures strive to ensure that they are sustained'[19] through the manipulation of food supply and means of food production.

Such emergency situations are called complex because there is no single factor that is the cause of the crisis. Food security, conflict, and environmental change are three 'sets of variables' that Cliffe tries to link conceptually.[20] He draws on the analysis of 'complex emergencies' and the idea of a 'political economy of internal war'[21] in which the occurrence of famine and war is explained as a result of complex relationships between several longer-term factors including the breakdown of the state, crisis in agriculture (i.e. degrading resource quality and availability), and 'triggers' such as the outbreak of conflict or drought. The coping mechanisms, and thus the resilience, of many people breaks down slowly and the triggers cause collapse, resulting in famine. But some people also gain in the situation, for example financially through illegal trade, and they may become a force for a kind of permanent emergency situation. Duffield argues that most of the thinking and acting in recent crises has focused on the 'losers' while it is the 'winners' who institutionalize the political economy of war. This political economy of war model may include further factors, and particularly land control (competition over land), that explain war and famine as an objective for some in maintaining the conflict situation.

Cliffe also argues that political economies of war lead to fundamental changes in people's livelihoods and survival strategies through migration, settlement of pastoralists, or the sale of assets (including land), so that the situation changes drastically and permanently.[22] This leads him to propose that instead of only addressing causes of conflicts once they subside or are over (in order to prevent them from re-emerging), we must also respond to the 'consequences' or 'outcomes' of conflicts. The complexity of the new situation that arises as a result of the crisis should not be looked upon as simply reversible.

Invoking concepts from natural sciences Roche also describes the increasing numbers of long-term emergency situations with words like 'chaos', 'complex', and 'turbulent', effectively meaning that the causes of crises are multiple and interlinked.[23] Events do not follow linear and smooth paths, i.e. from a normal development situation to a crisis to rehabilitation, and back to a normal development situation. Consequently 'solutions' cannot be singular, and he argues for an approach where in any one situation (severe crisis, a threatening crisis, a recovery, or a stable situation) the following 'groups of things' should be done, but in different proportions:

(a) (the focus in a stable situation): Income generation; support sustainable health and education systems; environmental protection; enterprise development; dialogue with governments; reinforcing women's entitlements; provide access to legal protection; etc.

(b) (the focus in a recovery situation): Support political stability and democracy; support institution building; secure and restart production; rehabilitate infrastructure; training; network building; etc.

(c) (the focus in a threatening crisis): Contingency planning and preparedness for crisis; secure production and diversify options; strengthen coping mechanisms; support organizational capacity; etc.

(d) (the focus in a severe crisis): Relief; preservation of local culture; strengthening of local coping mechanisms; political protection and lobbying; securing production; liaison between community and external providers; etc. Roche argues that the (conceptual) relief/development dichotomy is unhelpful and that development agencies have to collaborate in order to 'cover the whole range' from emergency to development and lobbying activities.

In practical terms, these analytical approaches lead to arguments for practical actions during conflict and famine that go far beyond humanitarian relief, i.e. responding to the symptoms, which is the focus of many international agencies. Responses should also go beyond addressing the causes of conflict and famine, which is the focus of several political lobbying groups. This would involve an approach with a wide variety of activities in any one 'complex emergency', i.e. practical 'hands-on' as well as lobbying activities which address both the multiple causes of the conflict, and/or famine *and* respond to the new situation. Responses should almost always include some form of institutional development, since the nation state may have all but collapsed and non-governmental organizations may have been weakened or suppressed before and during the conflict. Activities could also include the regeneration or the protection of particular environmental resources, for example sources for survival such as drinking-water, and sources for agricultural production. This in fact almost always happens to some extent. The analysis of famine by Sen and the ideas around complex emergencies of Duffield and others lead almost directly to the conclusion that rights and access issues need addressing *in particular* in times of war and environmental crisis, for example the control over land but also questions of access to salaries and markets, whilst permanent migration should become an option in some cases. For example, partial or local registration of land claims, which is currently most unusual in emergency response work, could be an example of a stabilizing factor in a turbulent situation.

Attempts to work in such holistic ways are vividly apparent in the concrete situations described in the next section, which will be looking at environmental resources as a potential cause for conflict, a source for conflict, and a source for survival.

5. Ecological Change: Cause for Conflict and Resource for Survival

In this section the spotlight is thrown on ecological change and the roles it can play with regard to conflict and survival. Some examples of concrete situations follow in which environmental resources played a prominent role (a) in causing a conflict and humanitarian crisis (Rwanda), (b) in fuelling a conflict (Sierra Leone); (c) in enabling the survival of victims (Sudan and Kivu and Kagera); and (d) in attempts to develop opportunities for longer-term survival and integration of refugees during a crisis (Uganda). The examples are not given in order to illustrate the 'how to' by agencies through showing success stories or failures; they are meant to highlight the difficulties and dilemmas that are met and the choices that might have to be made following an analysis of complex reality.

Rwanda—An Environmental Cause of Conflict

In a brief history of the events that led to the genocide of Tutsis and the gruesome violence against Hutus in Rwanda, Vassall-Adams mentions mounting population pressure and limited land for the predominantly rural population as important factors contributing to the tensions in Rwanda.[24] Fairhead looked at demographic developments in Rwanda and Kivu, and concluded 'There is unquestionably a land problem in the Great Lakes region related to demographic issues. But as everywhere, the land problem primarily relates to land value, and the social, economic and political mechanisms which distribute wealth in society.'[25] And in an overview of land tenure arrangements and dilemmas in current day Rwanda, Larbi reports the diminishing size of average family holdings, the fragmentation of plots, and the historically strongly centralized control of land combined with the effective existence of a local land market.[26]

Gasana sees ethnicity as an important factor in the history of Rwandan conflicts but stresses that the centralized control over the resources land and state are at the core of the power struggles that can explain the violence.[27] He explains the emergence of a cattle and land clientship relation between Tutsi elites and agriculturist Hutus and 'ordinary Tutsis' (centuries ago) that became highly exploitative. This went hand-in-hand with a strong military buildup, and over the years control over land resources and the state became strongly centralized. The Tutsi domination was not fundamentally challenged by the German and Belgian colonial powers, although the latter tried to support the emancipation of the Hutus towards the end of their control of Rwanda. In the run up to independence in 1962 ethnic tensions had reached very serious levels, causing displacement of hundreds of thousands of people, mainly Tutsis. Equal access to land, education and jobs (with the state) had become 'the rallying cry' of the elites arguing against the aristocratic domination, and after independence the Hutu government redistributed land, particularly to landless Hutus.

The resulting relative equality in land ownership (although still almost entirely controlled by men) led however over the following years to new inequality due to rapid partitioning of holdings, the emergence of a land market and land speculation. The state benefited initially from good earnings in agriculture too, but then coffee prices fell and the state was increasingly controlled by a corrupt elite, abusing their state powers in private business deals. Gasana warned even before the events of 1994 of an ensuing disaster in the making due to rapidly increasing population, stagnating agricultural production and large numbers of landless, malnourished peasants, and 'the systemic crisis became instrumental to generate the ethnic problem, where the basic focus of war was power'.[28] He goes on to explain that throughout history Rwandan military power has always been in the hands of just one ethnic group, and that the Hutu army had been used primarily to protect the State from former aristocrats and to protect the business deals of those in power. When the genocide of Tutsis and massacres of Hutus did happen in 1994 he believes people acted mainly out of fear, 'that if the other one gets more armed it will not only jump to power but exterminate the others as well'. Now the country is ruled again by a minority that controls the armed forces, the state, and natural resources. Gasana's proposals for 'instruments of a durable peace' must address 'structures and institutions that lead to inequality of access to land and state resources and that nourish ethnic fears'. His proposals include a radical decentralization of power, radical demilitarization, a federal connection with neighbouring states (particularly Tanzania) and moreover a kind of 'Marshall plan for Rwanda' because he believes economic growth and opportunity for non-agricultural livelihoods are essential to reduce the tensions.

The analysis that control over land, and thus livelihoods, is central in explaining the conflict is largely supported by André and Platteau.[29] They address the questions of land tenure and fragmentation and increased population based on detailed fieldwork in a community in north-west Rwanda. Over the 1988–93 study period they observed increased family sizes and decreased sizes of landholdings, as well as increased inequality in landholding within the community. The households with more land also have more access to off-farm income; in fact they seem to acquire land through their off-farm earnings. Most of the land purchase is formally illegal but the land market emerged anyhow. A large percentage of people who sell small plots do so for reasons of survival. The writers observe significant intra-family changes too, such as an increasing age for young adults to leave their parents (because of lack of independent livelihoods) and serious tensions between older and younger members of families. Reasons may include the fact that fathers do not feel obliged to hand the land that they bought to their sons (before or after their death), as they used to do with inherited land. Many marriages are now effectively 'illegal' in a traditional sense because young men fail to pay bride wealth under these circumstances. This means that children from that marriage will not inherit any land at all and nor will the wives (women traditionally have no ownership rights but can use the land of their children). The writers talk of 'inter-generational inequality' and of 'an increasingly exclusionary character of evolving customary rules of land tenure', affecting in particular separated and widowed women.

Longman also observed the interplay of soil degradation, short-age of land, migration and unemployment of youth, frustrations and conflict in two rural communities.[30] He writes about the situation before 1994: 'As opposition to existing structures of power emerged nationally, the poor peasants . . . found means to express their frustration and to challenge local . . . elites,' and he concludes that 'the massacres represented a calculated and systematic attempt by embattled elites to reassert their social, economic, and political dominance and to eliminate any challenges to their authority.'

André and Platteau do not claim that the issues of land, inequal-ity, and economic decline can explain fully the cause of the genocide, but argue that these factors contribute to intra-family and intra-community conflicts.[31] They also write 'it is illusionary to think that formal private property rights recorded in an official land registry following a procedure of land titling can provide a solution to the problem', mainly because of the bureaucratic (practical) complications and costs of such a system, and because of the severity of the problem, meaning there simply is not enough land for all to make a living from agriculture.

If the impossibility of a central registration system is accepted there would obviously have to emerge some form of local institution for the regulation of land access and control: deprivation and conflict are all too obvious results in situations of severe land scarcity. André and Platteau call however in particular for rapid technological development, increases in productivity and 'diversifying economic activities and sources of employment'[32] as the most plausible way out of the current problems, a conclusion very similar to Gasana's,[33] and a number of other writers.[34] Another aspect of a 'solution' to these problems seems to be migration, which may be the immediate result of a federation with neighbouring states such as Gasana suggests.

Sierra Leone—The Environment for War

Richards writes about the recent civil war in Sierra Leone and draws parallels with Liberia.[35] He shows that these are cases where population growth and environmental degradation are not amongst the causes for war, but that exploration and competition for natural resources like diamonds have contributed to social tensions and the recession of the state, whilst the ability to survive in rain forest (where much of the war has taken place) made an essential difference in the war. This ability to survive is explained in the historical context of people living with and in the forest with mineral resources (e.g. diamonds) and wildlife: '[in Sierra Leone] as in Liberia, war is a consequence of political collapse and state recession, not environmental pressure. In both countries war has been incubated in forest fastnesses,'[36] and 'rebel violence in Sierra Leone is no instinctive response to population pressure, but a mobilisation of youth on behalf of a small group of people angry at their exclusion from an opaque patrimonial system serving mineral extraction interests.'[37] Richards concludes that 'coping with war depends on cultural and institutional resourcefulness in civil society' and he suggests that that must be supported 'in order to build islands and archipelagos of peace.'[38]

An important parallel between his analysis and that of the Rwandan crisis by Longman[39] and Oxfam's analysis in Uganda[40] is the fact that local political objectives are served by violence and resource exploitation; indeed that there are winners as well as losers.[41] Richards argues against environmental determinism, but environmental degradation, drought, and population pressure are factors in the crises that affected Sudan (see below) and later Rwanda, so his thesis should not be simply extrapolated.

Sudan—The Environment for Survival

In a study of the interrelationships between environmental change, economic development, and human insecurity in the Horn of Africa, Spooner and Walsh[42] describe a wide range of livelihood and survival strategies that intricately link people and environments: 'Coping strategies and environmental management capabilities vary . . . men and women show highly specialized and intimate knowledge of their natural environment to serve their needs for reducing risks and their needs for construction, tools, human and animals medicines, spices, herbs, food supplements, famine products, seasonal forage and pest control. This knowledge is little tapped in any of the planning operations for modern development or relief schemes.'[43] Livelihood and survival strategies thus include the use of a very wide range of natural resources, and people in the Horn of Africa migrate for purposes of work, trade, or grazing of cattle, they build alliances between different ethnic groups, and in times of crisis they may sell assets and reduce their food intake before abandoning their livelihoods.

   Those strategies are disturbed by slow changes in markets and other institutions as well as natural environments, and by shocks that may occur in the form of livestock epidemics, political upheavals, drought, or otherwise. War and political changes that restrict the movement of pastoralists, or government policies that promote forms of modern agriculture are particular causes for diminishing resilience of local people. An important aspect of the analysis by Spooner and Walsh is that existing livelihood systems are incredibly complex and almost not knowable, yet authorities and intervening agencies can create or support conditions that offer people more opportunities instead of reducing their range of strategies.[44] They argue for rural development policies that help communication and support people's mobility, and that involve pastoralists and agriculturists in planning and decision-making. Pastoralist systems are evolving and the writers promote land tenure reform in order to enable herders to develop new forms of livelihood and advocate land reform and education in order to develop more viable forms of agriculture.

The importance of a bio-diverse environment in times of food crisis has been confirmed in a range of publications. For example, in Tokar, Sudan, in a large project that was part of rehabilitation efforts by Oxfam after droughts in the 1980s and early 1990s, several farmers were interviewed about the normal use of plants and trees and their use in times of food scarcity (for both people and animals) through ranking plants and their potential uses. An astonishing amount of knowledge was displayed in one big diagram which at a later stage was used by elders from the community to explain their use to youngsters. It is, however, questionable whether during the next drought they will be able to depend on 'wild foods' as previously. In this particular society of the Beja in north-east Sudan there are the twin problems of invasive mesquite (*Prosopis juliflora*)—a tree through which the original bio-diversity diminishes, and out-migration of youngsters, in particular to towns, so that knowledge of local environments is eroding.[45]

It seems, once again, that supporting the (local) management of access and control over natural resources and providing the wider conditions for their sustainable use in a changing world is paramount. This should happen in particular through education and local people's participation in development programmes in order to improve both prospects for short-term survival and long-term livelihoods.

The Environmental Impact of Refugees in Central Africa

Refugees fled from Rwanda to Kagera in Tanzania and Kivu in Zaire after April 1994 in extremely large numbers. Refugee camps of up to several hundreds of thousands of inhabitants were created overnight and large numbers died in the first weeks after crossing the international borders. The international community responded with food distributions, the installation of water provision and sanitation systems and distributed various other things, including fuel wood. Several camps were located in places of water scarcity, some were close to internationally renowned natural heritage sites (rain forests). There were camps on volcanic rock in North Kivu, rendering the digging of graves and pit latrines almost impossible, which caused major environmental health threats. There were also large numbers of refugees camped in local schools, parks, and churches.

The environmental impact of this enormous flux of people was significant, and it was largely negative: deforestation, water depletion, soil erosion, and city-scape destruction were among the impacts. Moving the refugees to other areas, where more resources and better conditions were available and environmental impact would be minimized proved to be extremely difficult and costly. Pressures for moving refugees out of towns were very strong, in particular because resentment about the presence of refugees was rising among the host population; the environmental destruction in the wake of their arrival played an important role in this.

Environmental changes such as depletion of confined aquifers or soil erosion did occur, which are environmental changes that are difficult to restore, but the most important impact is deforestation, which could be regenerated or mitigated through tree-planting, etc. Indeed, agencies did mitigate the impact through the distribution of fuel wood from other places, and some restoration did occur in e.g. Bukavu in South Kivu after refugees had been relocated. The large majority of refugees have now returned to Rwanda, but internal Congo-Zairian conflicts have prevented large-scale repair of damage and regeneration of the local production base.

Uganda—An Holistic and Environmental Response to a Crisis

An example of dealing with a temporary 'outcome' of conflict and displacement is work with refugees from southern Sudan in northwest Uganda, in an area known as Ikafe. Refugees have been moved since 1994 from 'care and maintenance camps' at the border with Sudan to a large area in the thinly populated Aringa County for security reasons. Exceptionally, the Ugandan government has adopted a policy that allows refugees access to reasonable amounts of agricultural land so that they can attempt to produce food for themselves and reach a degree of independence from aid efforts.

Aringa County has seen little infrastructure developed over the years and it is prone to violent national and international conflicts. Its population was itself displaced to southern Sudan in the 1980s. The natural resources are not particularly rich in terms of soil quality and water availability, there is tsetse fly (preventing the keeping of cattle), and some forest and wildlife. Careful land cultivation and some protective measures would enable production without devastating the environment, and infrastructure development would be beneficial for the host population as well as the refugees.

Oxfam, the main 'implementing agency', took a broad approach to the needs and problems of refugees and also local residents. In collaboration with the authorities and international agencies it aimed to achieve a minimum level of integration of refugees and a minimum level of (food) self-sufficiency by exploring the use of land for agricultural purposes, and supporting other income-generating activities. It helped in setting up representative structures of refugees parallel to the Ugandan representative system, allowed the host population access to health posts and schools, supplied locals with seedlings from a tree nursery, and the management of services (water, health) was being integrated with the local Ugandan administration.

The programme was designed with the intention of addressing the structural problems that are usually encountered in refugee programmes, such as a lack of refugee participation, in particular women, a lack of consultation with and support for local residents, and a continued dependency of refugees on handouts. Oxfam kept close contact with authorities at all levels, including traditional authorities. It also kept itself well informed about the movements of armies and rebels (at both sides of the international borders) in order to make the best decisions possible regarding security of refugees and staff and in order continuously to assess whether a structural approach to aid was realistic or whether a switch to emergency handouts with a maximum security alert was required. The logistical bases have been evacuated a number of times, and currently the military situation in Sudan has shifted whilst atrocities against them by Ugandan rebels have occurred regularly, causing the return to Sudan of most refugees. The programme is now almost phased out.

But these recent developments could not be predicted with any certainty almost until they actually happened. The programme worked under the assumption that a long term stay was a possible necessity, and that whatever happened politically it would be better to address the structural aspects that have so often been criticized elsewhere. A review of the programme was held in mid-1996 in order to assess the success of the different components of the programme, which included food, tools, utensils and other distributions, road repair and construction, water-well installation, school and health-post building and operation, and also the setting up of a 'refugee council'. During this review various local groups of residents including traditional authorities were consulted, as well as groups of refugees, members of staff and managers of the different international agencies, including Oxfam. Their perspectives on the success of the programme differed and they were brought together in various meetings in order to reach more mutual understanding and a minimum level of consensus about ways forward.

The review highlighted that fuel wood and sanitation, extreme deforestation and soil erosion were *not* of particular concern to refugees, the host population, local authorities or the international agencies, as is usually the case with crowded care and maintenance camps.[46] Some impacts were environmentally negative (like a reduction in wildlife and use by refugees of 'holy bushes' of the local residents), but deforestation was partly counteracted by tree planting, land was allocated and brought into cultivation by refugees without causing soil erosion, and wells were installed for both hosts and refugees. The presence of refugees had a positive impact on the local economy and availability of services. There remained, however, strong dissatisfaction among the host population, partly due to a limited funding commitment for local development activities of the international donors of the programme, and also because of strong distrust of the intentions of the national and district authorities: the dissatisfaction became entangled with the local political objectives of rebels.[47]

The claim of traditional and elected local leaders alike was that they had invited the refugees to come, they had offered land for their use, yet they felt that too few of their kinspeople were benefiting from schools, employment, water-supply, etc. On the contrary, some of their land would have been used against their will. It emerged that local leaders and possibly even warlords aimed to increase the status of Aringa County, a political objective that could be reached in part through infrastructure development. Formally however, the land was being allocated by a central ministry to the refugees through the mediation of international agencies like Oxfam, and the international community must focus its dealings with central government even where its authority is being disputed.

So how can such a complex situation be turned to the benefit of all, or minimally, how can violence be avoided? In one of many meetings that were organized to deal with the problems, local leaders suggested the setting up of extra legal negotiation forums between locals, officials, refugees and agencies that could help decide the actual allocation of land to refugees and infrastructure development. In this and many other cases, dealings with local leaders and even warlords may be crucial to the success of humanitarian relief. Furthermore, the review stressed that more efforts than Oxfam has so far made are required to involve local hosts and refugees in shared committees and forums so that they are all involved in management of services and infrastructure, and a contribution is made to constructive communication and collaboration.[48]

There could even be a more radical but politically less acceptable way to avoid all those complexities. Harrell-Bond warned the Ikafe programme against 'a refugee centric approach' and advised that good knowledge of and relationships with the local and refugee leadership was essential for success and would want to see the 'free movement and residence of refugees throughout the County'.[49] She also asks 'will the Ugandan Government permit the formalisation of such a flexible approach to developing Aringa County? Uganda's domestic legislation gives the government the right to insist on where refugees live. On the other hand, this provision contravenes international standards of human rights as

well as the 1951 Convention. Given Oxfam's established contact
with . . . it should be possible to persuade the Government to
adopt a flexible policy so long as it is not threatened with the
withdrawal of aid'.[50] Such free movement of refugees would have
forged a more real form of social integration than a refugee camp
or settlement area of any sort ever can.

6. Conclusions: Surviving Ecological Degradation and Conflicts

*Analyse 'complex emergencies' and their internal rationale, and
act accordingly.*

The world will not be destroyed in one environmental apocalyptic
disaster resulting from pollution and the overuse of resources, as
the Club of Rome may have suggested. Rather, the environmental
crisis has already started: we will see an increasing number of local
political crises which are extremely difficult to comprehend and to
deal with because they are caused by an array of interacting
phenomena in which environmental degradation and resource
distribution play an increasingly important role. This is happening
in particular in the poorer and politically more fragile parts of the
world. We need to understand more about the conditions under
which complex emergencies are building up, and learn about
how to prevent and act. Not least because they are also 'spilling
over' to other areas, in the form of refugees, political instability
(criminality), and environmental stress. It is no longer possible to
respond with blueprint relief solutions to famines and population
movements, but rather both causes and the new situation have to
be responded to in a structural manner.

*Peace is an important precondition for social justice and ecological
sustainability.*

Peace could be seen as a precondition for development, but
environmental quality and resource availability (control) play a
sometimes pivotal role in causation, prevention, and possibly
resolution of conflict. Watkins writes 'conflict prevention must,

as all the founders of the UN realised, start with national and
international policies, which are aimed at eradicating poverty and
giving all the world's people a stake in their society'.[51] Oxfam's
recommendations regarding conflict prevention and resolution
obviously include the reduction of arms sales, reorganizations in
the international system, etc. It could however be questioned
whether we can or should wait for (local) peace before addressing
issues of resource quality and control. Richards argued for support
to local 'islands' of peace in the conflict situation in Sierra Leone,
and indeed Oxfam pursued a broad development approach and
elaborate consultation with a range of stakeholders in a volatile
situation in Uganda, albeit with limited success.[52]

*Strong sustainability cannot be pursued in a situation of poverty,
rapid population growth, economic decline and weak systems of
governance, let alone in a situation of conflict and large population movements.*

Environmentalism and ecologically sustainable development
become unachievable goals in societies that find themselves in
downward spirals of economic decline, political controversy,
increased resource competition, etc. There is an increasing
number of examples around the world where the corresponding
erosion of central-level influence and/or the breakdown of values
and structures that hold communities and families together seems
to end the idea of a coherent nation state. Yet it is exactly in these
situations and in the 'complex emergencies' that may arise from
them, that environmental quality and access to environmental
resources is of critical importance to both the survival of local
people and to political stability.

   Macrae, Zwi, Duffield and others have argued that in a process
of ecological and economic decline, and amid the abuse of personal and political rights, 'political economies of war' emerge, i.e.
'predatory' political economies in which famines and social breakdown are generated.[53] They write that 'the social and civic costs'
of these conflicts are 'of far greater' importance than the 'formal
costs' which include loss of infrastructure, GNP, and lives. Warlords appropriate aid resources, manipulate markets, and we can

observe 'the loss of capacity at government and policy-making levels and the emergence of extra-legal forms of survival. Unless such issues are tackled, present relief strategies that focus on the delivery of commodities, and, at best, on physical repair, will simply continue to feed the emergency.'[54]

Economic growth is essential for 'substitution' to happen of capital for natural resources, otherwise no form of sustainability is possible, and no place is available within Dobson's typology.[55] In other words (ecological) exploitation by predatory political economies seems by definition ecologically unsustainable and thus only leads to more problems for large groups of people.

When a crisis has caused large numbers of people to move, such as in the case of Rwandan refugees who left for Tanzania and Zaire in 1994, environmental impact will be largely negative, at least initially. But aid efforts can mitigate this impact, and even reverse or regenerate most of it during or after the presence of large numbers of people.[56]

Economic growth is a precondition for peace and justice.

The need for economic growth as a central factor contributing to peace has been argued by Gasana and others for the case of Rwanda.[57] Economic growth is impossible without very rapid technology transfer, adaptation, and development, that is, technology that allows relatively high levels of material well-being without high levels of resource consumption and pollution.[58]

The international redistribution of claims on/use of natural and economic resources must be considered in various ways, in order to deal fairly, with population increase and the effects and causes of conflicts.

Different angles on the problem of population growth are, for example, an analysis of population control policies from an individual rights perspective[59] and the contribution that population growth makes to environmental change (locally and globally).[60] Both approaches seem to lead logically to the conclusion that international redistribution of resources and consumer rights is required. This has also been shown by Ekins under the premiss that we would want the majority of the world's population to have material lives that are close to those in the industrialized countries at present whilst achieving ecological sustainability.[61] This obviously begs the question *how* to redistribute consumption and pollution rights, but that question is beyond the scope of this chapter.[62]

Analysts like Harrell-Bond argue that asylum policies and practices must change so that refugees can integrate better and more often with host populations, to the benefit of both themselves and the local economy.[63] This must happen instead of being brought into camp-type settlements where they cannot be productive, where they remain a burden for the local authorities and the international community, and are the symbol for aspirations of returning to the pre-crisis situation, which is clearly not always possible without future violence and destruction.

In the case of Rwanda, Gasana argued in favour of a federation with neighbouring states, which would potentially make available vast, thinly populated parts of say Tanzania for the high-density population of Rwanda.[64]

The participation of local people and the development of democratic structures should be central to any policy, even in a situation of conflict or threatening conflict, in order to achieve some level of social justice and ecological sustainability through the strengthening of civil society.

Roche recommends that in complex and turbulent situations a broad mix of objectives and activities should indeed be pursued by aid agencies as we know it from 'development': preventive measures, welfare measures, capacity building, and institutional development efforts, political mediation and influencing activities, and much more.[65] This should be extended to the repair and regeneration of ecological resources in war- and famine-affected areas because their quality and the access that people have to them quite clearly play an important role in causing, perpetuating, and sustaining conflicts, famine, and mass migration.[66] This may often imply a choice of working with 'outcome' and not just with reference to the causes of the crisis.[67]

The case of the Ikafe settlement in Uganda is an example of a complex situation in which negotiations over natural resources, i.e. access to land, should happen at least partly locally, and not just with central authorities.[68] Duffield writes (on the basis of analysis of crises in Somalia, Angola, former Yugoslavia, and others) that, 'if predatory local political structures are the determining factor in a complex emergency, it follows that the situation can only be adequately addressed by an alternative indigenous political structure. International trusteeship of permanent refugee status cannot play this role. International efforts must therefore be geared to developing popular and alternative indigenous solutions'.[69]

These ideas of working with local people (i.e. not just the leaders and driving forces of the predatory political economy) are consistent with the ideas of participants in the seminar series that inspired this book. For example Norton argued that local people must be involved in the articulation of environmental values,[70] and Miller has also concluded that democratic processes are essential for the just distribution of environmental resources.[71] This should not necessarily assume that local involvement can only happen within the structure of a functioning nation-state that may be seen to be able to oversee the implementation of just environmental allocations. In its absence traditional and evolving local power relations and decision-making structures must be part of the picture.

NOTES

INTRODUCTION

1. A. Dobson, *Justice and the Environment: Conceptions of Environmental Sustainability and Dimensions of Social Justice* (Oxford: Oxford University Press, 1998), chs. 2 and 3.
2. Ibid. ch. 5.
3. Ibid.
4. A. Dobson, 'Environmental Sustainabilities: An Analysis and a Typology', *Environmental Politics*, 5 (1996a), 401–28; also Dobson (1998).
5. Dobson (1998), ch. 3.
6. J. Rawls, *A Theory of Justice* (Oxford: Clarendon Press, 1972).
7. J. Rawls, *Political Liberalism* (New York: Columbia University Press, 1993).

CHAPTER 1

1. These terms are now used more or less interchangeably. S. Lélé, 'Sustainable Development: A Critical Review', *World Development*, 19 (1991), 607–21, and M. Jacobs, *The Green Economy* (London: Pluto Press, 1991), distinguish between the narrower environmental meaning of 'sustainability' and the wider socio-political meaning of 'sustainable development'. This has not generally been followed elsewhere, but see Andrew Dobson, 'Environmental Sustainabilities: An Analysis and Typology', *Environmental Politics*, 5 (1996a), 401–28, and *id., Justice and the Environment: Conceptions of Environmental Sustainability and Dimensions of Social Justice* (Oxford: Oxford University Press, 1998), ch. 2. Sustainability now tends to be used effectively as an abbreviation of sustainable development. Recalling this distinction, I use the latter term in this chapter.
2. *Blueprint for Survival* 1972 ('sustainable' society, meaning 'stable') and *World Conservation Strategy* 1980.

3. United Nations Commission on Environment and Development, *Our Common Future* (Oxford: Oxford University Press, 1987).

4. See T. O'Riordan, *Environmentalism* (2nd edn.) (London: Pion Publishers, 1981).

5. See e.g. Lélé (1991).

6. Prominent among the 'ultra-green' opponents of the concept of sustainable development is *The Ecologist* magazine: see e.g. The Ecologist, *Whose Common Future? Reclaiming the Commons* (London: Earthscan, 1993). See also W. Sachs, *Global Ecology* (London: Zed Books, 1993), particularly the chapters by Sachs, Finger, and Worster; and T. de la Court, *Beyond Brundtland* (London: Zed Books, 1991).

7. P. Macnaghten, R. Grove-White, M. Jacobs, and M. Wynne, *Public Perceptions and Sustainability in Lancashire: Indicators, Institutions, Participation* (Report to Lancashire County Council, Centre for the Study of Environmental Change, Lancaster University, 1995); P. Macnaghten, 'Is Sustainability a Cultural Ghetto?', unpublished, Centre for the Study of Environmental Change, Lancaster University, 1993. See also R. Grove-White, 'Environment and Society; Some Reflections', speech given to the Green Alliance, November 1994.

8. Here 'Northern' refers to Northern Europe, and Canada and Australia. The analysis is derived principally from observation of the discourse and politics at work in Britain; similar general arguments apply to other countries, but no claims are made about the details.

9. M. Jacobs, 'Sustainable Development: Assumptions, Contradictions, Progress', in J. Lovenduski and J. Stanyer (eds.), *Contemporary Political Studies 1995* (Belfast: Political Studies Association, 1995), iii, 1,470–85.

10. In environmental economics, sustainability is defined in terms of 'maintaining the capital stock'. This is discussed further below. In effect, the debates in environmental economics can be characterized as arguments over the 'operational objectives' implied by the basic Brundtland and *Caring for the Earth* definitions. In practice these debates are of little interest to those involved in political or policy arguments over sustainable development.

11. World Commission on Environment and Development, *Our Common Future* (The Brundtland Report) (Oxford: Oxford University Press, 1987).

12. *Caring for the Earth* (Gland, Switz., World Conservation Union, UN Environment Programme and World Wide Fund for Nature, 1991).

13. H. Brooks, 'Sustainability and Technology', in *Science and Sustainability* (Vienna, International Institute for Applied Systems Analysis, 1992), cited (more or less approvingly) by W. Beckerman, '"Sustainable Development": Is It a Useful Concept?', *Environmental Values*, 3 (1994), 191–209.

14. Lélé, (1991), 618.

15. It should be said at once that this criticism is only directed at debates over the 'meaning of the concept', not over 'what the concept means in practice'. Clarification of the latter is extremely useful and important. It includes discussion of the *operational objectives* required to achieve sustainable development (such as limiting harvest rates of renewable resources to their regeneration rates), of the *management principles* needed to generate more sustainable policies (such as the precautionary principle), and—most important of all—of the *policies and practices* required to achieve sustainability (for example, approaches to forestry or agriculture). All these are essential components of making sustainable development 'meaningful' and operational in practice.

16. W. Gallie, 'Essentially Contested Concepts', *Proceedings of the Aristotelian Society*, 56 (1955–6), 167–98.

17. There *was*, of course, a period when even the first-level meaning was contested, and there was a genuine struggle to ensure that certain of the core ideas were included in it. But this time has now passed: ultimately linguistic meanings are socially constructed, not intellectually 'defined', and the prevalence of the discourse is now such that sustainable development means what its users take it to mean. This intellectual-political history would make a fascinating study, but not here.

18. Cf. D. Pearce, A. Markandya, and E. Barbier, *Blueprint for a Green Economy* (London: Earthscan, 1989); Jacobs (1991); Lélé (1991).

19. *Agenda 21* (New York, UNCED, 1992). Throughout, *Agenda 21* emphasizes that sustainable development requires the participation of every sector of society, including national governments, business, local government, trade unions, non-governmental and community organizations, women, indigenous people, and other disadvantaged groups.

20. It is interesting to compare in this regard the complacent response of the British Government in its original response to the Brundtland Report (Her Majesty's Government, *Our Common Future: A Perspective by the United Kingdom on the Report of the World Commission on Environment and Development* (London, Department of the Environment,

1988)), which basically argued that Britain was already pursuing sustainable development policies, with its much more probing understanding of the problem in its 1994 response to the Earth Summit, *Sustainable Development: The UK Strategy*.

21. The development of the UK's National Strategy was an interesting case in point.

22. See e.g. 'The Green Alliance Sets Twenty Key Tests for the Government's "Sustainable Development: The UK Strategy"', Press Release, 21 Jan. 1994.

23. M. Hajer, 'Ecological Modernization and Social Change', in S. Lash, B. Szerszynski, and B. Wynne (eds.), *Risk, Environment and Modernity: Towards a New Ecology* (London: Sage, 1995).

24. M. Hajer, *The Politics of Environmental Discourse: Ecological Modernization and the Regulation of Acid Rain* (Oxford: Oxford University Press, 1994).

25. Her Majesty's Government, *Sustainable Development: The UK Strategy*; Confederation of British Industry, *Statement of Principles*.

26. Michael Heseltine, MP, quoted in Local Government Management Board, *A Framework for Local Sustainability* (Luton: LGMB, 1993).

27. See e.g. D. Pearce and G. Atkinson, *Are National Economies Sustainable? Measuring Sustainable Development*, Working Paper (Centre for Social and Economic Research on the Global Environment, University College, London, 1992). For a discussion see P. Victor, *et al.*, 'How Strong is Weak Sustainability?', in S. Faucheux, M. O'Connor, and J. van der Straaten (eds.), *Sustainable Development: Analysis and Public Policy* (Dordrecht: Kluwer, 1995); and M. Jacobs, 'Sustainable Development, Capital Substitution and Economic Humility: A Response to Beckerman', *Environmental Values*, 4 (1995b), 57–68.

28. See e.g. T. Banuri, 'The Landscape of Diplomatic Conflicts' and S. Kothari and P. Parajuli, 'No Nature Without Social Justice', both in Sachs (1993).

29. See e.g. Her Majesty's Government, *Sustainable Development: The UK Strategy*; Local Government Management Board, *Framework for Local Sustainability*; World Wide Fund for Nature UK, *Changing Direction: Towards a Green Britain* (Godalming: WWF UK, 1994). It is notable that the Founding Statement of the 'Real World' coalition of British development, environment, and anti-poverty organizations is committed to 'environmental sustainability and social justice': the implication is clearly that the former does not include—or is not understood as including—the latter.

30. See e.g. F. Pearce, 'North–South Rift Bars Path to Summit', *New Scientist,* 23 (November 1991).
31. W. Rees and M. Wackernagel, 'Ecological Footprints and Appropriated Carrying Capacity: Measuring the Natural Capital Requirements of the Human Economy', in A. Jansson, M. Hammer, C. Folke, and R. Costanza (eds.), *Investing in Natural Capital: The Ecological Economics Approach to Sustainability* (Washington DC: Island Press, 1994); M. van Brakel, and M. Buitenkamp, *Sustainable Netherlands* (Rotterdam: Friends of the Earth Netherlands/Milieu Defensie, 1992); International Institute for Environment and Development, *Citizen Action to Reduce Ecological Footprints: A Review of Concepts and Methods,* Report for the Department of the Environment (London: IIED, 1995).
32. Department of the Environment, *Climate Change: Our National Programme for CO$_2$ Emissions* (London: DoE, 1992).
33. The term 'round table' is used differently in Canada; see below.
34. For a succinct description see J. Gordon, *Canadian Round Tables and Other Mechanisms for Sustainable Development in Canada* (Luton: Local Government Management Board, 1994). See also R. Doering, 'Canadian Round Tables on the Environment and the Economy: Their History, Form and Function', Working Paper, National Round Table on the Environment and the Economy, Ottawa, 1993.
35. C. Church and M. Lachowicz, *Towards Local Sustainability: A Review of Local Agenda 21 Activity* (London: United Nations Association, 1995).
36. Roger Levett, CAG Consultants, and Mark Roseland, School of Resource and Environmental Resource Management, Simon Fraser University, British Columbia, personal communications.
37. Local Government Management Board, *Sustainability Indicators Research Project: Report of Phase One* (Luton: LGMB, 1994).
38. Such a broad interpretation is common in Canada. See for example British Columbia Round Table on the Environment and the Economy, *Towards a Strategy for Sustainability* (Victoria: BCRTEE, 1992). The pioneering list of indicators produced by the 'Sustainable Seattle' project reflect a similarly broad interpretation. See *Indications for a Sustainable Seattle* (Seattle: Sustainable Seattle, 1993).
39. For an example of this formulation, see Local Government Management Board, *Framework for Local Sustainability.* It is interesting that some environmental organizations have started to refer only to 'environmental sustainability' or 'sustainable environments' in order to distinguish their narrow use from the broad one. See for example

M. Jacobs, *Sense and Sustainability: Land Use Planning and Environmentally Sustainable Development* (London: Council for the Protection of Rural England, 1993); English Nature, *Planning for Environmental Sustainability* (Peterborough: English Nature, 1994).

40. This was the reaction of a number of local authorities to the pilot list of indicators proposed by the Local Government Management Board 'Sustainability Indicators' project. Jan McHarry, United Nations Association Sustainable Development Unit, personal communication.

41. E. Barbier, 'The Concept of Sustainable Economic Development', *Environmental Conservation*, 14 (1987), defines social sustainability as 'The ability to maintain desired social values, traditions, institutions, cultures, or other social characteristics.' This idea is implicit, and sometimes used, in Canadian interpretations of sustainable development, where both social equity and the maintenance of community traditions and institutions are stressed along with economic viability and ecological health. See for example British Columbia Round Table, *Towards a Strategy for Sustainability*. However, though the idea is supported by many development organizations the term 'social sustainability' is not, because it implies that societies and cultures should not develop and change. See D. Satterthwaite.

42. See e.g. A. Agarawal and S. Narain, *Towards Green Villages: A Strategy for Environmentally Sound and Participatory Rural Development* (Delhi: Centre for Science and Environment, 1990), extracted in Sachs (1993).

43. Though arguably the model dominant in local government circles is non-egalitarian, and thus does not correspond to the full 'radical' position.

44. The Local Government Management Board, *Sustainability Indicators Research Project* is its first major expression.

45. Local Government Management Board, *Sustainability Indicators Research Project*.

46. Doering, 'Canadian Round Tables', and personal communication.

47. *Lancashire Environmental Action Plan* (Preston: Lancashire Environmental Forum, 1993).

48. This is discussed in M. Jacobs, 'Sustainable Development: Assumptions, Contradictions, Progress'.

CHAPTER 2

1. For ease of exposition only, I am adopting here, but not endorsing, a narrowly anthropocentric notion of 'morality'.

2. World Commission on Environment and Development, *Our Common Future* (The Brundtland Report) (Oxford: Oxford University Press, 1987), 43.

3. For anyone with a non-anthropocentric perspective, this can also, of course, be a moral concern.

4. I. Deutscher, *Stalin* (rev. edn.) (Harmondsworth: Penguin, 1966), 296.

5. W. Beckerman, 'Sustainable Development: Is It a Useful Concept?', *Environmental Values*, 3 (1994), 191–209.

6. R. K. Turner and D. Pearce, 'Sustainable Economic Development: Economic and Ethical Principles', in E. Barbier (ed.), *Economics and Ecology: New Frontiers and Sustainable Development* (London: Chapman & Hall, 1993), 180.

7. A. Clayton, 'The Reality of Sustainability', *ECOS*, 2/4 (1991), 14.

8. P. Shepherd and J. Gillespie, 'Developing Definitions of Natural Capital for Use Within the Uplands of England', *English Nature Research Report No. 197* (Peterborough: English Nature, 1996), 23.

9. D. Pearce, *Economic Values and the Natural World* (London: Earthscan, 1993), 51–3; W. Beckerman, 'How Would You Like Your Sustainability, Sir? Weak or Strong?', *Environmental Values*, 4 (1995*a*).

10. It is therefore sad to see English Nature, the statutory body whose job it is to protect nature in England, centring its policies around the concept of natural capital (English Nature, 1994).

11. H. Daly, 'On Wilfred Beckerman's Critique of Sustainable Development', *Environmental Values*, 4 (1995).

12. The present writer wholly endorses the view that environmental valuation is properly a matter of judgment not of measurement—or, more precisely, a matter of judgement applied to measurements rather than of measurement applied to judgements (A. Holland, 'The Foundations of Environmental Decision-Making', *International Journal of Environment & Pollution*, 7 (1997*a*)).

13. A. Holland, 'Substitutability: Or, Why Strong Sustainability is Weak and Absurdly Strong Sustainability is Not Absurd', in J. Foster (ed.) *Valuing Nature? Economics, Ethics and the Environment* (London: Routledge, 1997*b*). Essentially, the point is that there is no non-relational answer to the question: 'Is X a substitute for Y?' There are, of course, people for whom a cardboard box is no substitute for

a house. Unfortunately, there are also people for whom it *is* (and has to be).

14. But see Daly (1995).

15. 'Some ecological assets ('critical' Kn (= natural capital)) serve life-support functions. Removing them in a context where there is no man-made substitute means possible major harm for mankind' (Turner and Pearce (1993), 181). English Nature puts a slightly different slant on critical natural capital, which would need separate discussion: 'Critical Natural Capital is defined as those assets, stock levels or quality levels that are highly valued; and also either essential to human health, essential to the efficient functioning of life-support systems, or irreplaceable or unsubstitutable for all practicable purposes' (English Nature (1994)). It is notable that on this definition, being valued *by* humans is a necessary condition of being critical.

16. S. Gould, 'Kingdoms Without Wheels', in *Hen's Teeth and Horse's Toes* (Harmondsworth: Penguin, 1984). The two exceptions which Gould records are the bacterium *E. coli* and a single-celled organism that lives in the gut of termites.

17. Turner and Pearce (1993), 181.

18. It is unclear how far environmentalists can go in explaining such behaviour purely by reference to human 'greed' as distinct from ordinary and understandable attempts to alleviate and ameliorate the human condition.

19. From this perspective, the pursuit of sustainability understood in this way looks much more like a continuation of 'business as usual' than a departure from it. By the same token, hanging on to, or even reintroducing, natural ecosystems, if it is no longer misconstrued as the counsel of 'precaution', can be reconstrued as the more adventurous and risky path and therefore, as a departure from the pursuit of security.

20. Turner and Pearce (1993), 181.

21. There is an additional, conceptual point to be made here, which is that reversibility is itself a matter of which end you get hold of a process by. Species extinction is said to be irreversible. But looked at another way, it is simply the manifestation of the *reversibility* of the process of speciation.

22. J. Lawton, 'Are Species Useful?', *OIKOS*, 62 (1991), 4.

23. For the full, 'graphic' typology, see W. Fox, 'Why Care About the World Around Us?', *Resurgence*, 161 (1993). Notice that the idea of nature as 'storehouse' is every bit as metaphorical as the idea

of nature as 'gymnasium', although this fact tends to escape economists who treat the idea of nature as 'storehouse' (or 'resource') as
if it were a 'given'.

24. D. Defoe, *A Tour through England and Wales 1724–26* (London: Dent,
    1927), ii, 269.

25. How much (natural) capital there is, is a function of how much
    capability (to generate welfare) it represents, which is predominantly
    a function of available human-made and human capital.

26. Turner and Pearce (1993), 180.

27. Daly (1995).

28. M. Sagoff, 'Biotechnology and the Environment: What Is At Risk?',
    Agriculture and Human Values, 5 (1988*b*), 31.

29. The example is illustrative only; I ignore the fact that human-made
    capital has crept in.

30. J. C. V. Pezzey, 'Sustainability Constraints Versus "Optimality"
    Versus Intertemporal Concern, and Axioms Versus Data', *Land
    Economics*, 73 (1997), 5.

31. W. Beckerman, 'Sustainable Development and Our Obligations to
    Future Generations' (ch. 3, this volume).

32. P. Dasgupta and G. M. Heal, *Economic Theory and Exhaustible
    Resources* (Cambridge: Cambridge University Press, 1979), 299.

33. M. O'Connor and J. Martínez-Alier, 'Ecological Distribution and
    Distributed Sustainability', in S. Faucheux, M. O'Connor, and
    J. van der Straaten (eds.), *Sustainable Development: Concepts, Ration-
    alities and Strategies* (Dordrecht: Kluwer, 1996).

34. As advocated by Gillespie and Shepherd in their English Nature
    Research Report: 'selection [sc. of SSSIs] needs to be based on a
    realistic perception of the values which concerned society places on
    these features of nature rather than on the arcane concepts of
    theoretical ecology' ((1995), 34). They neither explain why it is
    relevant to allege that the concepts of ecology are arcane, nor
    stop to consider whether, if this is true, the answer might lie in
    educating society rather than denigrating ecology.

CHAPTER 3

1. See further discussion of the standard economist's disregard for
   distributional considerations in the context of optimal growth
   theory in W. Beckerman, 'Intergenerational Equity and the Environment', *Journal of Political Philosophy*, 5 (1997), 392–405.

2. It is for this reason that scattered throughout the vast literature on justice and equity are learned discussions of the relationship in the original Greek language between the words 'justice' and 'equality'. What it is that should be distributed equally is, of course, a subject of hot dispute and candidates for an appropriate equilisand include welfare, preference satisfaction, opportunities, capabilities, Rawlsian 'primary goods', functionings, economic resources, and so on—all with possible variations, such as the exclusion of allowance for 'expensive' tastes.

3. See the controversy between me and two of my critics, who disagreed with each other on major aspects of sustainable development, in W. Beckerman, '"Sustainable Development": Is it a Useful Concept?', *Environmental Values*, 3 (1994), 191–210; H. Daly, 'On Wilfred Beckerman's Critique of Sustainable Development', *Environmental Values*, 4 (1995), 49–56; M. Jacobs, 'Sustainable Development, Capital Substitution and Economic Humility: A Response to Beckerman', *Environmental Values*, 4 (1995), 57–68; and W. Beckerman, 'How Would You Like Your Sustainability, Sir? Weak or Strong? A Reply to My Critics', *Environmental Values*, 4 (1995*a*), 169–79.

4. J. Pezzey, *Sustainable Development Concepts: An Economic Analysis*, (Washington: World Bank Environment Paper No.2, 1992). In a more recent paper Pezzey has indicated that the variety of definitions of sustainable development has proliferated enormously since his 1992 survey and provides a useful classification of three most common sustainability 'contraints' encountered now in the literature (J. Pezzey, 'Sustainability Constraints versus "Optimality" versus Intertemporal Concern, and Axioms versus Data', *Land Economics*, 73 (1997)).

5. S. Faucheux, D. Pearce, and J. Proops (eds.), *Models of Sustainable Development* (Cheltenham: Edward Elgar, 1996), 4.

6. R. Nozick, *The Examined Life* (New York: Simon and Schuster, 1989), 99 ff. Pezzey, who is one of the most thoughtful commentators on sustainable development, specifically rebukes me, in Pezzey (1997), for failing to be convinced of the validity of this position.

7. Nozick (1989), 100.

8. Ibid. 101 n.

9. Ibid. 100.

10. As it happens I do not dissent from the view that certain values, including some environmental values, may well be incommensurate with most market values (see W. Beckerman and J. Pasek, 'Plural

Values and Environmental Valuation', *Environmental Values*, 6 (1997), 65–86).

11. Nozick's (1989) footnote to p. 101 discusses some other complicated issues that arise in making the sort of comparison attempted above, but it would be beyond the scope of this paper as well as of my own competence to embark on a discussion of them. But while I remain unconvinced I am particularly indebted to John Broome for persuading me that it may not be possible to dispose of the argument in the simple manner set out in the above model.

12. R. H. Tawney, *Equality*, (5th edn.) (London: Unwin 1964), 48.

13. J. Raz, *The Morality of Freedom* (Oxford: Oxford University Press, 1986), 234.

14. A mathematical proof—for the benefit of the very suspicious-minded—is contained in Beckerman (1997).

15. For an excellent recent survey of the different interpretations of *intrinsic* values and of their role in environmental ethics see J. O'Neill, *Ecology, Policy and Politics* (London: Routledge, 1993), ch. 2.

16. A. Margalit, *The Decent Society* (Cambridge, Mass.: Harvard University Press, 1996), 69.

17. Arne Naess, the father figure of the deep ecology movement, gives the first principle of the movement as 'The well-being and flourishing of human and non-human Life on earth have value in themselves (synonyms: intrinsic value, inherent value). These values are independent of the usefulness of the non-human world for human purposes' (A. Naess and G. Sessions, 'Basic Principles of Deep Ecology', *Ecophilosophy*, 6 (1984), 3–7.

18. This does not imply that Y is the person directly affected by X. Y may value X on account of the effect that it will have (good or bad) on some other person, Z, who may not even be aware that it is the X that is the cause of his good fortune or misfortune.

19. J. Broome, *Weighing Goods* (Oxford: Blackwell, 1991), 180–1. See also T. M. Scanlon, 'Rights, Goals, and Fairness', in J. Waldron (ed.), *Theories of Rights* (Oxford: Oxford University Press, 1984), 143.

20. It may, of course, also increase future inequality, including our own generation unless steps were taken to make corresponding reductions in future welfare levels as well.

21. H. Frankfurt, 'Equality and Respect', *Social Research*, 64 (1997), 3–16.

22. J. Raz (1986), 240.

23. W. Beckerman, *Small is Stupid* (London: Duckworth, 1995b), 15; T. Schelling, 'Intergenerational Discounting', in *Energy Policy*, 23 (1995), 396 ff.

24. L. Temkin, *Inequality* (Oxford: Oxford University Press, 1993), 247.
25. In my 1978 Presidential Address to Section F (Economics) of the British Association for the Advancement of Science (W. Beckerman, 'Does Slow Growth Matter? Egalitarianism versus Humanitarianism', in W. Beckerman (ed.), *Slow Growth in Britain: Causes and Consequences* (Oxford: Clarendon Press, 1979)), I also urged that humanitarianism replace egalitarianism as a central objective of distributive policy, but this was not in connection with future generations.
26. 'midfare' is Gerry Cohen's relatively recent addition to the usual list of suspects (G. Cohen, 'Equality of What? On Welfare, Goods, and Capabilities', in M. Nussbaum and A. Sen (eds.), *The Quality of Life* (Oxford: Clarendon Press, 1993).
27. Griffin's detailed analysis of the concept of well-being is an outstanding example of the scope for illuminating this concept without tying it to the question of what constitutes the 'well-being' (or some rival equilisand) that ought to be distributed equally (J. Griffin, *Well-Being* (Oxford: Clarendon Press, 1986)).
28. Margalit (1996).
29. Ibid. 1.
30. Ibid. 272–3.
31. M. R. Anderson, 'Human Rights Approaches to Environmental Protection: An Overview', in A. E. Boyle and M. R. Anderson (eds.), *Human Rights Approaches to Environmental Protection* (Oxford: Clarendon Press, 1996), 3.
32. L. Ferry, *The New Ecological Order* (Chicago: Chicago University Press, 1995, translated from French original, 1992), p. xxii and ch. 5.
33. M. Bowman, 'The Nature, Development and Philosophical Foundations of the Biodiversity Concept in International Law', in M. Bowman and C. Redgwell (eds.), *International Law and the Conservation of Biological Diversity* (London and The Hague: Kluwer Law International, 1996), 18.
34. See also O'Neill (1993), 148 ff., for a discussion of the unjustified attack on science in much deep ecology literature, in spite of its occasional appeals to a scientific basis for some of its claims.
35. *The Economist*, 27 Sept. 1998, p. 82.
36. Margalit (1986), 20.
37. Beckerman (1995b), 152. As Brian Barry has pointed out, it is perhaps in his treatment of our obligations to future generations that Rawls comes closest than anywhere else to his basic idea of justice as fairness (Barry (1989), 200).

38. In any case, if there are any truly 'finite' non-renewable resources that will always be 'needed' for survival then they can only last for ever if consumption of them is reduced to zero, in which case, as Streeten has pointed out, there would not be any future generations to worry about (P. Streeten, 'Mankind's Future: An Ethical View', *Interdisciplinary Science Reviews*, 11 (1986), 248–56.

39. Beckerman, (1995*b*) ch. 4; R. Cooper, *Environmental and Resource Policies for the World Economy* (Washington: Brookings Institution, 1994), ch. 2; Schelling (1995).

40. W. Beckerman, 'Economists, Scientists and Environmental Catastrophe', *Oxford Economic Papers*, 24/3, (1972), 327–44; W. Beckerman, *In Defence of Economic Growth* (London: Duckworth, 1974).

CHAPTER 4

1. J. S. Mill, *Utilitarianism* (Indianapolis: Bobbs-Merrill, 1971), ch. 5. Mill defines justice as equivalent to the performance of 'duties of perfect obligation', which presupposes 'a wrong done, and some assignable person who is wronged' (p. 47). This is close to my wide conception of justice (see below) in that it rules out obligations to non-human animals and obligations to 'nature'. However, the requirement that there should be assignable persons who are wronged would rule out the possibility of behaving unjustly with respect to future generations, since they can scarcely be regarded as assignable.

2. B. Barry, *Justice as Impartiality* (Oxford: Clarendon Press, 1995), esp. ch. 4.

3. In a paper presented to the first of the three seminars from which this book emerged, Andrew Dobson wrote of 'the privileging of human welfare over justice to nature'. But perhaps this was not intended to carry a lot of theoretical freight ('Sustainabilities: An Analysis and a Typology', paper presented to the Social Justice and Sustainability Seminars, Keele University, UK, (1996*b*), fo. 11). See also A. Dobson, *Justice and the Environment Conceptions of Environmental Sustainability and Dimensions of Social Justice* (Oxford: Oxford University Press, 1998).

4. Mill (1971), 55–6.

5. In *Justice as Impartiality* I have set out the criterion of reasonable agreement more fully and worked out some of its implications.

6. A. de-Shalit, *Why Posterity Matters: Environmental Politics and Future Generations* (London: Routledge, 1995).
7. J. S. Mill, *Principles of Political Economy*, ed. Donald Winch (Harmondsworth, Penguin Books, 1970 [1848]), Book IV, ch. 5, 115–16.
8. Ibid. 117.
9. G. E. Moore, *Principia Ethica* (Cambridge: Cambridge University Press, 1903), 81.
10. Ibid. 83–4.
11. R. Goodin, *Green Political Theory* (Cambridge: Polity Press, 1992).

CHAPTER 5

1. Initially, I will use the terms 'option' and 'opportunity' interchangeably, as do most writers on this subject. See e.g. B. Barry, 'Intergenerational Justice in Energy Policy', in D. MacLean and P. Brown (eds.), *Energy and the Future* (Totowa, NJ: Rowman and Littlefield, 1983), 17. Below, I show how they might usefully be distinguished.
2. This formulation of the problem owes much to a private conversation with Brian Barry. Also see Barry (1983, 243 f) and, especially, B. Barry, 'The Ethics of Resource Depletion', in B. Barry, *Democracy, Power, and Justice* (Oxford: Clarendon Press, 1989a). Barry provides an eloquent argument for comparison of opportunities rather than comparing aggregated utilities. We differ, however, in that Barry sets out to explicate opportunities across time in terms of equality of 'productive potential', defined in terms of non-declining income. I argue below (section 4) that reduction of future opportunity to compensable losses to income fails to capture the full meaning of 'sustainable opportunities'.
3. R. Solow, 'An Almost Practical Step Toward Sustainability', Invited Lecture on the Occasion of the Fortieth Anniversary of Resources for the Future, Resources for the Future, Washington, 8 Oct. 1992, 15.
4. R. Howarth, 'Sustainability Under Uncertainty: A Deontological Approach', *Land Economics, 71* (1995), 421.
5. B. Barry, 'Circumstances of Justice and Future Generations', in R. I. Sikora and B. Barry (eds.), *Obligations to Future Generations* (Philadelphia: Temple University Press, 1978); Barry (1989a), 511–19.
6. See e.g. most of the essays in Sikora and Barry (1978) and in P. Laslett and J. Fishkin (eds.), *Justice between Age Groups and Genera-*

tions (New Haven: Yale University Press, 1992). An important exception among philosophers is Derek Parfit, who argues that we do, intuitively, care about our impacts on the distant future, and who seems willing, if necessary, to give up the 'person-regarding principle' if this step is necessary to support intuitively felt obligations.

7. Following B. Norton, 'Future Generations, Obligations to', *Encyclopedia of Bioethics*, 2nd edn. (New York: Macmillan Reference, 1995*b*); B. Norton, 'Intergenerational Fairness and Sustainability', unpublished manuscript in preparation.

8. See T. Page, *Conservation and Economic Efficiency* (Baltimore: Johns Hopkins University Press for Resources for the Future, 1977), and 'Intergenerational Justice as Opportunity', in MacLean and Brown (1983), for clear formulations of, and creative reactions to, this problem.

9. H. Daly and J. Cobb, *For the Common Good* (Boston: Beacon Press, 1989); Norton, 1995*a*; Norton, in preparation.

10. B. Norton and M. Toman, 'Sustainability: Ecological and Economic Perspectives', *Land Economics* (1997).

11. R. Solow, 'Intergenerational Equity and Exhaustible Resources', *Review of Economic Studies: Symposium on the Economics of Exhaustible Resources*, 41 (Edinburgh: Longman Group, 1974); id., 'On the Intergenerational Allocation of Natural Resources', *Scandinavian Journal of Economics*, 88 (1986), 141–9; id., (1992); id., 'Sustainability: An Economist's Perspective', in R. Dorfman and N. Dorfman (eds.), *Selected Readings in Environmental Economics*, 3rd edn. (New York: Norton, 1993).

12. Solow (1993), 181.

13. Ibid.

14. Ibid.

15. Solow does not explicitly endorse presentism and, indeed, in one of his early papers (1974), he endorsed a zero social discount rate. It is difficult, however, once one has reduced all concern for the future to a matter of maintaining general capital over time, to specify any particular concerns for the distant future. See B. Barry, *Theories of Justice* (Berkeley and Los Angeles: University of California Press, 1989*b*), 193.

16. As Barry (ibid.) and others have noted, John Rawls, who has set the terms of the debate regarding the nature of social justice for the past two decades, assumes that a present generation can improve the lot of subsequent generations by saving, but he never considers the possibility that earlier generations can harm the future. So, in

philosophical discussions carried out in these terms, problems of intergenerational justice are, as for Solow, reduced to a matter of specifying a just savings rate.

17. H. Daly, 'On Wilfred Beckerman's Critique of Sustainable Development', *Environmental Values*, 4 (1995).
18. Daly and Cobb (1989).
19. Ibid.
20. Ibid. 71.
21. Ibid. 410.
22. Ibid. 411.
23. I have been reinforced in this judgement by several helpful discussions of this topic in the Working Group that led to this book. In particular, I credit Alan Holland (see, for example, ch. 2, this volume) for convincing me that the very concept of capital—even when used in the phrase, 'natural capital', encourages a collapse of strong into weak sustainability.
24. Norton, in preparation.
25. Ibid.
26. See Solow (1974) for a brief discussion and also D. Farber and P. Hemmersbaugh, 'The Shadow of the Future: Discount Rates, Later Generations, and the Environment', *Vanderbilt Law Review*, 46 (1993), for a detailed analysis that supports the broad argument of this paper—that the obligation to the future is mainly to avoid specifiable harms rather than to maintain any particular level of welfare.
27. F. Ramsey, 'A Mathematical Theory of Saving', *Economic Journal*, 38 (1928); A. Pigou, *The Economics of Welfare* (London: Macmillan, 1932); Page (1977); id., 'Intergenerational Equity and the Social Rate of Discount', in V. K. Smith (ed.), *Environmental Resource and Applied Welfare Economics* (Washington: Resources for the Future, 1988); B. Norton, 'Evaluating Ecosystem States: Two Competing Paradigms', *Ecological Economics*, 14 (1995a).
28. Farber and Hemmersbaugh (1993).
29. Solow (1974).
30. See Page (1983) for a clear statement of requirements with this logical force.
31. Definitions are based on *Webster's New Universal Unabridged Dictionary*.
32. But I do not mean to rest any important theoretical points on this speculation—it is intended only to motivate the distinction between options and opportunities, a distinction I believe has merit in its own right.

33. It thereby becomes clear that there is no conflict between actions to improve the access of contemporaries to resources—concerns of intragenerational justice—and actions to protect the opportunities of future generations. Since we can only act in the present, we should act to create fair *and lasting* institutions for distribution of nature's resources.

34. Risk Decision Squares were introduced in B. Norton, 'Sustainability, Human Welfare, and Ecosystem Health', *Environmental Values*, 1 (1992), and elaborated in Norton (1995); also see Toman, (1994).

35. These problems are explored in more detail in B. Norton and B. Hannon, 'Environmental Values: A Place-Based Theory', *Environmental Ethics*, 19 (1997), and id., 'Democracy and Sense of Place Values', *Philosophy and Geography* (Forthcoming).

36. C. Holling, *Adaptive Environmental Assessment and Management* (London: John Wiley, 1978); C. Walters, *Adaptive Management of Renewable Resources* (New York: Macmillan, 1986); K. Lee, *Compass and Gyroscope: Integrating Science and Politics for the Environment* (Covelo, Calif.: Island Press, 1993).

37. L. Gunderson, C. Holling, and S. Light, *Barriers and Bridges* (New York: Columbia University Press, 1995).

38. T. Allen and T. Starr, *Hierarchy: Perspectives for Ecological Complexity* (Chicago: University of Chicago Press, 1982); B. Norton and R. Ulanowicz, 'Scale and Biodiversity Policy: A Hierarchical Approach', *Ambio*, 21 (1992).

39. C. Holling, 'Cross-Scale Morphology, Geometry, and Dynamics of Ecosystems', *Ecological Monographs*, 62 (1992).

40. C. Holling, 'Engineering Resilience versus Ecological Resilience', in P. C. Schulze (ed.), *Engineering within Ecological Constraints* (Washington: National Academy Press, 1996).

41. See also M. Common and C. Perrings, 'Towards an Ecological Economics of Sustainability', *Ecological Economics*, 6 (1992), 7–34.

42. K. Arrow *et al.*, 'Economic Growth, Carrying Capacity, and the Environment', *Science*, 268 (1995), 520–1; B. Norton, 'Resilience and Options', *Ecological Economics*, 15 (1996).

43. See R. Solow, 'Sustainability: An Economist's Perspective', in R. Dorfman and N. Dorfman (eds.), *Selected Readings in Environmental Economics*, (3rd edn.) (New York: Norton, 1993), 184, for an application of this reasoning to a specific non-renewable resource, North Sea oil.

44. It is arguable that this model describes what has actually happened (Actual Path), as Portland and Seattle have developed high-tech

industries, providing high-paying jobs to replace jobs in exploitational industries. But, again, the point of this and the next idealization, is to avoid controversies about the actual case.

45. C. Clark, 'The Economics of Over-Exploitation', *Science* (1974).

46. Daly and Cobb (1989).

47. T. Power, *Lost Landscapes and Failed Economies: The Search for a Value of Place* (Covelo, Calif.: Island Press, 1996).

48. The negative aspects of this spiral, and some of the antidotes to it, are discussed interestingly by D. Kemmis, *Community and the Politics of Place* (Norman, Okla.: University of Oklahoma Press, 1990).

49. Ibid.

CHAPTER 6

1. In this respect I agree with John Rawls, some of whose ideas are discussed later in the chapter See J. Rawls, *A Theory of Justice* (Cambridge, Mass.: Harvard University Press, 1971), sect. 2; J. Rawls, *Political Liberalism* (New York: Columbia University Press, 1993), lecture vii.

2. Perhaps the assumption is that members of the present generation have renounced their claims by consenting to government policies that inflict environmental damage for the sake of jobs and economic growth, whereas for obvious reasons members of future generations cannot (yet) give such consent. But this would be highly controversial. Until we know what environmental justice requires, we cannot even know what our contemporaries can *legitimately* consent to in this area.

3. See W. Baumol, 'Environmental Protection and Income Distribution', in H. M. Hochman and G. E Peterson (eds.), *Redistribution through Public Choice* (New York and London: Columbia University Press, 1974).

4. Rawls (1993), 244–5.

5. See also here Rawls (1971), 512: '[Animals] are outside the scope of the theory of justice, and it does not seem possible to extend the contract doctrine so as to include them in a natural way.' Despite this disavowal some green philosophers have explored possible ways of extending Rawls' theory: there is a helpful review in D. Thero, 'Rawls and Environmental Ethics: A Critical Examination of the Literature', *Environmental Ethics*, 17 (1995), 93–106.

6. Rawls (1993), 246.
7. Rawls (1971), sect. 42
8. Ibid. 282–3.
9. As Rawls acknowledges, this principle was first proposed by Knut Wicksell in 'A New Theory of Just Taxation', repr. in R. A. Musgrave and A. T. Peacock (eds.), *Classics in the Theory of Public Finance* (Basingstoke: Macmillan, 1994).
10. Rawls (1971), 283.
11. R. Dworkin, 'What is Equality? Part 3: The Place of Liberty', *Iowa Law Review*, 73 (1987), 1–73, esp. sect. iv.
12. R. Dworkin, 'Liberalism', in *A Matter of Principle* (Oxford: Clarendon Press, 1986), 202.
13. For a parallel critique of Dworkin, see A. de-Shalit, *Why Posterity Matters: Environmental Policies and Future Generations* (London: Routledge, 1995), 126.
14. R. Dworkin, 'What is Equality? Part 1: Equality of Welfare', *Philosophy and Public Affairs*, 10 (1981), 202.
15. Rawls does not say this explicitly, but it seems a reasonable extrapolation from what he does say about e.g. national defence.
16. Dworkin (1981), 203.
17. Cost-benefit analysis is defended in D. Pearce, A. Markandya, and E. B. Barbier, *Blueprint for a Green Economy* (London: Earthscan, 1989) and attacked by J. Knetsch, 'Environmental Valuation: Some Problems of Wrong Questions and Misleading Answers', and D. Vadnjal and M. O'Connor, 'What is the Value of Rangitoto Island?', both in *Environmental Values*, 3 (1994), 351–68 and 369–80 respectively. See also J. O'Neill, *Ecology, Policy and Politics* (London: Routledge, 1993) and M. Jacobs, 'Environmental Valuation, Deliberative Democracy and Public Decision-Making Institutions', in J. Foster (ed.), *Valuing Nature* (London: Routledge, 1997).
18. Pearce, Markandya, and Barbier (1989), ch. 3.
19. Mark Sagoff makes considerable use of this observation in *The Economy of the Earth* (Cambridge: Cambridge University Press, 1988a), esp. ch. 4.
20. Vadnjal and O'Connor give a parallel interpretation of many respondents' refusal to specify how much they would be willing to pay to keep Rangitoto Island out of the hands of the developers in 'What is the Value of Rangitoto Island?'.
21. In principle it would be possible for someone to express a consistent set of preferences as between various combinations of environmental goods, but refuse to make choices as between those goods

and different quantities of money. They would be organizing their valuations into two separate compartments and refusing to compare items drawn from different compartments. In practice, however, such rigid compartmentalization will be very difficult to sustain. Partly this is because of the heterogeneity of environmental goods: it surely does make sense to ask someone whether they would prefer a piece of waste ground to be developed as a golf course, and that immediately creates a bridge between environmental and recreational values (and from there further bridges can be built to other forms of consumption, and so on). Partly also the compartmentalization will be challenged by the presence of values of other kinds, for instance human life and health: how many deaths would it take to make you agree to the draining of a malaria-ridden swamp? For a more sceptical view of attempts to use measures other than money to commensurate environmental goods, see J. O'Neill, 'Value Pluralism, Incommensurability and Institutions', in J. Foster (ed.), *Valuing Nature* (London: Routledge, 1997).

22. O'Neill (1993), 78–9.
23. R. Goodin, *Green Political Theory* (Cambridge: Polity Press, 1992), 37.
24. It is worth pointing out here that for many people a sense of historical place is an important part of the context in which their lives are set, and that responding to this need may require the preservation of landscapes shaped by centuries of human activity and bearing little resemblance to the results of 'natural processes'. There may in other words be sharp conflicts between those who value untouched nature and those who value a certain historical heritage when environmental decisions have to be made.
25. Sagoff (1988), *passim*.
26. Should this worry supporters of cost-benefit analysis, given that, as I noted earlier, they want their analysis to capture the value of environmental goods to individuals in a broad sense, not a narrowly instrumental one? I think it should worry them, for two reasons. First, if people are recording valuations of environmental goods that reflect their judgements about the worth of these goods to others, then such valuations must be regarded as fallible in the extreme. Even if I know what it is worth to me to preserve the Dartford Warbler, how can I tell what it is worth to others? Second, the appeal of cost-benefit analysis is that, by aggregating individual valuations on an equal basis, it promises to establish the social value of an environmental good in a fair way. If however the valuations that are going into the calculus are radically heterogeneous—not merely in

the sense that A may regard an environmental feature as having only use value while B regards it as having existence value, but in the sense that C records a personal valuation while D records a social valuation, incorporating his (true or false) beliefs about the value of the feature to everyone else as well—there is no reason to think that the resulting 'value' will be a fair reflection of individual valuations. See also here R. Keat, 'Values and Preferences in Neo-classical Environmental Economics', in Foster (1997), who makes a similar point in the course of a penetrating analysis of cost-benefit analysis as a technique of environmental valuation.

27. B. Barry, *Justice as Impartiality* (Oxford: Clarendon Press, 1995), ch. 6, sect. 23.

28. See D. Miller, 'Deliberative Democracy and Social Choice', *Political Studies*, Special Issue, 40 (1992), 54–67, and D. Miller, 'Citizenship and Pluralism', *Political Studies*, 43 (1995), 432–50.

29. On this, see Sagoff (1988), ch. 6, and R. Nash, *Wilderness and the American Mind* (New Haven: Yale University Press, 1982). For reasons why national cultures in general are worth preserving, see my *On Nationality* (Oxford: Clarendon Press, 1995), esp. chs. 2 and 4.

30. It is wrong to assume that adopting the citizen perspective necessarily entails giving priority to environmental goods over benefits of other kinds. As Russell Keat has pointed out in a powerful critique of Sagoff, we may value increased opportunities for consumption *from the citizen perspective*, since this corresponds to a leading cultural value in contemporary societies. See R. Keat, 'Citizens, Consumers and the Environment', *Environmental Values*, 3 (1994), 333–51.

31. As I have suggested, it would be wrong to take these judgements too literally. In opinion surveys, between one-half and two-thirds of those with a view agree with the statement that 'Protecting the environment is so important that requirements and standards cannot be too high, and continuing environmental improvements must be made regardless of cost'. But when asked to choose between 'protecting the environment' and 'ensuring an adequate supply of energy' as objectives, opinion divides roughly equally as to which should have priority. There is a considerable degree of tension between these two findings, which it seems to me is best resolved by treating 'regardless of cost' in the first declaration as a hyperbolic way of saying 'I care a great deal about the environment'. For these findings see J. Gillroy and R. Shapiro, 'The Polls: Environmental Protection', *Public Opinion Quarterly*, 50 (1986), 270–9.

32. Michael Jacobs has suggested that citizens' juries might be used as a

guide to environmental policy as a substitute for cost-benefit analysis (see Jacobs (1997)). In general I am sympathetic to citizens' juries as instruments of policy-making, but the problem here is that a conscientious jury faced with a difficult environmental decision would want to see a good deal of evidence about how the public at large valued the environmental features in question as an essential input to its deliberations. It is possible however that a jury large enough to be reasonably representative of the general public might be able to 'internalize' the first stage of my proposed two-stage procedure by using its own members' individual valuations as the relevant evidence—in which case the jury will effectively be carrying out an informal cost-benefit analysis as a preliminary to reaching its verdict.

33. If the claim is that the preservation of ecosystem E is essential to the preservation of human life or health, then that is a testable empirical claim which can be verified or rebutted by methods that everyone must accept. But here I am contemplating a different possibility: the claim being made is simply that the ecosystem is valuable for its own sake. *From the perspective of social justice,* this has to be treated as on a par with the claim that church C is the true church, since it is a claim with which others may reasonably disagree.

CHAPTER 7

1. J. Rawls, *A Theory of Justice* (Oxford: Oxford University Press, 1971), 128.
2. J. Rawls, *Political Liberalism* (New York: Columbia University Press, 1993), 274.
3. Rawls (1971), 128.
4. Ibid.
5. Ibid.
6. Ibid. 287.
7. Cf. S. Okin, *Justice, Gender and the Family* (New York: Basic Books, 1989).
8. The credits for this idea should go to Sasja Tempelman.
9. Cf. N. Daniels (ed.) *Reading Rawls: Critical Studies on Rawls' A Theory of Justice* (Oxford: Basil Blackwell, 1975); B. Barry, 'Justice between Generations', in P. M. S. Hacker and J. Raz (eds.), *Law, Morality and Society: Essays in Honour of H. L. A. Hart* (Oxford: Clarendon Press, 1977).

10. Rawls (1993), 274 n.
11. Ibid. 274.
12. They still do in one respect: Rawls discounts distant future genera-
    tions. So will I. As I hope to show below, the question of the relative
    weight of our obligations to distant respectively close future
    generations is one we do not need to discuss.
13. Rawls (1971), 567.
14. Andrew Dobson, personal communication.
15. Robert Goodin, personal communication.
16. As criticized by, amongst others, Brian Barry (Barry (1977), 268, 271)
    and J. Narvesen, 'Future People and Us', in R. I. Sikora and B. M.
    Barry (eds.), *Obligations to Future Generations* (Philadelphia: Temple
    University Press, 1978), 56.
17. Rawls (1993), 274.
18. Rawls (1971), 92, 441.
19. Cf. Narvesen (1978), 58.
20. Another way to represent this problem is to point to the fact that we
    enter the real world, finding goods and institutions bequeathed to us
    by our predecessors without the express condition that we do the
    same for those who come after us. Why then, the critic would ask,
    should we feel obliged to do the same for our own descendants?
21. Cf. Barry (1977), 280.
22. All this is not to say that an appeal to self-interest and mutual
    advantage offer the only way to give rise to principles of justice
    between generations. Justice is perhaps 'a good thing quite apart
    from its general long-run tendency to be in everyone's interest'
    (Barry (1978), 217) and there may be other arguments leading to
    such principles—but all I want to show here is that self-interest is a
    sufficient condition for their existence.
23. Rawls (1993), 274, his italics.
24. Cf. W. Kymlicka, *Liberalism, Community, and Culture* (Oxford: Oxford
    University Press 1989); id., *Multicultural Citizenship: A Liberal Theory
    of Minority Rights* (Oxford: Clarendon Press, 1995).
25. However, the fact that moral principles may be difficult to satisfy
    under harsh empirical conditions does not *invalidate* them (cf.
    B. Barry, 'Circumstances of Justice and Future Generations', in
    Barry and Sikora (1978).
26. e.g. D. Wells, *Environmental Policy: A Global Perspective for the Twenty-
    First Century* (Upper Saddle River: Prentice Hall, 1996).
27. I use the term 'property right' in a technical sense: a property right
    is the sum of (1) a set of user rights indicating what one is permitted

to do with an object, including or excluding rights to let or lend, and
(2) a right to irrevocably transfer these user rights, i.e. to sell, give,
or bequeath.

28. M. Walzer, 'Interpretation and Social Criticism', in S. M. McMurrin
    (ed.), *The Tanner Lectures on Human Values 1985* (Salt Lake City:
    University of Utah Press, 1988).
29. M. Sandel, *Liberalism and the Limits of Justice* (Cambridge: Cambridge
    University Press, 1982), 77.
30. Cf. R. Nozick, *Anarchy, State, and Utopia* (New York: Basic Books,
    1974).
31. For a detailed critique of Nozick's theory of entitlement see
    O. O'Neill, 'Nozick's Entitlements', in P. Jeffrey (ed.), *Reading
    Nozick: Essays on Anarchy, State, and Utopia* (Oxford: Basil Blackwell,
    1981).
32. W. Galston, *Liberal Purposes: Goods, Virtues, and Diversity in the Liberal
    State* (Cambridge: Cambridge University Press, 1991), 131.
33. *Our Common Future*, World Commission on Environment and Devel-
    opment, quoted in N. Nelissen, J. van der Straaten, and L. Klinkers
    (eds.), *Classics in Environmental Studies: An Overview of Classic Texts in
    Environmental Studies* (Utrecht: International Books, 1997), 282.
34. Barry (1977), 284.
35. Ibid. 281.
36. Cf. W. Beckerman, '"Sustainable Development": Is It a Useful
    Concept?', *Environmental Values*, 3 (1994), 200; id., 'Sustainable
    Development and Intergenerational Egalitarianism', paper presented at
    the Environmental Sustainability and Social Justice Seminars, Keele
    University, UK, 19 Nov. 1996.
37. Barry (1977), 277.
38. Ibid. 284.
39. Cf. Barry's conception of crucial goods (B. Barry, *A Treatise on
    Social Justice, ii, Justice as Impartiality* (Oxford: Clarendon Press,
    1995), 11, 84).

CHAPTER 8

1. See M. Redclift, *Sustainable Development: Exploring the Contradictions*
   (London and New York: Methuen, 1987) and A. Dobson, 'Environ-
   mental Sustainabilities: An Analysis and a Typology' *Environmental
   Politics*, 5 (1996a), 401–28.

2. W. M. Adams, *Green Development: Environment and Sustainability in the Third World* (London and New York: Routledge, 1990), ch. 2 and 3.
3. P. Ehrlich, *The Population Bomb* (New York: Ballantine, 1970).
4. D. H. Meadows, D. L. Meadows, J. Randers, and W. W. Behrens III, *The Limits to Growth* (London and Sydney: Pan, 1974).
5. International Union for Conservation of Nature and Natural Resources, *The World Conservation Strategy* (Geneva: IUCN, UNEP, WWF).
6. World Commission on Environment and Development (WCED), *Our Common Future* (Oxford: Oxford University Press, 1987).
7. Ibid. 8.
8. Ibid. 1.
9. Ibid. 8.
10. Cf Brian Barry's 'essential interests', ch. 4, this volume
11. A. H. Maslow, *Motivation and Personality* (New York: Harper, 1954). See also K. Soper, *On Human Needs* (Brighton: Harvester, 1981) and L. Doyal and I. Gough, *A Theory of Human Need* (London: Macmillan, 1991).
12. See T. Benton, *Natural Relations: Ecology, Animal Rights and Social Justice* (London: Verso, 1993), for further development of some theoretical and political implications of this way of thinking.
13. J. Rocha, 'Floods of Tears', *Guardian*, 12 Mar. 1997.
14. P. McCully, *Silenced Rivers* (London: Zed Books, 1997).
15. See e.g. M. A. Jaimes (ed.), *The State of Native America: Genocide, Colonization, and Resistance* (Boston: South End Press, 1992), esp. chs. 6, 7 and 8.
16. See e.g. S. Whatmore, 'From Farming to Agribusiness', in R. J. Johnston, P. J. Taylor, and M. J. Watts (eds.), *Geographies of Global Change* (Oxford: Blackwell, 1995). J. N. Pretty, *Regenerating Agriculture* (London: Earthscan, 1995), and P. McMichael and L. T. Raynolds, 'Capitalism, Agriculture and World Economy', in L. Sklair (ed.), *Capitalism and Development* (London and New York: Routledge, 1994).
17. See C. Jackson, 'Radical Environmental Myths: A Gender Perspective', *New Left Review*, 210 (1995), 124–140.
18. Convention on Biological Diversity, Article 8.
19. A. Rowell, 'Crude Operators', *The Ecologist*, 27 (1997), 99–106.
20. Convention on Biological Diversity, Article 16(2).
21. R. McNally and P. Wheale, 'Biopatenting and Biodiversity: Comparative Advantages in the New Global Order', *The Ecologist*, 26 (1996), 222–8.

22. A. Levy, C. Scott-Clark, and D. Harrison, 'Save the Rhino, Kill the People', *Observer* (23 Mar. 1997), 9.
23. J. Habermas, *Legitimation Crisis* (London: Heinemann, 1975).
24. See J. O'Connor, *Natural Causes: Essays on Ecological Marxism* (New York: Guilford, 1997) also T. Benton (ed.), *The Greening of Marxism* (New York: Guilford, 1996).
25. See especially C. Hay, 'Environmental Security and State Legitimacy', *Capitalism, Nature, Socialism*, 5 (1994), 83–97.
26. See M. O'Connor (ed.), *Is Capitalism Sustainable? Political Economy and the Politics of Ecology* (New York: Guilford, 1994).
27. D. Pearce, A. Markandya, and E. B. Barbier, *Blueprint for a Green Economy* (London: Earthscan, 1989).
28. M. Jacobs, *The Green Economy* (London: Pluto Press, 1991), ch. 12.
29. A. Giddens, *The Consequences of Modernity* (Cambridge: Polity Press, 1990), ch. 1.
30. S. Retallack, 'The WTO's Record So Far', *The Ecologist*, 27 (1997), 136–7.
31. See Giddens (1990), ch. 4, and A. Giddens, *Beyond Left and Right: The Future of Radical Politics* (Cambridge: Polity Press, 1994), ch. 8; U. Beck, *Risk Society: Towards a New Modernity* (London: Sage, 1992), chs. 1 and 2.
32. See T. Benton, 'Beyond Left and Right? Ecological Politics, Capitalism and Modernity', in M. Jacobs (ed.), *Greening the Millennium? The New Politics of the Environment* (Oxford: Blackwell, 1997a).
33. McNally and Wheale (1996).
34. I am here drawing on the work of Wil Gibson ('*Sustainable Development and Caribbean Island States*' (Unpub. Ph. D. thesis, Essex University, 1998)).
35. D. Pearce *et al.* (1989), P xiv.
36. Ibid. 7.
37. Ibid. 50.
38. M. Grubb, M. Koch, A. Munsen, F. Sullivan, and K. Thomson *The 'Earth Summit' Agreements: A Guide and Assessment* (London: Earthscan, 1993), 26–7.
39. An informative account of the record of the oil industry in this respect is Rowell (1997).
40. See P. Blaikie, *The Political Economy of Soil Erosion in Developing Countries* (London: Longman, 1985); R. L. Bryant and S. Bailey, *Third World Political Ecology* (London: Routledge, 1997); M. L. Mellor, *Breaking the Boundaries* (London: Virago, 1992); and S. Amin *Delinking: Towards a Polycentric World* (London and New Jersey: Zed Books, 1990).

41. See L. J. Bunin, E. Yuen and T. Stroshane, 'Multicultural Ecology: An Interview with Carl Anthony', *Capitalism, Nature, Socialism,* 31 (1997), 41–62; and B. Epstein, 'The Environmental Justice / Toxics Movement: Politics of Race and Gender', *Capitalism, Nature, Socialism,* 31 (1997), 63–87.

42. P. Rosset *et al.,* 'Cuba's Nationwide Conversion to Organic Agriculture', *Capitalism, Nature, Socialism,* 19 (1994), 41–62.

43. T. Radford, 'Chronicle of Deaths Foretold', *Guardian,* (1992) 30 (n.d).

44. World Commission on Environment and Development (1987), 13.

45. R. Eckersley, *Environmentalism and Political Theory* (London: UCL Press, 1992).

CHAPTER 9

1. See M. Jacobs, ch. 1, this volume.

2. S. Lansley and D. Gowan, *Fair Taxes* (London: Campaign for Fair Taxation, 1994).

3. D. Corry, 'Indirect Taxation is Not as Bad as You Think', in S. Tindale, and G. Holtham, *Green Tax Reform* (London: IPPR, 1996).

4. S. Hutton and G. Hardman, *Assessing the Impact of VAT on Fuel on Low-Income Households: Analysis of the Fuel Expenditure Data from the 1991 Family Expenditure Survey* (York: Social Policy Research Unit, University of York, 1993).

5. DTI, *Energy Projections for the UK: Energy Use and Energy-Related Emissions of Carbon Dioxide in the UK 1995–2020,* Energy Paper 65 (London: HMSO, 1995).

6. e.g. J. Meade, *Agathopia: The Economics of Partnership* (Aberdeen: Aberdeen University Press / David Hulme Institute, 1988).

7. S. Smith and M. Pearson, *The European Carbon Energy Tax Proposal* (London: Institute for Fiscal Studies, 1991).

8. P. Johnson, S. McKay, and S. Smith, *The Distributional Consequences of Environmental Taxes,* IFS Commentary 23 (London: Institute for Fiscal Studies, 1990).

9. Confederation of British Industry (CBI), *Moving Forward: A Business Strategy for Transport* (London: CBI, 1995).

10. S. Tindale and G. Holtham, *Green Tax Reform* (London: Institute for Public Policy Research, 1996).

11. J. Bradshaw, *Household Budgets and Living Standards* (York: Joseph Rowntree Foundation., 1993).

12. M. Jacobs, *Sustainability and Socialism* (London: Socialist Environment & Resources Association, 1995*a*).

CHAPTER 10

1. Norton, paper presented to the Social Justice and Sustainability Seminars, Keele University, UK 1996.

2. Dobson, paper presented to the Social Justice and Sustainability Seminars, Keele University UK, 1996, see also A. Dobson, 'Environmental Sustainabilities: An Analysis and a Typology', *Environmental Politics*, 5 (1996), 401–28, and *Justice and the Environment* (Oxford: Oxford University Press, 1998), ch. 2.

3. Miller, paper presented to the Social Justice and Sustainability Seminars, Keele University, UK, 1996.

4. M. Wissenburg, paper presented to the Social Justice and Sustainability Seminars, Keele University, UK, 1996.

5. C. Ponting, *A Green History of the World; The Environment and the Collapse of Great Civilisations* (Harmondsworth: Penguin Books, 1991).

6. Ibid. 53–4

7. B. Slicher van Bath, *De agrarische geschiedenis van West-Europa 500–1850* (Utrecht/Antwerp: Het Spectrum, 1960) (The Agrarian History of Western Europe 500–1850).

8. A. Sen, *Poverty and Famines: An Essay on Entitlements and Deprivation* (Oxford: Clarendon Press, 1981).

9. P. Harrison, *The Third Revolution: Population, Environment and a Sustainable World* (Harmondsworth: Penguin Books, 1992).

10. See also Ponting (1991)

11. Harrison (1992).

12. P. Ekins, 'Making Development Sustainable', in W. Sachs (ed.), *Global Ecology. A New Arena of Political Conflict* (London: Zed Books, 1993).

13. C. LeQuesne, 'Ecological Footprints', in K. Watkins (ed.), *The Oxfam Poverty Report* (Oxford: Oxfam, 1995).

14. K. Meyer-Abich, 'Winners and Losers in Climate Change', in Sachs (ed.), *Global Ecology. Arena of Political Conflict* (London: Zed Books, 1993).

15. Ekins (1993).
16. N. Myers, 'Environmentally Induced Displacements: The State of the Art', paper presented to International symposium on Environmentally-Induced Population Displacements and Environmental Impacts Resulting from Mass Migrations, Geneva, April 1996, IOM/UNHCR/RPG.
17. Watkins (1995).
18. R. Kaplan, 'The Coming Anarchy: How Scarcity, Crime, Overpopulation, Tribalism and Disease are Rapidly Destroying the Social Fabric of Our Planet', *Atlantic Monthly* (1994).
19. J. Macrae and A. Zwi with M. Duffield and H. Slim, *War and Hunger: Rethinking International Responses to Complex Emergencies* (London: Zed Books, 1994), 21
20. L. Cliffe, '*War and Environment in the Horn of Africa: Sorting Out Causes and Consequences*', draft paper presented to the Conference on Environment and Development in Africa: Challenging the Orthodoxies, University of Leeds, African Studies Unit, 1995.
21. M. Duffield, 'The Political Economy of Internal War: Asset Transfer, Complex Emergencies and International Aid', in Macrae *et al.* (1994)
22. Cliffe (1995).
23. C. Roche, 'Operationality in Turbulence: The Need for Change', *Development in Practice*, 4 (1994).
24. G. Vassall-Adams, *Rwanda—un programme d'action internationale* (Oxford: Oxfam, Insight Series, 1994).
25. J. Fairhead, '*Demographic Issues in the Great Lakes Region*', short paper for presentation at the SCF Conference, March 1997.
26. W. Odame Larbi, *Land Reform Potential in Rwanda: Report of the Relationships Foundation* (Cambridge: Newick Park Initiative, 1995).
27. J. Gasana, *Factors of Ethnic Conflict in Rwanda and Instruments For a Durable Peace*, International Conference of Experts on Federalism against Ethnicity: Institutional, Legal and Democratic Instruments to Prevent or Resolve Minority Conflicts (Basle, 1995).
28. Ibid.
29. C. André and J.-P. Platteau, *Land Relations Under Unbearable Stress: Rwanda Caught in the Malthusian Trap* (CRED. University of Namur, Belgium, 1996).
30. T. Longman, 'Genocide and Socio-Political Change: Massacres in Two Rwandan Villages', *Issue: A Journal of Opinion*, 23/2 (1995).
31. André and Platteau (1996).
32. Ibid.
33. Gasana (1995).

34. See K. Neefjes, *Displacement and Environmental Change in the Great Lakes Region: Do We Need to Respond?* discussion paper for Novib and Oxfam (UK & I) (The Hague/Oxford 1997).

35. P. Richards, *Fighting For the Rain Forest: War, Youth and Resources in Sierra Leone,* African Issues Series (Oxford: James Currey: Portsmouth: Heinemann/London: International Africa Institute, 1996).

36. Ibid. 124.

37. Ibid. 164.

38. Ibid. 163.

39. Longman (1995).

40. K. Neefjes and R. David, *A Participatory Review of the Ikafe Refugee Response,* Oxfam-(UK & I) report (1996), see the Ugandan example in this chapter.

41. M. Duffield, 'The Political Economy of Internal War: Asset Transfer, Complex Emergencies and International Aid', in Macrae *et al.* (1994).

42. B. Spooner and N. Walsh, *Fighting for Survival: Insecurity, People and the Environment in the Horn of Africa,* IUCN Sahel Programme Study Report, vol. 1, (Gland, Switz., 1991).

43. Ibid. 122.

44. Ibid. (1991)

45. K. Neefjes, '*Ecological Needs in Community Based Dryland Development*', paper for the Dryland Symposium at the Royal Botanic Gardens: Botany, what's in it for Drylands Development? (July 1996*b*).

46. See e.g. T. Hoerz, *Refugees and Host Environments: A Review of Current and Related Literature* (Oxford: GTZ, RSP, 1995).

47. Neefjes and David (1996).

48. Ibid.

49. B. Harrell-Bond, 'The Ikafe Refugee Settlement Project in Aringa County', draft consultancy report to Oxfam, 1994.

50. Ibid.

51. K. Watkins (1995), 70.

52. Richards (1996).

53. Macrae *et al.* (1994).

54. Ibid. 225.

55. Dobson (1996).

56. Neefjes (1997).

57. Gasana (1995).

58. See e.g. P. Harrison, *The Third Revolution: Population, Environment and a Sustainable World* (Harmondsworth: Penguin Books, 1992).

59. Wissenburg (1996).
60. Harrison (1992).
61. Ekins (1993).
62. See e.g. C. LeQuesne, 'Ecological Footprints', in Watkins (1995).
63. B. Harrell-Bond, 'Refugees and the International System: The Evolution of Solutions', paper presented to the conference The Third World after the Cold War: Ideology, Economic Development and Politics, Oxford, July 1995.
64. Gasana (1995).
65. Roche (1994).
66. Neefjes (1996); Gasana (1995); André and Platteau (1996); Hoerz (1995) for areas hosting refugees; Neefjes and David (1996).
67. Cliffe (1995).
68. Neefjes and David (1996).
69. Duffield (1994).
70. Norton (1996).
71. Miller (1996).

BIBLIOGRAPHY

Adams, W. M., *Green Development: Environment and Sustainability in the Third World* (London and New York: Routledge, 1990).

Agarawal, A. and Narain, S., *Towards Green Villages: A Strategy for Environmentally Sound and Participatory Rural Development* (Delhi: Centre for Science and Environment, 1990).

Agenda 21 (New York: UNCED, 1992)

Allen, T. and Starr, T., *Hierarchy: Perspectives for Ecological Complexity* (Chicago: University of Chicago Press, 1982).

Amin, S., *Delinking: Towards a Polycentric World* (London and New Jersey: Zed Books, 1990).

Anderson, M. R., 'Human Rights Approaches to Environmental Protection: An Overview', in A. E. Boyle and M. R. Anderson (eds.), *Human Rights Approaches to Environmental Protection* (Oxford: Clarendon Press, 1996).

André, C. and Platteau, J.-P., *Land Relations Under Unbearable Stress: Rwanda Caught in the Malthusian Trap* (CRED: University of Namur, Belgium 1996).

Arrow, K., Bolin, B., Costanza, R., Dasgupta, P., Folke, C., Holling, C. S., Jansson, B.O., Levin, S., Maler, K.-G., Perrings, C., and Pimentel, D., 'Economic Growth, Carrying Capacity, and the Environment', *Science,* 268 (1995), 520–1.

Banuri, T., 'The Landscape of Diplomatic Conflicts', in W. Sachs, *Global Ecology* (London: Zed Books, 1993).

Barbier, E., 'The Concept of Sustainable Economic Development', *Environmental Conservation,* 14 (1987).

Barry, B., 'Justice Between Generations', in P. M. S. Hacker and J. Raz (eds.), *Law, Morality and Society: Essays in Honour of H. L. A. Hart* (Oxford: Clarendon Press, 1977).

—— 'Circumstances of Justice and Future Generations', in R. I. Sikora and B. Barry (eds.), *Obligations to Future Generations* (Philadelphia: Temple University Press, 1978).

—— 'Intergenerational Justice in Energy Policy', in D. MacLean and P. Brown (eds.), *Energy and the Future* (Totowa, NJ: Rowman and Littlefield, 1983).

—— *Theories of Justice* (London: Harvester-Wheatsheaf, 1989a).

—— 'The Ethics of Resource Depletion', in B. Barry, *Democracy, Power, and Justice* (Oxford: Clarendon Press, 1989a).

—— *A Treatise on Social Justice. ii. Justice as Impartiality* (Oxford: Clarendon Press, 1995).

Baumol, W., 'Environmental Protection and Income Distribution', in H. Hochman and G. Peterson (eds.), *Redistribution through Public Choice* (New York and London: Columbia University Press, 1974).

Beck, U., *Risk Society: Towards a New Modernity* (London: Sage, 1992).

Beckerman, W., 'Economists, Scientists and Environmental Catastrophe', *Oxford Economic Papers*, 24/3 (1972), 327–44.

—— *In Defence of Economic Growth* (London: Duckworth, 1974).

—— 'Does Slow Growth Matter? Egalitarianism versus Humanitarianism', in W. Beckerman (ed.), *Slow Growth in Britain: Causes and Consequences* (Oxford: Clarendon Press, 1979).

—— '"Sustainable Development": Is it a Useful Concept?', *Environmental Values*, 3 (1994), 191–209.

—— 'How Would You Like Your Sustainability, Sir? Weak or Strong?', *Environmental Values*, 4 (1995a), 169–79.

—— *Small is Stupid* (London: Duckworth, 1995b)

—— 'Sustainable Development and Inter-Generational Egalitarianism', paper presented to the Environmental Sustainability and Social Justice Seminars, Keele University, UK, 19 Nov. 1996.

—— 'Intergenerational Equity and the Environment', *Journal of Political Philosophy*, 5 (1997), 392–405.

—— and Pasek, J., 'Plural Values and Environmental Valuation', *Environmental Values*, 6 (1997), 65–86.

Benton, T., *Natural Relations: Ecology, Animal Rights and Social Justice* (London: Verso, 1993).

—— (ed.), *The Greening of Marxism* (New York: Guilford, 1996).

—— 'Beyond Left and Right? Ecological Politics, Capitalism and Modernity', in M. Jacobs (ed.), *Greening the Millennium? The New Politics of the Environment* (Oxford: Blackwell, 1997a).

—— 'Ecology, Community and Justice', in T. Hayward and J. O'Neill (eds.), *Justice, Property and the Environment* (Aldershot: Ashgate, 1997b).

Blaikie, P., *The Political Economy of Soil Erosion in Developing Countries* (London: Longman, 1985).

Bowman, M., 'The Nature, Development and Philosophical Foundations of the Biodiversity Concept in International Law', in M. Bowman and C. Redgwell (eds.), *International Law and the Conservation of Biological Diversity* (London and The Hague: Kluwer Law International, 1996).

Bradshaw, J., *Household Budgets and Living Standards* (York: Joseph Rowntree Foundation, 1993).

British Columbia Round Table on the Environment and the Economy, *Towards a Strategy for Sustainability* (Victoria, BC: BCRTEE, 1992).

Brooks, H., 'Sustainability and Technology', in *Science and Sustainability* (Vienna: International Institute for Applied Systems Analysis, 1992).

Broome, J., *Weighing Goods* (Oxford: Blackwell, 1991).

Bryant, R. L. and Bailey, S., *Third World Political Ecology* (London: Routledge, 1997).

Bunin, L. J., Yuen, E., and Stroshane, T., 'Multicultural Ecology: An Interview With Carl Anthony', *Capitalism, Nature, Socialism*, 31 (1997), 41–62.

Church, C. and Lachowicz, M., *Towards Local Sustainability: A Review of Local Agenda 21 Activity* (London: United Nations Association, 1995).

Clark, C., 'The Economics of Over-Exploitation', *Science* (1974).

Clayton, A., 'The Reality of Sustainability', *ECOS*, 2/4 (1991), 8–14.

Cliffe, L., 'War and Environment in the Horn of Africa: Sorting Out Causes and Consequences', draft paper presented to the Conference on Environment and Development in Africa: Challenging the Orthodoxies, University of Leeds, African Studies Unit (1995).

Cohen, G., 'Equality of What? On Welfare, Goods, and Capabilities', in M. Nussbaum and A. Sen (eds.), *The Quality of Life* (Oxford: Clarendon Press, 1993).

Common, M. and Perrings, C., 'Towards an Ecological Economics of Sustainability', *Ecological Economics*, 6 (1992), 7–34.

Confederation of British Industry (CBI), *Moving Forward: A Business Strategy for Transport* (London: CBI, 1995).

Cooper, R., *Environmental and Resource Policies for the World Economy* (Washington: Brookings Institution, 1994).

Corry, D., 'Indirect Taxation is not as Bad as you Think', in S. Tindale and G. Holtham, *Green Tax Reform* (London: IPPR, 1996).

Daly, H., 'On Wilfred Beckerman's Critique of Sustainable Development', *Environmental Values*, 4 (1995), 49–56.

—— and J. Cobb, *For the Common Good* (Boston: Beacon Press, 1989).

Daniels, N. (ed.) *Reading Rawls: Critical Studies on Rawls' A Theory Of Justice* (Oxford: Basil Blackwell, 1975).

Dasgupta, P. and Heal, G. M., *Economic Theory and Exhaustible Resources* (Cambridge: Cambridge University Press, 1979).

Defoe, D., *A Tour through England and Wales 1724–26* (London: Dent, 1927).

de la Court, T., *Beyond Brundtland* (London: Zed Books, 1991).

Department of the Environment, *Climate Change: Our National Programme for CO₂ Emissions* (London: DoE, 1992).

de-Shalit, A., *Why Posterity Matters: Environmental Policies and Future Generations* (London: Routledge, 1995).

Deutscher, I., *Stalin* (rev. edn.) (Harmondsworth: Penguin, 1966).

Dobson, A., 'Environmental Sustainabilities: An Analysis and a Typology', *Environmental Politics*, 5 (1996a), 401–28.

—— 'Sustainabilities: An Analysis and a Typology', paper presented to the Social Justice and Sustainability Seminars, Keele University, UK, (1996b).

—— *Justice and the Environment: Conceptions of Environmental Sustainability and Dimensions of Social Justice* (Oxford: Oxford University Press, 1998).

Doering, R., 'Canadian Round Tables on the Environment and the Economy: Their History, Form and Function', Working Paper, National Round Table on the Environment and the Economy, Ottawa (1993).

Doyal, L. and Gough, I., *A Theory of Human Need* (London: Macmillan, 1991).

DTI, *Energy Projections for the UK: Energy Use and Energy-Related Emissions of Carbon Dioxide in the UK 1995–2020*, Energy Paper 65 (London: HMSO, 1995).

Duffield, M., 'The Political Economy of Internal War. Asset Transfer, Complex Emergencies and International Aid', in Macrae and Zwi, with Duffield and Slim, *War and Hunger: Rethinking International Responses to Complex Emergencies* (London: Zed Books, 1994).

Dworkin, R., 'What is Equality? Part 1: Equality of Welfare', *Philosophy and Public Affairs*, 10 (1981), 202.

—— *A Matter of Principle* (Oxford: Clarendon Press, 1986),

—— 'What is Equality? Part 3: The Place of Liberty', *Iowa Law Review*, 73 (1987), 1–73.

Eckersley, R., *Environmentalism and Political Theory* (London: UCL Press, 1992).

Ehrlich, P., *The Population Bomb* (New York: Ballantine, 1970).

Ekins, P., 'Making Development Sustainable', in W. Sachs (ed.), *Global Ecology: A New Arena of Political Conflict* (London: Zed Books, 1993).

English Nature, *Planning for Environmental Sustainability* (Peterborough: English Nature, 1994).

—— *Sustainability in Practice: Planning for Environmental Sustainability* (Peterborough: English Nature, 1994).

Epstein, B., 'The Environmental Justice/Toxics Movement: Politics of Race and Gender', *Capitalism, Nature, Socialism*, 31 (1997), 63–87.

Fairhead, J., 'Demographic Issues in the Great Lakes Region' short paper for presentation at the SCF Conference, March 1997.

Farber, D. and Hemmersbaugh, P., 'The Shadow of the Future: Discount Rates, Later Generations, and the Environment', *Vanderbilt Law Review*, 46 (1993), 267–304.

Faucheux, S., Pearce, D., and Proops, J., (eds.), *Models of Sustainable Development* (Cheltenham: Edward Elgar, 1996).

Ferry, L., *The New Ecological Order* (Chicago: Chicago University Press, 1995, translated from French original, 1992).

Fox, W., 'Why Care About the World Around Us?', *Resurgence*, 161 (1993), 10–12.

Frankfurt, H., 'Equality and Respect', *Social Research*, 64 (1997), 3–16.

Gallie, W., 'Essentially Contested Concepts', *Proceedings of the Aristotelian Society*, 56 (1955–56), 167–98.

Galston, W., *Liberal Purposes: Goods, Virtues, and Diversity in the Liberal State* (Cambridge: Cambridge University Press, 1991).

Gasana, J., *Factors of Ethnic Conflict in Rwanda and Instruments For a Durable Peace*. International Conference of Experts on Federalism against Ethnicity. Institutional, Legal and Democratic Instruments to Prevent or Resolve Minority Conflicts (Basle, 1995).

Gibson, W., *Sustainable Development and Caribbean Island States* (unpub. Ph. D. thesis, Essex University, 1998).

Giddens, A., *The Consequences of Modernity* (Cambridge: Polity Press, 1990).

—— *Beyond Left and Right: The Future of Radical Politics* (Cambridge: Polity Press, 1994).

Gillespie, J. and Shepherd, P., 'Establishing Criteria for Identifying Critical Natural Capital in the Terrestrial Environment', English Nature Research Report No. 141 (Peterborough: English Nature, 1995).

Gillroy, J. and Shapiro, R., 'The Polls: Environmental Protection', *Public Opinion Quarterly*, 50 (1986), 270–9.

Goodin, R., 'Ethical Principles for Environmental Protection', in R. Elliot and A. Gare (eds.), *Environmental Philosophy* (Queensland: University of Queensland Press, 1983).

—— *Green Political Theory* (Cambridge: Polity Press, 1992).

Gordon, J., *Canadian Round Tables and Other Mechanisms for Sustainable Development in Canada* (Luton: Local Government Management Board, 1994).

Gould, S., 'Kingdoms Without Wheels', in *Hen's Teeth and Horse's Toes* (Harmondsworth: Penguin, 1984).

Griffin, J., *Well-Being* (Oxford: Clarendon Press, 1986).

Grubb, M., Koch, M., Thomson, K., Munsen, A., and Sullivan, F., *The 'Earth Summit' Agreements: A Guide and Assessment* (London: Earthscan, 1993).

Gunderson, L., Holling, C., and Light, S., *Barriers and Bridges* (New York: Columbia University Press, 1995).

Habermas, J., *Legitimation Crisis* (London: Heinemann, 1975).

Hajer, M., *The Politics of Environmental Discourse: Ecological Modernization and the Regulation of Acid Rain* (Oxford: Oxford University Press, 1994).

—— 'Ecological Modernisation and Social Change', in S. Lash, B. Szerszynski, and B. Wynne (eds.), *Risk, Environment and Modernity: Towards a New Ecology* (London: Sage, 1995).

Harrell-Bond, B., 'The Ikafe Refugee Settlement Project in Aringa County.' Draft Consultancy Report to Oxfam (1994).

—— 'Refugees and the International System: The Evolution of Solutions.' Paper presented to the Conference The Third World after the Cold War: Ideology, Economic Development and Politics, Oxford, July 1995.

Harrison, P., *The Third Revolution: Population, Environment and a Sustainable World* (Harmondsworth: Penguin Books, 1992).

Hay, C., 'Environmental Security and State Legitimacy', *Capitalism, Nature, Socialism* 5 (1994), 83–97.

Her Majesty's Government, *Our Common Future: A Perspective by the United Kingdom on the Report of the World Commission on Environment and Development* (London: DOE, 1988).

Hoerz, T., *Refugees and Host Environments: A Review of Current and Related Literature* (Oxford: GTZ, RSP, 1995).

Holland, A., 'The Foundations of Environmental Decision-Making', *International Journal of Environment & Pollution*, 7 (1997a), 483–96.

—— 'Substitutability: Or, Why Strong Sustainability is Weak and Absurdly Strong Sustainability is Not Absurd', in J. Foster (ed.), *Valuing Nature? Economics, Ethics and the Environment* (London: Routledge, 1997b).

Holling, C., *Adaptive Environmental Assessment and Management* (London: John Wiley, 1978).

—— 'Cross-Scale Morphology, Geometry, and Dynamics of Ecosystems', *Ecological Monographs*, 62 (1992), 447–502.

—— 'Engineering Resilience versus Ecological Resilience,' in P. C. Schulze (ed.), *Engineering within Ecological Constraints* (Washington: National Academy Press, 1996).

Howarth, R., 'Sustainability Under Uncertainty: A Deontological Approach', *Land Economics*, 71 (1995), 417–26.

Hutchison, R., (ed.) *Fighting for Survival: Insecurity, People and the Environ-ment in the Horn of Africa* (Gland, Switz.: IUCN, 1991).

Hutton, S. and Hardman, G., *Assessing the Impact of VAT on Fuel on Low-Income Households: Analysis of the Fuel Expenditure Data from the 1991 Family Expenditure Survey* (York: Social Policy Research Unit, University of York, 1993).

International Institute for Environment and Development, *Citizen Action to Reduce Ecological Footprints: A Review of Concepts and Methods,* Report for the Department of the Environment (London: IIED, 1995).

International Union for Conservation of Nature and Natural Resources. *The World Conservation Strategy.* (Geneva: IUCN, UNEP, WWF).

Jackson, C., 'Radical Environmental Myths: A Gender Perspective', *New Left Review,* 210 (1995), 124–40.

Jacobs, M., *The Green Economy* (London: Pluto Press, 1991).

—— *Sense and Sustainability: Land Use Planning and Environmentally Sustainable Development* (London: Council for the Protection of Rural England, 1993).

—— *Sustainability and Socialism* (London: Socialist Environment & Resources Association, 1995 *a*).

—— 'Sustainable Development, Capital Substitution and Economic Humility: A Response to Beckerman', *Environmental Values,* 4 (1995*b*), 57–68.

—— 'Sustainable Development: Assumptions, Contradictions, Progress', in J. Lowenduski and J. Stanyer (eds.), *Contemporary Political Studies 1995* (Belfast: Political Studies Association, 1995 iii, 1, 470–85).

—— 'Environmental Valuation, Deliberative Democracy and Public Decision-Making Institutions', in J. Foster (ed.), *Valuing Nature?* (London: Routledge, 1997).

Jaimes, M. A., (ed.), *The State of Native America: Genocide, Colonization, and Resistance* (Boston: South End Press, 1992).

Johnson, P., McKay, S., and Smith, S., *The Distributional Consequences of Environmental Taxes,* IFS Commentary 23 (London: Institute for Fiscal Studies, 1990).

Kaplan, R., 'The Coming Anarchy: How Scarcity, Crime, Overpopulation, Tribalism and Disease are Rapidly Destroying the Social Fabric of Our Planet', *Atlantic Monthly* (1994).

Keat, R., 'Citizens, Consumers and the Environment', *Environmental Values,* 3 (1994), 333–51.

—— 'Values and Preferences in Neo-classical Environmental Economics', in Foster (ed.), *Valuing Nature?*

Kemmis, D., *Community and the Politics of Place* (Norman, Okla.: University of Oklahoma Press, 1990).

Knetsch, J., 'Environmental Valuation: Some Problems of Wrong Questions and Misleading Answers', *Environmental Values*, 3 (1994), 351–68

Kothari, S. and Parajuli, P., 'No Nature Without Social Justice', in Sachs, *Global Ecology.*

Kymlicka, W., *Liberalism, Community, and Culture* (Oxford: Oxford University Press 1989).

—— *Multicultural Citizenship: A Liberal Theory of Minority Rights* (Oxford: Clarendon Press, 1995).

Lancashire Environmental Forum, *Lancashire Environmental Action Plan* (Preston: Lancashire Environmental Forum, 1993).

Lansley, S. and Gowan, D., *Fair Taxes* (London: Campaign for Fair Taxation, 1994).

Larbi, W., Odame, *Land Reform Potential in Rwanda: Report of the Relationships Foundation* (Cambridge: Newick Park Initiative, 1995).

Laslett, P. and Fishkin, J. (eds.), *Justice between Age Groups and Generations* (New Haven: Yale University Press, 1992).

Lawton, J., 'Are Species Useful?', *OIKOS*, 62 (1991), 3–4.

Lee, K., *Compass and Gyroscope: Integrating Science and Politics for the Environment* (Covelo, Calif.: Island Press, 1993).

Lélé, S., 'Sustainable Development: A Critical Review', *World Development*, 19 (1991), 607–21.

LeQuesne, C., 'Ecological Footprints', in K. Watkins (ed.), *The Oxfam Poverty Report.* (Oxford: Oxfam, 1995).

Levy, A., Scott-Clark, C., and Harrison, D., 'Save the Rhino, Kill the People', The *Observer* (23 Mar. 1997), 9.

Local Government Management Board, *A Framework for Local Sustainability* (Luton: LGMB, 1993).

—— *Sustainability Indicators Research Project: Report of Phase One* (Luton: LGMB, 1994).

Longman, T., 'Genocide and Socio-Political Change: Massacres in Two Rwandan Villages', *Issue: A Journal of Opinion*, 23/2 (1995).

McCully, P., *Silenced Rivers* (London: Zed Books, 1997).

McMichael, P. and Raynolds, L. T., 'Capitalism, Agriculture and World Economy', in L. Sklair (ed.), *Capitalism and Development* (London and New York: Routledge, 1994).

McNally, R. and Wheale, P., 'Biopatenting and Biodiversity: Comparative Advantages in the New Global Order', *The Ecologist*, 26 (1996), 222–8.

MacNaghten, P., 'Is Sustainability a Cultural Ghetto?', unpub. seminar paper, Centre for the Study of Environmental Change, Lancaster University, 1993.

—— Grove-White, R., Jacobs, M., and Wynne, M., *Public Perceptions and Sustainability in Lancashire: Indicators, Institutions, Participation* (Report to Lancashire County Council, Centre for the Study of Environmental Change, Lancaster University, 1995).

Macrae, J. and Zwi, A., with M. Duffield and H. Slim, *War and Hunger: Rethinking International Responses to Complex Emergencies* (London: Zed Books, 1994).

Margalit, A., *The Decent Society* (Cambridge, Mass.: Harvard University Press, 1996).

Martínez Alier J., 'Environmental Justice (Local and Global)', *Capitalism, Nature, Socialism* 8 (1997), 91–107.

Maslow, A. H., *Motivation and Personality* (New York: Harper, 1954).

Meade, J., *Agathopia: The Economics of Partnership* (Aberdeen: Aberdeen University Press/David Hulme Institute, 1988).

Meadows, D. H., Meadows, D. L., Randers, J., and Behrens III, W. W., *The Limits to Growth* (London and Sydney: Pan, 1974).

Mellor, M., *Breaking the Boundaries* (London: Virago, 1992).

Meyer-Abich, K., 'Winners and Losers in Climate Change', in Sachs *Global Ecology*.

Mill, J. S., *Principles of Political Economy,* ed. Donald Winch (Harmondsworth: Penguin Books, 1970 [1848]).

—— *Utilitarianism* (Indianapolis: Bobbs-Merrill, 1971).

Miller, D., 'Deliberative Democracy and Social Choice', *Political Studies,* Special Issue, 40 (1992), 54–67.

—— *On Nationality* (Oxford: Clarendon Press, 1995).

—— 'Social Justice and Environmental Goods', paper presented to the Environmental Sustainability and Social Justice Seminars, Keele University, UK (1996).

Moore, G. E., *Principia Ethica* (Cambridge: Cambridge University Press, 1903).

Myers, N., Environmentally Induced Displacements: The State of the Art, paper presented to the International Symposium on Environmentally induced Population Displacements and Environmental Impacts Resulting from Mass Migrations, Geneva April 1996, IOM/UNHCR/RPG.

Naess, A. and Sessions, G., 'Basic Principles of Deep Ecology', *Ecophilosophy,* 6 (1984), 3–7.

Narvesen, J., 'Utilitarianism and New Generations', *Mind,* 76 (1967).

—— 'Future People and Us', in Sikora and Barry (eds.), *Obligations to Future Generations*.

Nash, R., *Wilderness and the American Mind* (New Haven: Yale University Press, 1982).

Neefjes, K., *Resettlement in Northern Mutara: A Report of a Participatory Planning Exercise*, Report for Oxfam (UK & I) (Kigali: Oxfam 1995).

—— '*Ecological Needs in Community-Based Dryland Development*', paper for the Dryland Symposium at the Royal Botanic Gardens: Botany, What's in it for Drylands Development? (Oxford, July 1996*b*).

—— *Displacement and Environmental Change in the Great Lakes Region: Do We Need to Respond?* Discussion paper for Novib and Oxfam (UK & I) (The Hague/Oxford, 1997).

—— and David, R., *A Participatory Review of the Ikafe Refugee Response*, Oxfam (UK & I) Report (Oxford, 1996*a*).

Nelissen, N., van der Straaten, J., and Klinkers, L., (eds.), *Classics in Environmental Studies: An Overview of Classic Texts in Environmental Studies* (Utrecht: International Books, 1997).

Norgaard, R., *Sustainability and the Economics of Assuring Assets for Future Generations* (Washington: World Bank Policy Research Working Paper, WPS 832, 1992)

Norton, B., 'Sustainability, Human Welfare, and Ecosystem Health', *Environmental Values*, 1 (1992), 97–111.

—— 'Evaluating Ecosystem States: Two Competing Paradigms', *Ecological Economics*, 14 (1995*a*), 113–27.

—— 'Future Generations, Obligations to', *Encyclopedia of Bioethics*, 2nd edn. (New York: Macmillan Reference, 1995*b*).

—— 'Ecology and Freedom: Toward a Theory of Sustainable Opportunities', Paper presented to the Environmental Sustainability and Social Justice Seminars, Keele University, UK (1996).

—— 'Resilience and Options', *Ecological Economics*, 15 (1996), 133–6.

—— 'Intergenerational Fairness and Sustainability', unpublished MS, in preparation.

—— and Ulanowicz, R., 'Scale and Biodiversity Policy: A Hierarchical Approach', *Ambio*, 21 (1992), 244–9.

—— and Hannon, B., 'Environmental Values: A Place-Based Theory', *Environmental Ethics*, 19 (1997), 227–45.

—— and Toman, M., 'Sustainability: Ecological and Economic Perspectives', *Land Economics* (1997).

—— and Hannon, B., 'Democracy and Sense of Place Values' Philosophy and Geography (Forthcoming).

Nozick, R., *The Examined Life* (New York: Simon and Schuster, 1989).

—— *Anarchy, State, and Utopia* (New York: Basic Books, 1974).

O'Connor, J., *Natural Causes: Essays on Ecological Marxism* (New York: Guilford, 1997).

O'Connor, M., (ed.), *Is Capitalism Sustainable? Political Economy and the Politics of Ecology* (New York: Guilford, 1994).

—— and Martínez Alier, J., 'Ecological Distribution and Distributed Sustainability', in S. Faucheux, M. O'Connor, and J. van der Straaten (eds.), *Sustainable Development: Concepts, Rationalities and Strategies* (Dordrecht: Kluwer, 1996).

Okin, S., *Justice, Gender and the Family* (New York: Basic Books, 1989).

O'Neill, J., *Ecology, Policy and Politics* (London: Routledge, 1993).

—— 'Value Pluralism, Incommensurability and Institutions', in J. Foster (ed.), *Valuing Nature* (London, Routledge, 1997 *a*).

—— 'Environmental Values, Anthropocentrism and Speciesism', *Environmental Values*, 6 (1997 *b*).

O'Neill, O., 'Nozick's Entitlements', in P. Jeffrey (ed.), *Reading Nozick: Essays on Anarchy, State, and Utopia* (Oxford: Basil Blackwell, 1981).

O'Riordan, T., *Environmentalism* (2nd edn.) (London: Pion Publishers, 1981).

Page, T., *Conservation and Economic Efficiency* (Baltimore: Johns Hopkins University Press for Resources for the Future, 1977).

—— 'Intergenerational Justice as Opportunity', in D. MacLean and P. Brown (eds.), *Energy and the Future* (Totowa, NJ: Rowman and Littlefield, 1983).

—— 'Intergenerational Equity and the Social Rate of Discount', in V. K. Smith (ed.), *Environmental Resource and Applied Welfare Economics* (Washington: Resources for the Future, 1988).

Parfit, D., 'Energy Policy and the Further Future: The Identity Problem', in D. Maclean and P. Brown (eds.), *Energy and the Future.*

—— *Reasons and Persons* (Oxford: Oxford University Press, 1984).

Pasek, J., 'Obligations to Future Generations: A Philosophical Note', *World Development*, 20 (1992), 513–21.

Passmore, J., *Man's Responsibility for Nature* (London: Duckworth, 1974).

Pearce, D., *Economic Values and the Natural World* (London: Earthscan, 1993).

—— and Atkinson, G., *Are National Economies Sustainable? Measuring Sustainable Development*, Working Paper (Centre for Social and Economic Research on the Global Environment, University College, London, 1992)

—— Markandya, A., and Barbier, E., *Blueprint for a Green Economy* (London: Earthscan, 1989).

Pearce, F., 'North–South Rift Bars Path to Summit', *New Scientist*, 23 November 1991.

Pezzey, J., *Sustainable Development Concepts: An Economic Analysis*, (Washington, World Bank Environment Paper no. 2, 1992).

—— 'Sustainability Constraints versus 'Optimality' Versus Intertemporal Concern, and Axioms Versus Data', *Land Economics*, 73 (1997).

Pigou, A., *The Economics of Welfare* (London: Macmillan, 1932).

Ponting, C., *A Green History of the World: The Environment and the Collapse of Great Civilisations* (Harmondsworth: Penguin Books, 1991).

Power, T., *Lost Landscapes and Failed Economies: The Search for a Value of Place* (Covelo, Calif.: Island Press, 1996).

Pretty, J. N., *Regenerating Agriculture* (London: Earthscan, 1995).

Radford, T., 'Chronicle of Deaths Foretold.' the *Guardian*, (1992), 30, n.d.

Ramsey, F., 'A Mathematical Theory of Saving', *Economic Journal*, 38 (1928), 543–59.

Rawls, J., *A Theory of Justice* (Oxford: Clarendon Press, 1972).

—— *Political Liberalism* (New York: Columbia University Press, 1993).

Raz, J., *The Morality of Freedom* (Oxford: Oxford University Press, 1986).

Redclift, M., *Sustainable Development: Exploring the Contradictions* (London and New York: Methuen, 1987).

Rees, W. and Wackernagel, M., 'Ecological Footprints and Appropriated Carrying Capacity: Measuring the Natural Capital Requirements of the Human Economy', in A. Jansson, M. Hammer, C. Folke, and R. Costanza (eds.), *Investing in Natural Capital: The Ecological Economics Approach to Sustainability* (Washington DC: Island Press, 1994).

Retallack, S., 'The WTO's Record So Far', *The Ecologist*, 27 (1997), 136–7.

Richards, P., *Fighting For the Rain Forest: War, Youth and Resources in Sierra Leone*, African Issues Series (Oxford: James Currey Portsmouth: Heinemann/London: International Africa Institute, 1996).

Rocha, J., 'Floods of Tears', the *Guardian*, 12 Mar. 1997.

Roche, C., 'Operationality in Turbulence: The Need for Change', *Development in Practice*, 4 (1994).

Rosset, P., et al., 'Cuba's Nationwide Conversion to Organic Agriculture', *Capitalism, Nature, Socialism*, 19 (1994), 41–62.

Rowell, A., 'Crude Operators', *The Ecologist*, 27 (1997), 99–106.

Sachs, W., *Global Ecology* (London: Zed Books, 1993).

Sagoff, M., *The Economy of the Earth* (Cambridge: Cambridge University Press, 1988a).

—— 'Biotechnology and the Environment: What Is At Risk?', *Agriculture and Human Values*, 5 (1988b), 26–35.

Sandel, M., *Liberalism and the Limits of Justice* (Cambridge: Cambridge University Press, 1982).

Scanlon, T. M., 'Rights, Goals, and Fairness', in, J. Waldron (ed.), *Theories of Rights* (Oxford: Oxford University Press, 1984).

Schelling, T., 'Intergenerational Discounting', *Energy Policy*, 23 (1995).

Sen, A., *Poverty and Famines: An Essay On Entitlements and Deprivation* (Oxford: Clarendon Press, 1981).

Shepherd, P. and Gillespie, J., 'Developing Definitions of Natural Capital For Use Within the Uplands of England', *English Nature Research Report* No. 197 (Peterborough: English Nature, 1996).

Slicher van Bath, B., *De agrarische geschiedenis van West-Europa 500–1850* (Utrecht/Antwerp: Het Spectrum, 1960) (The Agrarian History of Western Europe 500–1850).

Smith, S. and Pearson, M., *The European Carbon Energy Tax Proposal,* (London: Institute for Fiscal Studies, 1991).

Solow, R., 'Intergenerational Equity and Exhaustible Resources', *Review of Economic Studies: Symposium on the Economics of Exhaustible Resources,* 41 (Edinburgh: Longman 1974), 29–45.

—— 'On the Intergenerational Allocation of Natural Resources', *Scandinavian Journal of Economics*, 88 (1986), 141–9.

—— 'An Almost Practical Step Toward Sustainability', Invited Lecture on the Occasion of the Fortieth Anniversary of Resources for the Future, Resources for the Future, Washington, 8 Oct. 1992.

—— 'Sustainability: An Economist's Perspective', in R. Dorfman and N. Dorfman (eds.), *Selected Readings in Environmental Economics* (3rd edn.) (New York: Norton, 1993).

Soper, K., *On Human Needs* (Brighton: Harvester, 1981).

Spooner, B. and Walsh, N., *Fighting for Survival: Insecurity, People and the Environment in the Horn of Africa,* IUCN Sahel Programme Study Report, vol. 1 (1991).

Streeten, P., 'Mankind's Future: An Ethical View', *Interdisciplinary Science Reviews*, 11 (1986), 248–56.

Sustainable Seattle, *Indications for a Sustainable Seattle* (Seattle: Sustainable Seattle, 1993).

Tawney, R. H., *Equality* (5th edn.) (London: Unwin 1964).

Temkin, L., *Inequality* (Oxford: Oxford University Press, 1993).

The Ecologist, *Whose Common Future? Reclaiming the Commons* (London: Earthscan, 1993).

Thero, D., 'Rawls and Environmental Ethics: A Critical Examination of the Literature', *Environmental Ethics*, 17 (1995), 93–106.

Tindale, S. and Holtham, G., *Green Tax Reform* (London: Institute for Public Policy Research, 1996).

Toman, M. 'Economics and "Sustainability": Balancing Trade-Offs and Imperatives', *Land Economics* 70 (1994), 399–413.

Turner, R. K. and Pearce, D., 'Sustainable Economic Development: Economic and Ethical Principles', in E. Barbier (ed.), *Economics and Ecology: New Frontiers and Sustainable Development* (London: Chapman & Hall, 1993).

Vadnjal, D. and O'Connor, M., 'What is the Value of Rangitoto Island?', *Environmental Values*, 3 (1994), 369–80.

van Brakel, M. and Buitenkamp, M., *Sustainable Netherlands* (Rotterdam: Friends of the Earth Netherlands/Milieu Defensie, 1992).

Vassall-Adams, G., *Rwanda: Un Programme d'action internationale* (Oxford: Oxfam, Insight Series, 1994).

Victor, P., *et al.,* 'How Strong is Weak Sustainability?', in S. Faucheux, M. O'Connor, and J. van der Straaten (eds.), *Sustainable Development: Analysis and Public Policy,* (Dordrecht: Kluwer, 1995).

Walters, C., *Adaptive Management of Renewable Resources* (New York: Macmillan, 1986).

Walzer, M., 'Interpretation and Social Criticism', in S. M. McMurrin (ed.), *The Tanner Lectures on Human Values 1985* (Salt Lake City, University of Utah Press, 1988).

Watkins, K., *The Oxfam Poverty Report* (Oxford: Oxfam, 1995).

Wells, D., *Environmental Policy: A Global Perspective for the Twenty-First Century* (Upper Saddle River: Prentice Hall, 1996).

Whatmore, S., 'From Farming to Agribusiness', in R. J. Johnston, P. J. Taylor, and M. J. Watts (eds.), *Geographies of Global Change* (Oxford: Blackwell, 1995).

Wicksell, K., 'A New Theory of Just Taxation', in R. Musgrave and A. Peacock (eds.), *Classics in the Theory of Public Finance* (Basingstoke: Macmillan, 1994).

Wissenburg, M., 'The Rapid Reproducers Paradox', paper presented to the Social Justice and Sustainability Seminars, Keele University, UK (1996).

—— *Green Liberalism: The Free and the Green Society* (London: UCL Press, 1998).

World Commission on Environment and Development, *Our Common Future* (The Brundtland Report) (Oxford: Oxford University Press, 1987).

World Conservation Union, UN Environment Programme, and World

Wide Fund For Nature, *Caring for the Earth* (Gland, Switz.: WCU, UNEP and WWF, 1991).

World Wide Fund for Nature UK, *Changing Direction: Towards a Green Britain* (Godalming: WWF UK, 1994).

INDEX